MOLIÈRE

MOLIÈRE

Mignard

MOLIÈRE

BY

ARTHUR TILLEY, M.A.

FELLOW AND LECTURER OF KING'S COLLEGE, CAMBRIDGE

CAMBRIDGE
AT THE UNIVERSITY PRESS
1921

CAMBRIDGE UNIVERSITY PRESS
Cambridge, New York, Melbourne, Madrid, Cape Town,
Singapore, São Paulo, Delhi, Tokyo, Mexico City

Cambridge University Press
The Edinburgh Building, Cambridge CB2 8RU, UK

Published in the United States of America by
Cambridge University Press, New York

www.cambridge.org
Information on this title: www.cambridge.org/9781107600089

© Cambridge University Press 1921

First published 1921
First paperback edition 2011

A catalogue record for this publication is available from the British Library

ISBN 978-1-107-60008-9 Paperback

PREFACE

MY excuse for adding to the number of books on Molière is that I have been a lover of his comedies for more than forty-five years. I have made no attempt to add to our knowledge of his life; indeed, the field has been so carefully gleaned that there is little hope of further harvest. Nor can I pretend to have introduced any startling novelty into the interpretation of his comedies. But there are one or two features of his dramatic genius upon which it has seemed worth while to insist. I would urge in particular that he is before all things a writer of comedy—not of tragedy dressed up as comedy to suit the tastes of a half-educated *parterre*, but of real comedy, meant to evoke laughter and resting upon the broad and secure foundations of humour and common sense. The man who understood Molière least was Jean-Jacques Rousseau, and he was conspicuously lacking in both these qualities. He failed utterly to realise, as some modern readers and critics of Molière fail to realise, that you can laugh at those with whom you sympathise. and even at those whom you love and admire,

We can sympathise with Orgon and George Dandin and Argan, with Sosie and Sganarelle (the valet of Don Juan); yet at the same time we laugh at them. Our love and admiration for Alceste are none the less sincere because we are not blind to his ridiculous side.

But Molière is not only a true humourist; he is also an apostle of common sense. He looks at life from the point of view of the average man, not of the intellectual and the high-brow. He takes the verdict of the community rather than that of a few superior persons. Like the other great writers of his age, he makes no exalted claim on behalf of human nature, but he has a kindly feeling for its shortcomings, as one who is conscious of his own frailty. He is a healthy rather than a lofty moralist, unsparing of the grasping, the insolent, and the self-opinionated, but tolerant towards ignorance, folly, and credulity.

In the note appended to my first chapter I have given an account of the authorities for Molière's life. For the criticism of his dramatic art the most helpful work, at any rate of recent date, is the *Molière* of M. Eugène Rigal, 2 vols. 1908. M. Lafenestre's little book in the series of *Les grands écrivains français* shews, perhaps, a juster appreciation of Molière's character and moral teaching, and he rightly insists that Molière creates living men and women and not mere abstract types. The best book in English is that by Professor Brandes Matthews, New York, 1910. Nor must I forget Francisque Sarcey, one of whose volumes of *Quarante ans de Théâtre* is devoted to Molière and classical comedy, and whose unfailing common sense makes him a sound interpreter of our author. Reference to books dealing with special features of Molière's work will be found in my notes.

Finally I must offer my grateful thanks to Mr E. O. Vulliamy of King's College for reading the greater part of my book in proof.

The frontispiece is from a photograph, kindly supplied by the Director of the Musée Condé, of the portrait attributed to Mignard on the authority of J.-B. Nolin, who engraved it in 1685, about fifteen years after it was painted.

A. T.

Cambridge,
February, 1921.

CONTENTS

CORRIGENDA

pp. 12, 18, 63, 64.
  For Le Dépit amoureux read the *Dépit amoureux*.
p. 18, l. 17. *For* two months *read* three months.
p. 22, l. 18. *For* comédie-ballets *read* comédies-ballets.

CHAPTER I

LIFE[1]

Jean-Baptiste Poquelin, whom the world knows as Molière, was, like Regnard and Beaumarchais and Scribe, the son of a well-to-do Parisian *bourgeois*. He was the eldest child of Jean Poquelin, a *tapissier* or upholsterer, who lived in a house at the corner of the Rue Saint-Honoré and the Rue des Vieilles-Étuves (now the Rue Sauval). It was near the Halles and the Pont-Neuf, and it was known as the *Maison des Singes* from the figures of monkeys which were carved on a wooden pillar at the corner of the first and second storeys. Molière was baptised in the church of Saint-Eustache on January 15, 1622, and we may assume that he was born on the same day, for otherwise, in accordance with the usual practice, the date of his birth would have been inserted in the certificate. In 1631 Jean Poquelin the elder purchased from his brother the post of *tapissier et valet de chambre du roi*. The stipend was 300 *livres* a year, and the duties consisted in making the royal bed when on service, which was for three

[1] See for authorities the note at the end of this chapter.

months in the year, and in providing and taking charge of the tapestries, bed-hangings, and other furniture, when the Court travelled.

In 1632, when his eldest son was ten years old, Jean Poquelin lost his wife, Marie Cressé, and in the following year he married again. The inventory made after his first wife's death shews that he was at this time a prosperous man. The family plate was valued at 866 *livres*, and Marie Cressé's jewellery at 1650 *livres*[1]. It also appears from this inventory that he did a little business in money-lending, but there is no reason for supposing, as has been rashly conjectured, that he was the original either of Harpagon or of other close-fisted old gentlemen who appear in his son's comedies. Nor need we regard it as an example of the great dramatist's love of first-hand observation that there are few mothers in his plays, and that there are two notable step-mothers, Elmire and Béline. This is rather to be accounted for by the difficulty in getting actresses to take the part of an elderly woman[2]. In Molière's time such parts were usually played by men, as, for instance, that of Mme Pernelle by Louis Béjart and those of Mme Jourdain and Philaminte by Hubert.

In October 1636—this at least is the probable

---

[1] Soulié, *Recherches*, pp. 138 and 139.
[2] Il est de l'art du poëte de ne produire des mères que dans un bel âge, et de ne leur pas donner des fils qui puissent les convaincre d'avoir plus de quarante ans. (S. Chappuzeau, *Le théâtre français*, 1674, cited by E. Despois, *Le théâtre français*, 4th ed. 1894, p. 148.)

date—Molière was sent to the Jesuit College of Clermont, afterwards Louis-le-Grand[1], at that time the most fashionable and probably the best school in Paris. Two years later it numbered 2000 *externes* or out-students, and 300 *internes* or boarders. Molière, who was an *externe*, probably remained there for the full five years prescribed for the humanities, and he became a good Latin scholar. Then for a short time he shared the lessons in philosophy which the distinguished physicist, Pierre Gassendi, was giving to Claude-Emmanuel Chapelle, the natural son of his friend Pierre Lhuilier. The class was also joined by François Bernier, who seems to have acted as Gassendi's secretary, and according to some, but the evidence is doubtful, by Cyrano de Bergerac, the fantastic author of *L'histoire comique de l'Empire de la Lune* and *Le Pédant joué*. Bernier became later a distinguished traveller, and spent several years in India, partly as physician to the Emperor Aurangzib, for the early part of whose reign he is the most important contemporary European authority. Besides his writings on the Mogul empire he published an abridgement of Gassendi's philosophy. On his return to France he became a well-known figure in Parisian society and made numerous friends, who nicknamed him the Mogul and *Le joli philosophe*.

Gassendi had given many years to the study

---

[1] Its name was changed in 1682. It is now the Lycée Louis-le-Grand.

of Epicurus's philosophy and had carried on a
notable controversy with Descartes. The two
men represented diametrically opposite stand-
points. Descartes was a metaphysician and an
idealist, Gassendi was a man of science—a
follower of Bacon and a friend of Galileo—and
in philosophy at any rate a materialist. Among
his intimates at Paris were Gabriel Naudé, the
librarian of the Bibliothèque Mazarine, who was
a decided free-thinker, the physician Guy Patin,
who, though he hated an atheist worse than a
Jesuit, was at least a *frondeur* in religion, and
the English philosopher Hobbes. Gassendi,
however, combined his materialistic philosophy
with the regular and devout performance of his
duties as a priest.

From Gassendi Molière learnt at any rate to
appreciate the poetry, if not the philosophy, of
Lucretius, and he amused himself by translating
into verse such passages of his poem as especially charmed him, and the rest into prose. But
this translation has completely vanished, and all
that remains to testify to Molière's interest in
the great Roman poet is the free imitation of
twenty lines from the Fourth Book which he
has put in the mouth of Éliante in the Second
Act of *Le Misanthrope*[1].

Molière was now in his twenty-first year and

[1] The evidence for the existence of this translation consists of
a letter of Chapelain to Bernier, a note by Brossette on Boileau's
Second Satire, and the prefaces to the 2nd (1659) and 3rd edition
(1677) of the Abbé de Marolles's translation of Lucretius. See
Molière, *Œuvres* V, 558–61.

it was time to decide on his profession. In 1637 his father had obtained for him the succession to his post of *tapissier du roi*, but this was merely a formal proceeding and did not necessarily imply that the lad was intended for a *tapissier*. La Grange and Vivot say that he studied law, and according to other early biographers of less authority he took his licence at Orleans[1] and was received as an advocate at Paris[2].

After he had finished his studies, he was called upon, says Grimarest, to act as deputy for his father "on account of his great age," and in that capacity accompanied Louis XIII to Narbonne, 1642. As Jean Poquelin was then only forty-seven, the statement does not carry conviction. But there is documentary evidence to shew that he was at Paris on July 3, which he could not have been, seeing that the Court was at Lyons on July 1, if he had fulfilled his duties in person for the second quarter of the year, when he was normally on service. If this is the case, his son would naturally have acted as his

---

[1] *Élomire hypocondre ou les Médecins vengés*, Paris, 1670. Though the author of this libellous comedy, Le Boulanger de Chalussay, is ill-disposed towards Molière, he seems to be fairly well-informed. There are two reprints, one of 1869 in the *Collection Moliéresque*, and the other of 1878 ed. Ch. Livet. Soulié (p. 23) quotes from Charles Perrault's *Mémoires* a lively account of how he and two friends took their degrees at Orleans a few years later, i.e. in 1651. At this time Orleans and Poitiers were the only two Universities in France which had a Faculty of Civil Law.

[2] Grimarest, on the authority, he says, of Molière's 'family.'

deputy, and if so he was on duty at the time of Cinq Mars's arrest—June 13, 1642[1].

But Molière's heart was neither in humanistic studies nor in upholstering ; it was wholly given to the stage. According to Grimarest this passion was implanted in him by his maternal grandfather, who often took him to the neighbouring Hôtel de Bourgogne. However this may be, we know that from about the year 1635 the drama in France received a great impetus and entered on a long period of flourishing success. Molière in his boyhood and early youth may well have paid frequent visits both to the Hôtel de Bourgogne and to the Théâtre du Marais, but of this part of his education more will be said in the next chapter.

Molière's love of the stage brought him into close relations with some young people of his own age who lived in his neighbourhood and shared his tastes. They were the three elder children of Joseph Béjart, a *huissier* in the department of the *Eaux et Forêts*, and Marie Hervé, who, not altogether unjustly, has been likened to Halévy's Mme Cardinal. The leading spirit seems to have been the elder sister, Madeleine, who was five years older than Molière, and who as early as 1636, when she was just eighteen, had embarked on a theatrical career. She was good-looking, attractive, and intelligent, and she had a remarkable business capacity. Of the other two, her brother Joseph was her senior

[1] See Soulié, p. 24.

by one or two years, while her sister Geneviève was six and a half years younger[1].

As a result of this friendship Molière and the three Béjarts determined to form a theatrical company, and accordingly on January 6, 1643 he formally renounced in favour of his next brother, also called Jean[2], the succession to his father's office, and at the same time persuaded his father to advance him the sum of 630 *livres* out of the share in his mother's estate which would fall due to him at the age of twenty-five. We do not need the anecdote related by Charles Perrault and repeated by Grimarest to assure us of the grief which Molière's choice of a profession caused his family. Actors at this time were regarded in France almost as social and religious pariahs. " I have learnt with sorrow," writes Sister Agnes of Port-Royal to her nephew Racine, "that you associate more than ever with persons whose name is an abomination to all who have the smallest grain of piety[3]." "The qualities of a writer of romances and plays," says Nicole in answer to Desmarets de Saint-Sorlin, "are not regarded as very honourable by the world, but they are horrible from the point of view of the Christian religion and the precepts of the Gospel[4]."

[1] A. Jal, *Dictionnaire critique de biographie et d'histoire.*
[2] Molière received the name of Jean only at his baptism ; the name of Baptiste was doubtless added after his younger brother was born.   [3] Cited by G. Larroumet, *Racine*, p. 32.
[4] *Ib.* p. 34, and cp. Nicole's *Traité de la Comédie*, written in 1659 and first printed at the end of *Les Visionnaires* in 1667 and again in vol. III of his *Essais de Morale*, 1671 ff.

In his treatise, *De l'Éducation Chrestienne des Enfans*, published in 1669, Varet, a Port-Royalist and a historian of the Jansenist movement, inveighs in no measured terms against stage-plays. "You must then, my sister, inspire your children with a horror of the theatre, for it is a dangerous pastime, and unworthy of a Christian[1]." These quotations all come from Jansenist writers, but they only represent in a more austere form the general opinion of the Church. We may therefore look with suspicion on the story that it was for the *beaux yeux* of Madeleine Béjart that Molière became an actor. Nothing short of an inborn passion for the stage could have given him courage to defy the opposition of his family and his friends.

So on June 30, 1643 Molière signed an agreement which made him, together with the three Béjarts and six others, a member of a theatrical company called the *Illustre Théâtre*[2]. They hired a *tripot* or tennis-court—the ordinary substitute for a theatre in those days—near the Porte de Nesle, and after a few performances at Rouen, pending the necessary alterations, they opened their theatre in the following December. From the first the venture was a failure. The patronage of the young king's uncle, Gaston, Duke of Orleans, who gave them a small subvention, did not save them from financial difficulties, and Molière—so for the first time he signed his name

---

[1] H. C. Barnard, *The Port-Royalists on Education*, Cambridge, 1918.   [2] Molière, *Œuvres* x, 462–3.

to an agreement of June 28, 1644[1]—who had come
to be recognised as the leader of the troop, was
three times imprisoned for debt. With his re-
lease in August 1645, followed by a bond given
by the whole company to the friend who had
guaranteed payment of his debt[2], the career of
the *Illustre Théâtre*, the numbers of which had
dwindled to seven, came to an end. Nothing
daunted, Molière and the Béjarts determined to
try their luck in the provinces.

In spite of the patient investigations of devoted researchers the history of this provincial
Odyssey, which lasted for thirteen years, is but
imperfectly known. There is good reason for
believing that before the close of the year 1645
what was left of the *Illustre Théâtre* amalga-
mated with another strolling company, which
had for its chief one Charles Dufresne and for
its patron the Governor of Guyenne, the Duc
d'Épernon[3]. But it is not till April 23, 1648 that
we come upon a definite trace of Molière himself.
On that day the register of the Hôtel de Ville
at Nantes records that the Sieur Morlierre
[*sic*], one of the comedians of the troop of the
Sieur Dufresne, humbly petitioned the municipal
officials to allow them to give representations
in the theatre. There were various delays and
it was not till May 17 that the representations
began. They met with little success. In the course
of the year 1649 we hear of the company at

---

[1] Soulié, p. 176.   [2] *Ib.* p. 190.
[3] Molière, *Œuvres* x, 106.

Toulouse (May 16) and Narbonne (December 26 or 27), and in February 1650 they visited Agen by order of the Duc d'Épernon. From October 24, 1650 to January 14, 1651 they were at Pézenas in the service of the Estates of Languedoc, and Molière received on their behalf the sum of 4000 *livres* for their performances. There is also evidence to shew that they played at Carcassonne, where the Estates were in session from July 31, 1651 to January 10, 1652.

We can form some idea of the life led by Molière and his troop from Scarron's entertaining *Roman comique*, the First Part of which was published in 1651. The actors of the strolling company whose fortunes he relates were no doubt inferior in social status to Molière and his friends, but, allowing for a certain amount of comic exaggeration, the picture may be regarded as on the whole a faithful one. It corresponds very closely to that drawn by Cervantes some forty years earlier of strolling players in Spain. "In the sweat of their brows they gain their bread by insupportable toil, learning constantly by heart, leading a perpetual gipsy life from place to place and from inn to tavern, and staying awake to please others, for in other men's pleasure lies their profit[1]."

The ordinary difficulties and hardships that provincial companies had to encounter were increased in the case of Molière's company by the

[1] *El Licenciado Vidriera* (*Exemplary Novels*, translated by N. Maccoll, 1902, I, 191).

state of disorder and misery to which the Fronde had reduced the greater part of France. Marauding soldiers, famine prices, inundations, and plague had brought the provinces of Guyenne, Languedoc, and Provence, which were the scenes of Molière's chief activity, to the utmost pitch of desolation[1]. In November 1649 a request by Molière to the town council of Poitiers to allow his company to spend two months in that city was refused "attendu la misère du temps et cherté des blés[2]." Yet, in spite of these adverse circumstances, the patronage of the Estates of Languedoc during their session of 1650–1651 marks the turning-point in the fortunes of the company. At the end of 1652 we find them at Lyons, and they seem to have made this city their headquarters for the next five years. There in 1653 they presented Corneille's new and highly popular spectacular play of *Andromède* (1650), which from the part played in it by machinery must have been expensive to produce. Here too—but not before 1655, if we accept the date definitely given by La Grange in his *Registre*—Molière presented *L'Étourdi*, his first regular play[3]. In September 1653 the company entered the service of Armand, Prince de Conti, who, having submitted to Mazarin at Bordeaux in the

[1] See A. Feillet, *Les misères au temps de la Fronde*, 5th ed. 1886.
[2] H. Chardon, *M. de Modène, ses deux femmes et Madeleine Béjart*, 1886.
[3] In the *Vie en abrégé* La Grange and Vivot say that "Molière came to Lyons in 1653, and it was there that he presented to the public his first play; it was *L'Étourdi*."

previous July had retired to his château of La Grange-des-Prés near Pézenas, pending his marriage with the minister's niece. An interesting passage in the memoirs of Daniel de Cosnac, Archbishop of Aix, describes how in his young days, as the prince's treasurer for his *menus plaisirs*, he engaged "the troop of Molière and la Béjart" to play before him, and how after a second representation the prince took them into his service[1]. During the next four winters they again played before the Estates, twice at Montpellier, then at Pézenas, and lastly at Béziers, where *Le Dépit amoureux* was presented in November or December 1656. We also encounter the company at Narbonne (February and May 1656), Dijon (June 1657), and Avignon (November or December 1657), where Molière met the celebrated painter Pierre Mignard, and struck up with him a durable friendship. "In 1658," say La Grange and Vivot, "Molière's friends advised him to come into the neighbourhood of Paris," with a view to getting into touch with persons of consideration, who might procure for him the patronage of the Court. Accordingly, after spending the carnival at Grenoble, he established his company at Rouen for the summer, and from that city made several preliminary trips to the capital. Then in October the whole company, having obtained permission to assume the title of "Troupe de Monsieur, frère unique du Roi," moved to Paris.

[1] *Mémoires*, 2 vols. 1852, I, 126–8.

So Molière, after his long absence of thirteen years, returned to the city of his birth. He had "seen the towns and learnt the minds of many men," and he had, we may be sure, "suffered many woes." The hardships and annoyances incidental to his profession, the petty tyranny of local magistrates, the caprices of patrons, the coarsely expressed displeasures of the *parterre*, all this must have struck deep into the heart of an educated and sensitive man. And upon his shoulders the chief burden must have fallen. As the acknowledged leader of the troop it must have been his task to interview the authorities, to placate persons of importance, to charm a noisy audience into good humour, and, not least, to compose the differences of his comrades. How often must he have exclaimed—

Ah! les étranges animaux à conduire que les comédiens.

But to an observer of the comedy of life all this must have been a first-rate experience, and to an actor an invaluable training. According to Samuel Chappuzeau, whose *Théâtre français* was printed in the year following Molière's death, it was in such strolling companies that actors as a rule served their apprenticeship, and it was from these companies that the Paris theatres drew their recruits.

Molière's career at Paris as a theatrical manager began on October 28, 1658, when his company played Corneille's *Nicomède* and a farce called *Le Docteur amoureux* in the Louvre

before the king. His Majesty, who was then a lad
of seventeen, expressed his pleasure at the performance, especially at that of the farce, and he
assigned to the new arrivals the Salle du Petit-
Bourbon, which stood between Saint-Germain-
l'Auxerrois and the Louvre, and was connected
with the latter by long galleries. They had,
however, to share this improvised theatre with
an Italian company, to whom Molière paid 1500
livres for its use on the 'extraordinary' days of
the week, that is to say Mondays, Tuesdays,
Thursdays, and Saturdays. The troop now consisted of eleven persons, namely, Molière, Joseph
Béjart and his younger brother Louis, who had
joined it since the migration to the provinces,
Dufresne, René Berthelot, called Du Parc, Edme
Villequin de Brie, Madeleine Béjart and her
sister Geneviève, who acted under her mother's
name of Hervé, Mlle Du Parc, Mlle de Brie,
and a *gagiste* named Croisac, who did not share
in the profits but was paid at the rate of two
livres a day. Du Parc was possibly a member of
Dufresne's company at the time of the amalga-
mation. His acting name of Gros-René was
suggested by his rotund figure, to which there
is an evident allusion in *Le Dépit amoureux*,
when the valet, played by Gros-René and bearing his name, says—

Je suis homme fort rond de toutes les manières.

In February 1653 this popular actor had married Marquise-Thérèse de Gorla, the daughter of

an Italian amateur or vendor of quack medicines, whose remarkable beauty captivated in turn Molière, Corneille, and Racine. Being a fairly good actress in comedy, she proved a useful addition to the troop, but her wayward and imperious temper added greatly to Molière's difficulties as a manager. In the same year, 1653, the company was also joined by De Brie and his wife, a pretty woman who retained for many years her youthful appearance and who with her gentle and conciliating disposition formed a welcome contrast to Mlle Du Parc.

If we may trust the authority of *Élomire hypocondre*, the new actors began their tenure at the Petit-Bourbon with five tragedies by Corneille, none of which was well received. Then, renouncing tragedy, Molière scored two brilliant successes with *L'Étourdi* and *Le Dépit amoureux*. At Easter 1659 there were changes in the company; Dufresne retired, and Mlle Du Parc with her husband deserted Molière for the Théâtre du Marais. A little later (May 21) Joseph Béjart died, and his comrades marked the sense of their loss by closing the theatre for a fortnight. The vacant places were filled by the popular low comedian whose acting name was Jodelet, and his brother Lespy, both from the Marais, by Du Croisy and his wife, and by La Grange. Jodelet, whose name in real life was Julien Bedeau, had made his mark as the valet Cliton in Corneille's *Le Menteur*, and in several plays by Scarron—*Jodelet ou le Maître-Valet*

(1645), *Jodelet souffleté* (1646), *Don Japhet d'Ar-
ménie* (1652), and *Le Marquis ridicule* (1656).
His large nose, powdered face, and nasal accent
were admirably suited to broad farce, but he was
past sixty when he threw in his lot with Molière. Du Croisy was a gentleman by birth, good-
looking but somewhat stout. He was a merito-
rious actor, and, as we shall see, Molière entrusted
to him the part of Tartuffe. His wife, on the
other hand, had little talent, and was of no great
assistance to the company.

The most valuable of the recruits was La
Grange. He was only twenty, young enough to
be trained by Molière for the lovers' parts, in
which he took the place of Joseph Béjart. He
not only became an actor of singular grace and
charm, but he rendered great services to the
company as treasurer and secretary, and later
as 'orator,' in which office he succeeded Molière
in 1664. The two chief functions of the orator
were to compose the *affiche* and to make an-
nouncements to the audience, the latter duty
often demanding considerable tact and *esprit*.
La Grange also kept a private register of events
which concerned the company. It has happily
been preserved and forms a brief but thoroughly
reliable history of Molière's theatre from 1658
to 1685[1].

On November 18, 1659 the new company

---

[1] *Registre de Lagrange*, ed. Ed. Thierry, 1876. It is preceded
by a biographical notice, which was published separately in the
same year.

presented Corneille's *Cinna* and with it a farcical comedy entitled *Les Précieuses ridicules*, which Molière had written since his return to Paris. It was very well received, but it gave offence in some quarters and an "*alcôviste* of quality" prevented its repetition for a fortnight. It was given again on December 2, and between that date and the close of the theatrical year, a fortnight before Easter, La Grange records thirty-two performances, or more than two a week[1]. After the Easter holidays it was played again, but without Jodelet, who had died on the previous Good Friday (March 28). His part was taken by Gros-René, who with his wife now returned to Molière's company. The same actor played the valet's part in the new one-act comedy of *Sganarelle, ou le Cocu imaginaire*, which Molière produced on May 26, and which was repeated with hardly an intermission till the middle of August.

On August 26 Louis XIV returned to Paris with his Spanish bride, and plans for the completion of the Louvre, which involved the demolition of the Salle du Petit-Bourbon, were approved. In exchange, the theatre of the Palais-Royal, which Richelieu had constructed in 1639, was assigned to Molière's company. But it required certain repairs, and for three months they were homeless and had to maintain themselves by giving representations in private houses and in the Louvre.

[1] The Italians having left Paris in July 1659, Molière's company took the 'ordinary' days.

In this year (1660) Molière's younger brother, who had been associated with his father in the office of *tapissier du roi*, died (April 6), and Molière took his place. La Grange tells us that he was "very assiduous" in the performance of his duties, and that in this way he brought himself into notice with the Court as a civil and well-bred man.

On January 20, 1661 the newly repaired theatre opened with a performance of *Le Dépit amoureux* and *Sganarelle*. On February 4 Molière produced his first and last tragi-comedy, *Don Garcie de Navarre*. It was a failure, and he withdrew it after seven performances[1]. Returning to his true bent he achieved a fresh success with *L'École des Maris*, which was presented on June 24, two months after the death of Mazarin. On July 11 it was played at Fouquet's princely seat at Vaux before the Queen of England and her daughter Henrietta, who had just married *Monsieur*, the king's only brother. In the middle of August, three weeks before his arrest, Fouquet gave a series of magnificent entertainments, to which Molière contributed on August 17 the dramatic portion of a *comédie-ballet*, entitled *Les Fâcheux*. The boldness of its satire marks his growing favour with the Court and the public, and the dedication to

[1] It was performed at the Palais-Royal for the king on September 29, 1662, at Chantilly by order of Condé on September 29, 1663, twice at Versailles in October of the same year, and finally twice in public at the Palais-Royal in the following November.

the king of the printed play is that of a man who is confident of his position. We have an interesting confirmation of this in a letter written by La Fontaine, partly in prose and partly in verse, to his friend Maucroix, in which he gives an account of the proceedings at Vaux, including *Les Fâcheux*.

> C'est un ouvrage de Molière.
> Cet écrivain par sa manière
> Charme à présent toute la cour.
> De la façon que son nom court,
> Il doit être par delà Rome:
> J'en suis ravi, car c'est mon homme.

On February 20, 1662 Molière, now a man of forty, married Armande-Grésinde Béjart, the youngest sister of Madeleine, who was barely twenty[1]. There was a fairly widespread rumour in Molière's day that Armande was Madeleine's daughter, but, in 1821, Beffara found the certificate of her marriage, in which it is stated that she was the daughter of Joseph Béjart and Marie Hervé and the sister of Madeleine[2]. Moreover Madeleine, both in her will made on January 9, 1672, when she was mortally ill, and in a codicil of February 14, which she added three days before her death, calls Armande her sister[3]. One would have thought that this put the question beyond doubt, but it is easier to start a scandal than to stop it, and there are still biographers and critics of Molière who with more ingenuity

---

[1] She was almost certainly the *petite non baptisée* who is mentioned in the document of March 10, 1663, in which Marie Hervé, the widow of Joseph Béjart *père*, renounces on behalf of her children the succession to his estate (Soulié, pp. 172–3).

[2] Soulié, pp. 203–5. [3] *Ib.* pp. 243–7.

than common sense propound elaborate theories, no two of which agree, to shew that Molière's wife was the daughter of Madeleine Béjart, that both families conspired to make a false statement in the marriage contract, and that Madeleine Béjart on her death-bed confirmed the lie in a legal document[1].

In June 1662 Molière's company received some useful additions in the persons of Brécourt, La Thorillière, and Hubert, all from the Théâtre du Marais. Brécourt was a good actor both in comedy and tragedy, and he made his mark in such very different parts as Alain in the *École des Femmes* and Antiochus in Racine's *Bérénice*. He was turbulent and quarrelsome, and it was doubtless on this account that he only remained with the company for two years. He was the author of a few pieces, one of which, *L'Ombre de Molière*, a one-act comedy in prose, played in 1674, may be regarded as an act of reparation to the memory of his former chief. François Le Noir, Sieur de la Thorillière, was a tall handsome man, who had been a captain in the army. He was for a time secretary and treasurer to the company and in that capacity[2] kept the register of receipts and expenses. His son was a distinguished actor and he had two daughters, both of whom married actors and dramatists,

[1] See Trollope, pp. 298–307, where the question is discussed with fairness and common sense.

[2] He has left two Registers, covering the period from April 6, 1663 to January 6, 1665, which have been edited by G. Monval for the *Nouvelle Collection Moliéresque* (Nos. XVII and XVIII).

the one Baron, and the other Dancourt. André Hubert has been already mentioned as a successful actor of elderly women's parts. He kept a Register from April 28, 1672 to March 21, 1673[1].

In *L'École des Maris* Molière had taken for his theme the intended marriage of a middle-aged man with a young girl, and he returned to it again in his next comedy, *L'École des Femmes*, which he produced on December 26, 1662. It was immensely successful. At the Palais-Royal it ran almost without interruption till the Easter holidays, and the receipts for the first eighteen days averaged 1187 *livres*. There were also performances at the Court and in private houses. But the play, partly by reason of this very success, roused violent opposition in many quarters —from the Hôtel de Bourgogne whose receipts must have suffered from the rivalry of the new company, from the *précieuses* who stigmatised the play as indecent, from the *dévots* who complained of its irreligion, from the critical pedants who detected in it violations of the rules, and from the *marquis* who resented their rough handling in *Les Fâcheux*. On the other hand it was nobly defended by Boileau, who sent his well-known *Stances à Molière* as a New-Year's gift to the poet. Molière too had a powerful supporter in the king, who on March 12, 1663 made the company a present of 4000 *livres*, while soon after

[1] See above, p. 2. His Register is printed in the *Nouvelle Collection Moliéresque*.

Easter Molière's name was added to the list of pensions for that year, with the sum of 1000 *livres* attached to it[1].

Thus encouraged, Molière on June 1, 1663 replied to his critics in a one-act comedy, *La Critique de l'École des Femmes*, which still remains the best exposition of the principles of his art; and when the Hôtel de Bourgogne commissioned a young author, named Edme Boursault[2], to make a counter-attack with a piece entitled *Le Portrait du Peintre ou la Contre-critique de l'École des Femmes*, he avenged himself in *L'Impromptu de Versailles*, in which he held up to ridicule not only the rival actors, but the *marquis*, the *précieuses*, and Boursault himself.

One result of Molière's favour with Louis XIV was that he was called on from time to time to produce *comédie-ballets* at short notice. The first of these was *Les Fâcheux*; the second was *Le Mariage forcé*, which was played at the Louvre on January 29, 1664, the king taking part in the ballet as a gipsy. Molière's services were again called upon for the splendid fêtes held at Versailles from May 7 to 12, which Voltaire has thought worthy of commemoration in his *Siècle de Louis XIV*. For these Molière wrote *La Princesse d'Élide*, *comédie galante*, which he began in verse, but from want of time finished in prose. It was presented on May 8. On the

---

[1] Chapelain received 3000 *livres*, Corneille 2000.
[2] According to the 'keys' he was the original of La Bruyère's Capys in his chapter, *Des Ouvrages de l'esprit*.

11th there was a performance of *Les Fâcheux*, and on the 12th Molière produced the first three acts of *Tartuffe*. Of the fortunes of the play and of the long struggle which Molière had to go through before it was played in public without let or hindrance I shall speak later. It need only be said here that the complete play in five acts was first given on November 29, 1664 at Raincy, the seat of the Princess Palatine, in honour of Condé, who from this time accorded to Molière the same steadfast and judicious protection that he gave to Racine and Boileau. The performance shews that Molière was occupied with the last two acts of the play during the summer and autumn of 1664.

His next play, *Don Juan*, which was produced on February 15, 1665 and which bears evident traces of hurried composition, is in a sense a sequel to *Tartuffe*. The subject may have been suggested to him by his comrades, but his treatment of it, and of the principal character, perhaps the strongest that he ever drew, clearly indicates the militant character of the play. It was well received by the public, the receipts for the first nine representations being very high, and on one occasion reaching 2390 *livres*. But the boldness of some of its strokes called forth fresh protests from the religious zealots, and after the fifteenth performance (March 20) it was withdrawn. The attack on the medical profession, initiated in *Don Juan*, was pushed home in *L'Amour Médecin*, another *comédie-ballet*, which, written and rehearsed in five days, was presented at Versailles on September 15, 1665, and at the Palais-Royal on September 22.

During the previous seven months Molière seems to have written nothing; probably because he was discouraged by the unfair attacks of the last two years. Instead of a new piece from his own pen he produced a tragi-comedy entitled *La Coquette ou le Favori* by Mlle Des Jardins, or, as she called herself, Mme de Villedieu, and revived old plays like Desmarets de Saint-Sorlin's *Les Visionnaires*, Scarron's *Don Japhet*, and Tristan L'Hermite's *Marianne*. After *L'Amour Médecin* he presented *La Mère coquette* by Donneau de Visé (October 23), and Racine's *Alexandre* (December 4). But except Molière's own play, which ran till the end of November, and *Alexandre*, none of these pieces met with more than a moderate success, and the receipts of the company for 1665–1666 were lower than in any year since their return to Paris. A single share came only to 2243 *livres*, whereas in the year 1663–1664 it had reached 4554 *livres*. On the other hand, in August 1665 the company received a fresh pledge of the royal favour. Louis XIV sent for them to Saint-Germain, and, promising them an annual subvention of 6000 *livres*, expressed a wish that they should change their title to that of *Troupe du Roi*.

Besides the king's support Molière had another source of encouragement in this difficult year

1664. This was his friendship with Racine, Boileau, and La Fontaine. That with Boileau probably dates from the latter's championship of *L'École des Femmes* at the beginning of 1663. That with Racine seems to have begun rather later; in November of 1664 Racine refers to Molière in terms which bespeak a certain intimacy. It was probably through Racine, who had known La Fontaine, a relation of his wife's, since 1659, that both Molière and Boileau were introduced to *le bonhomme*; at any rate it must have been in the years 1664 and 1665 that the four great writers used to meet either at Boileau's lodgings in the Rue du vieux Colombier or at the taverns of the *Mouton blanc* or the *Croix de Lorraine*. Molière's old friend Chapelle and Antoine Furetière, the author of *Le Roman bourgeois*, with whom Boileau lodged, were sometimes of the party. At the beginning of his *Amours de Psyché* La Fontaine draws a charming picture of these meetings and of the conversations which took place at them. " They adored the works of the ancients, but they did not refuse to the moderns the praise that was their due. They spoke of their own writings with modesty, and gave one another sincere advice when any of them, which was a rare event, succumbed to the fashionable malady and became an author." It is true that among the four friends referred to by La Fontaine Molière does not find a place, for Gelaste stands certainly for Chapelle and not, as some suppose, for Molière. But La Fontaine's words will apply equally to occasions when Molière was present, and it is reasonable to conjecture that their conversations contributed in no small degree to that general unanimity of aim which marks the whole literature of the classical age, and not least the writings of Molière and his three friends.

The five years from May 1664 to February 1669, during which Molière fought for the production of *Tartuffe*, are among the most important, as they are among the most glorious, in the whole annals of French literature. *Tartuffe*, *Don Juan*, Boileau's first *Satires* (I–VII), *Le Misanthrope*, *Andromaque*, La Fontaine's *Fables* (I–VI), *Les Plaideurs*, Boileau's eighth and ninth *Satires*, all belong to this great *lustrum*. And to complete the tale of masterpieces we must add La Rochefoucauld's *Maximes* and some of Bossuet's sermons. Each of these works marks a victory in a crucial struggle. Molière with his great trilogy, La Fontaine with his fables, Racine with his tragedies, Boileau with his satires, were all fighting for the cause of nature and truth in art. Boileau's ninth *Satire* (1668), in which he scattered his feeble foes in one fierce onslaught, and the removal of the interdict on *Tartuffe* in February 1669, gave the victory to the allies. They had won over the public; it only remained for them to storm the citadel of the *Académie française*. The first breach was made by the election of Racine in 1673.

But at the close of the year 1665 Molière fell upon evil days. On the 4th of December he scored a success with Racine's new play of *Alexandre*, and it ran for a fortnight. Then on the 18th he and his company "were surprised"— such is La Grange's temperate expression—to find that there was a simultaneous performance of it at the Hôtel de Bourgogne. It appeared that Racine, dissatisfied with the acting of the Palais-Royal company, had without notice transferred his play to the rival theatre. At the beginning of the next year (1666) Molière, while still smarting from the ingratitude of his friend, had a serious illness, either pleurisy or pneumonia, which left his lungs permanently affected. He had a perpetual cough, of which he makes fun in a well-known passage of *L'Avare*. "Je n'ai pas de grandes incommodités," says Harpagon, "il n'y a que ma fluxion qui me prend de temps en temps," to which Frosine replies, "Votre fluxion ne vous sied pas mal, et vous avez grâce à tousser." Owing to this illness, and then on account of the death of the Queen-Mother, Anne of Austria, which took place on January 20, the Palais-Royal was closed till February 21. Molière must at this time have been at work on his new play, *Le Misanthrope*, which he produced on June 4. Though, like *Tartuffe*, it is essentially a comedy, it contains a large element of seriousness, and even an under-current of tragedy, which is clearly inspired by Molière's own condition. For to the interdict on *Tartuffe* the perfidy of Racine, and his own ill-health, was added what affected him more than all—his estrangement from his wife. The warm-hearted, but irritable and jealous husband, who loved her with the tenderness of a highly sensitive nature, but who knew that his love was not returned, had found his wife's coquetry—there is no evidence to shew that it was anything worse[1]—more than he could endure, and in the previous October, or thereabouts, they had agreed to separate.

In complete contrast to *Le Misanthrope*, with its serious tone and lack of external action, is *Le Médecin malgré lui*, with its broad and often boisterous fun, which was acted with it from September 3. In the winter there were brilliant fêtes at Saint-Germain, which lasted from December 2, 1666 to February 19, 1667. They included a *Ballet des Muses* to which Molière successively contributed *Mélicerte, comédie pastorale héroïque*, of which he only wrote two acts, a *pastorale comique*, of which only a few unimportant fragments have come down to us, and a little comedy of much charm, entitled *Le Sicilien*.

On his return to Paris he had a fresh lung attack, which kept him away from the theatre for two months. When he began to act again, the War of Devolution had begun, and on May 16 the king, followed by the Court, set out

[1] No credence is to be placed on the anonymous libel, *La fameuse comédienne ou Histoire de La Guerin, auparavant Femme et Veuve de Molière*, Frankfort, 1688.

for Flanders. During his absence, while Paris, according to Mme de Sévigné, was " a desert," Molière, on August 5 with the king's permission, produced *Tartuffe*, and promised to repeat it on the following day. But the second performance was forbidden by the first President of the *Parlement*, and though two members of Molière's company went to see the king in Flanders, bearing a petition skilfully worded by their chief, they could not obtain a reversal of the sentence. In this same year the company suffered another blow in the defection of Mlle Du Parc, who after Easter transferred her services to the Hôtel de Bourgogne. Her desertion was naturally attributed to the influence of Racine, who was passionately in love with her, and in whose play of *Andromaque* she appeared in the following November. Her part was the title-rôle, though she was more fitted in temperament for that of Hermione. But if we may believe Boileau, as reported by Brossette, she was not a great actress in tragedy, and had to be carefully coached by Racine. The difficult part of Hermione would have been beyond her powers, but we may hazard a conjecture that the psychological knowledge displayed by Racine in his study of that character was largely derived from his intimacy with this haughty, passionate, and capricious actress. She did not remain long at the Hôtel de Bourgogne, for she died in December 1668.

The whole year, 1667, was anything but a prosperous one for Molière's company. Cor-

neille's play of *Attila*, which they bought for
2000 *livres* on March 4, though it ran for twenty
days, was far from a financial success. When
La Grange and La Thorillière went to Lille in
August, the theatre again closed its doors and
did not reopen them till September 25, when
Molière reappeared in *Le Misanthrope*.

> Molière reprenant courage,
> Malgré la bourrasque et l'orage,
> Sur la scène se fait revoir.

But he did not act for long, and in a new play
by Donneau de Visé, which was produced on
October 28, he had no part.

It seems clear that at this time he was seriously
contemplating retirement. In August of this
year (1667) he acquired a *pied de terre* in the
pretty village—as it then was—of Auteuil. It
consisted of three rooms on the ground-floor—
a dining-room, a kitchen, and a bed-room which
also served as a sitting-room—and two attics in
the second storey, which he rented for 400 *livres*
a year from Jacques de Grou, Sieur de Beaufort,
of whose considerable mansion they practically
formed part. Molière also had the right to walk
in the adjoining park[1]. His friend Chapelle
rented a bed-room in an adjoining building. In
Molière's bed-room were a few books, which at
the time of his death consisted of the *Works* of
Balzac in two volumes, the *Lives* and other
works of Plutarch also in two volumes, Montaigne's *Essays*, Ovid's *Metamorphoses*, He-

[1] See J. Loiseleur, *Les points obscurs de la vie de Molière*,
1877, pp. 318 ff.

liodorus, Herodotus, Diodorus Siculus (two volumes), and Valerius Maximus. All these were folios. Caesar's *Commentaries*, Horace, Rohault's *Traité de physique* (1671), and a book of Travels in the Levant represented the quartos. There were also eighteen volumes in octavo or duodecimo, the titles of which are not stated in the inventory[1]. Here the great dramatist forgot his troubles in the society of his friends. These included Boileau, La Fontaine, Chapelle, who contributed greatly to the gaiety of the gatherings, Lulli, Mignard, Rohault the distinguished physicist, and others of lesser fame.

But if Molière seriously thought of spending the rest of his days in this quiet retreat he changed his mind before the end of the year, and on January 3, 1668 he reappeared on the boards of the Palais-Royal.

> Veux-tu, lecteur, être ébaudi?
> Sois au Palais-Royal Mardi:
> Molière, qu'on idolâtre,
> Y remonte sur son théâtre.

Ten days later he took the part of Sosie in his new play of *Amphitryon*, and in his first speech spoke some lines which, whether they were intended or not, exactly represent his own situation.

> Vers la retraite en vain la raison nous appelle,
> En vain notre dépit quelquefois y consent;
>   Leur vue a sur notre zèle
>   Un ascendant trop puissant,
> Et la moindre faveur d'un coup d'œil caressant
>   Nous rengage de plus belle.

[1] Soulié, p. 284.

His quarrel with the stage was only a lover's quarrel or *dépit amoureux*. He could not resist its call, nor could he desert his company, who looked to him for guidance and encouragement and who largely depended on him for the favour of the public.

The year 1668 was a busy one for Molière. In the course of it he produced besides *Amphitryon*, *George Dandin* (July 18) and *L'Avare* (September 9), the former at Versailles and the latter at his own theatre. It has been remarked that in all three plays a large proportion of the characters are knaves or fools. Moreover, in all three there is an underlying suggestion of tragedy. Amphitryon's dishonour, the unhappy matrimonial venture of George Dandin, the disruption of Harpagon's family life, are tragic themes, though Molière has chosen to look at them, as far as possible, from the comic side. In these plays Molière not only takes a more pessimistic view than he usually does of human nature, but he seems to be deeply impressed, even oppressed, by a sense of the power of evil, and especially of its power to sever the natural bonds of humanity.

But early in 1669 there was a rift in the clouds. On February 5 the king gave permission for *Le Tartuffe* to be performed in public, and that very afternoon it was presented to a crowded house. The receipts amounted to 2860 *livres*, the highest figures ever recorded by La Grange in his Register. It ran without intermission till the Easter holidays, when the accounts shewed that the receipts for the year 1668–1669 were higher than they had been since 1663–1664, and that the share of each actor amounted to 5477 *livres*, a figure which it never reached before or since in Molière's lifetime, and which was more than twice that for the preceding year. After Easter there were fifteen public performances up to June 25, and then, after three performances in August and two in September, it made way for a new piece, *Monsieur de Pourceaugnac*, which was presented at Chambord before the king on October 6 and at the Palais-Royal on November 15.

The festivities at Chambord were followed four months later by similar ones at Saint-Germain, for which Molière provided on February 4 a great spectacular display entitled *Le Divertissement royal* and, as part of this, a *comédie-héroïque* called *Les Amants magnifiques*, which contains at least one scene of delicate comedy and an admirable comic character in the person of Moron, the court buffoon.

After Easter there were some changes in the *personnel* of Molière's company. Louis Béjart, Sieur de l'Éguisé, though he was only in his fortieth year, retired and was voted a yearly pension of 1000 *livres*. His retirement was apparently due to a wound which had left him permanently lame. When Harpagon says of his son's valet, La Flèche "Je ne me plais point à voir ce chien de boiteux-là," there is an evident allusion to the lameness of the actor who created the part. The additions to the company were M. and Mlle Beauval, and Baron. Mlle Beauval was an extremely useful accession ; she was the Nicole of *Le Bourgeois gentilhomme* and the Toinette of *Le Malade imaginaire*. There is a story that at one of the rehearsals for the latter play she complained to Molière that he found fault with everybody except her husband, who was cast for the part of that immortal simpleton, Thomas Diafoirus. "If I did so," replied Molière, "I should spoil his acting ; nature has given him better instruction than mine for the part." This simple minded person had begun his connexion with the stage as a snuffer of candles, and it is said that it was his wife's energy that first made him her husband and then got him an engagement as an actor in a provincial company. More than twenty years later she created the part of Nérine in Regnard's *Le Joueur* (1696). Alike as *soubrette* and as tragedy-queen she maintained her reputation till her retirement in 1704. Her last part was that of Lisette in Regnard's *Les folies amoureuses*. She died in 1720.

Michel Boyron, called Baron, was the son of an actor, and was only in his seventeenth year. Left an orphan at the age of nine, he had been engaged in a juvenile troop, of which the manager was one Raisin. In 1665 Molière, having lent his theatre to them for three performances, and having been struck by the boy's precocity, secured him for his own company, took great

pains with his education, and entrusted him with
the part of Myrtil in *Mélicerte* (1666). But
Mlle de Molière having, it is said, boxed his
ears at a rehearsal, he took offence and after
the performances were over joined a provincial
company. Three and a half years later Molière
brought him back to Paris by means of a *lettre
de cachet* signed by the king and countersigned
by Colbert. The same convenient method pro-
cured him the Beauvals. Baron developed into
a fine actor and an insufferable coxcomb.

Molière was still in high favour with the king,
and the fulfilment of the royal commands took
up nearly his whole time. The *comédie-ballet*
of *Le Bourgeois gentilhomme* was presented at
Chambord on October 14, 1670, *Psyché*, a
tragédie-ballet in which Molière collaborated
with Corneille and Quinault, at the Tuileries on
January 17, 1671, and *La Comtesse d'Escarbagnas*, a little comedy which with a lost *pastorale*
formed part of a great spectacular representation
entitled *Le Ballet des Ballets*, at Saint-Germain
on December 2 of the same year. Between
the two last pieces Molière brought out at the
Palais-Royal on May 24 a new comedy, *Les
Fourberies de Scapin*. It is a free imitation from
the *Phormio* of Terence, but the main influences
are partly national and partly Italian. Nowhere
does Molière's genius for gay comedy of a farcical
type display itself more convincingly.

On February 17, 1672 Molière and his company suffered a great loss by the death of

Madeleine Béjart. After certain charitable bequests and small annuities to her brother Louis and her sister Geneviève[1], she left all her property, amounting to 17,800 *livres* in ready money, besides plate and jewels to the value of 3000 *livres*, to Molière's wife. Before her death, probably about the end of the year 1671, a reconciliation had taken place between the ill-matched couple, and a son was born to them on September 15, 1672, but he only survived till October 11[2]. Molière was now a rich man, and on October 1 he moved into a large house in the Rue Richelieu, of which he rented the greater portion for 1300 *livres*. The only comedy from his own pen that he produced in 1672 was *Les Femmes savantes*, which ran at the Palais-Royal from March 11 to the Easter holidays, and after the holidays till the middle of May. In the summer his health became worse, and La Grange notes that the theatre was closed from August 9 to 12 owing to "the indisposition of M. de Molière." According to a well-known story, the authority for which is Cizeron Rival[3], the editor of the correspondence between Boileau and Brossette, Boileau paid him a visit in December,

[1] Soulié, pp. 258–9.

[2] Molière's eldest boy, Louis, to whom the king stood godfather, was born on January 17, 1664, and died in the following November. He also had a daughter, Esprit Madeleine, baptised on August 4, 1665, who married in 1705 Claude Rachel, Sieur de Montalant, and died without issue in 1723.

[3] *Recréations littéraires ou anecdotes et remarques sur différents sujets*, recueillis par M. C. R***, Lyons, 1765, pp. 19–20. Pages 1–26, 64, 65, 153–155 relate to Molière.

and noticing his cough and distressed breathing urged him to leave the stage. But Molière replied that it was a point of honour with him not to give up, revealing in these simple words his passion for his art and his devotion to the interests of his company. So with the same courage and defiance with which he had met the attacks of his opponents he now faced the last enemy—death. Just as in *Le Misanthrope* he had mocked at his own misanthropic humour, so now he made sport of his own malady, and on Feb. 10, 1673 he produced at the Palais-Royal the *comédie-ballet* of *Le Malade imaginaire*.

This admirable play shews him in full possession of his dramatic powers. The execution is large and easy; the characters and the dialogue are extraordinarily true to life, and the wealth of comic action makes it an excellent acting play. Moreover in that lyricism of laughter, as Sainte-Beuve calls it, in that exuberance of comedy in which Molière's only rivals are Aristophanes and Rabelais, it is the equal of *M. de Pourceaugnac* and *Le Bourgeois gentilhomme.* The attack on the doctors is fiercer than ever; as La Grange says, after laughing at doctors individually in several plays Molière now laughed at the whole Faculty of Medicine. But, underneath all this boisterous gaiety lay a grim and cruel humour. The actor, who played the part of the imaginary invalid, who excited the laughter of the audience, as he now ran shouting about the stage, now dropped exhausted into his chair,

was in reality a dying man. On February 17,
the fourth representation of the comedy, he
was suffering more than usual, and his wife and
Baron urged him not to act. "What would you
have me do?" he said, "there are fifty poor
workmen who have nothing to live on but their
day's wages. What will happen to them, if I do
not act?"[1] So he went to the theatre, but just
before the close of the piece he had a sudden
seizure, and it was only by a great effort that
he got through his part. When the play was
over he was carried in a chair to his house in
the Rue Richelieu accompanied by Baron.
The play had begun punctually at four o'clock,
so that it must by this time have been nearly
seven. He asked for some bread and Parmesan
cheese, and when he had eaten them he had himself put to bed. His cough then redoubled in
violence, and he broke a blood-vessel in his
lungs. Baron went to fetch his wife, and a servant was told to find a priest to administer the
Sacrament. But in about three-quarters of an
hour after the attack, before the arrival of either
wife or priest, he died in the arms of two Sisters
of Charity, who were staying in the house as
his guests. He was only fifty-one years of age.

Since Molière was an actor and had died
unshriven, the *curé* of Saint-Eustache, in accordance with the ordinances of the Church,

---

[1] Grimarest, evidently on the authority of Baron. And cp. the
shorter accounts of La Grange and Vivot in the *Vie en abrégé* and
of La Grange in his Register.

refused him Christian burial. Thereupon his widow appealed to the Archbishop of Paris, representing to him that Molière had died with Christian sentiments, that he had received the Sacrament at the Easter before his death from the Abbé Bernard of Saint-Germain l'Auxerrois, who was his confessor[1], that immediately he felt himself to be dying he had sent for a priest, that two had declined to answer the summons, and that the third had arrived too late. Mlle Molière also addressed a petition to the king, and it was almost certainly by his wishes that the Archbishop so far overruled his subordinates as to permit a religious ceremony of the barest kind. The funeral was to be after dark and without any pomp; the body was to be taken straight to the cemetery, and there was to be no service in any church. A touch of irony was added to this grudging concession by the fact that Harlay de Champvallon, the Archbishop, was a notorious evil-liver[2].

[1] Strictly the Sacrament should not have been administered unless Molière had renounced his profession. "On prive des sacraments, et à la vie et à la mort, ceux qui jouent la comédie, s'ils ne renoncent à leur art;...par une suite infaillible, la sepulture ecclésiastique leur est déniée" (Bossuet, Maximes et réflexions sur la comédie). But before the repeal of the Edict of Nantes, the clergy were laxer in these matters, and we may be sure that no such renunciation was exacted from Molière. Doubtless, also, it was not exacted from either Joseph or Madeleine Béjart on their death-beds. (See Despois, op. cit. p. 219; Brunetière, Études critiques I, 141-3.)

[2] When John Kemble died in 1823, Talma sent a subscription to his proposed monument in Westminster Abbey, with the remark: "Pour moi, je serai heureux si les prêtres me laissent enterrer dans un coin de mon jardin" (Fanny Kemble, Record of

Such is the bare outline of Molière's life. A few details may be added by way of an attempt to fill in the picture. The only written description of his outward appearance that we have from a contemporary appeared in the *Mercure de France* nearly seventy years after his death. The author, Mlle Poisson, a daughter of the actor Du Croisy, had acted with him in *Psyché*, and had joined his company in 1673. " He was," she says, " neither too fat nor too thin ; he was tall rather than short ; he had a noble bearing and a well-turned leg. He walked with a grave and serious air. He had a large nose and mouth, thick lips, and a dark complexion. His eye-brows were black and strongly-marked, and the way he moved them made his physiognomy extremely comic[1]." This description is borne out by the portrait at Chantilly, which is generally ascribed to his friend Mignard, and which is certainly the best that exists. One is particularly struck by its serious and sad expression. We know indeed from other sources that Molière often wore a melancholy look, and that he was usually silent in general company. " Il ne parlait guère en compagnie," says La Grange, "à moins qu'il ne se trouva avec quelqu'un pour qui il eût une estime particulière. Cela faisait dire à ceux qui ne le connaissaient pas qu'il

a Girlhood I, 106). About the same time, records the same writer, there was a serious riot at the funeral of an actor named Philippe, to whom the Archbishop of Paris had refused burial in consecrated ground, and the Archbishop had to give way.

[1] *Mercure de France*, May 1740 (cited in *Œuvres* III, 383).

était rêveur et mélancolique," and with this we may compare a passage from *La Critique de l'École des Femmes*, in which Molière says of himself "vous connaissez l'homme et sa naturelle paresse à soutenir la conversation." But it will be observed that La Grange says it was those who did not know him who thought he was a dreamer and melancholy. Molière, in fact, was an observer and a thinker rather than a dreamer, and though the vicissitudes of his life and his observation of human nature had given him no little cause for sadness, he was at bottom a laughing and not a weeping philosopher. The following passage from Chappuzeau's *Le Théâtre français*, which, as has been said, was published in 1674, shews in what a high estimation he was held as a man by his contemporaries. After praising him as a writer and an actor, Chappuzeau goes on to say: "In addition to these great qualities necessary to a poet and an actor, he had those of a true gentleman ; he was generous and a good friend, polite and honourable in all his actions, modest in the reception of praise, learned without wishing to appear so, and he talked with such charm and ease that the first men of the Court and the Town were delighted to converse with him."

In Grimarest's anecdotes—some of which, as coming from Baron and relating to the last years of Molière's life when the young actor was living in his house, may be accepted as substantially true—Molière is always on the side of reason and moderation and common sense. The most improbable of these anecdotes, but the best authenticated, for it is also told by Louis Racine, is the well-known one of the supper-party at Auteuil. It tells how Chapelle unexpectedly brought Boileau, Lulli, and two other friends to supper with Molière, and how the latter, being on a milk diet, drank his glass of milk and retired early to bed, leaving Chapelle to do the honours. Hard drinking followed, till the friends, becoming more and more gloomy, instead of more and more hilarious, finally decided to get rid of life altogether by drowning themselves in the river. On some countrymen trying to prevent them a free fight ensued, till Molière, who had been summoned by Baron, persuaded them that so noble a design should be carried out in the full light of day. So they went quietly to bed[1]. Another story, in which figure Molière, Chapelle, and a lay-friar, represents Molière as disputing with his friend on the respective merits of Descartes and Gassendi as philosophers, Molière being for Descartes and Chapelle for Gassendi[2].

Molière was generous with his money and charitable to the poor. His pecuniary relations with his father testify not only to his generosity, but to his delicacy. He not only did not claim

---

[1] Grimarest, pp. 82–9; Racine, ed. P. Mesnard, *Œuvres* I, It is a little puzzling that Louis Racine says that Boileau used to refer to this incident as a *folie de jeunesse*. Grimarest does not mention Boileau as being one of the party.

[2] Grimarest, pp. 116–20.

from his father the residue, amounting to about
1500 *livres*, of his share in his mother's fortune,
but he repaid 2800 *livres* of what he had
already received from him[1]. Further, in 1668,
six months before his father's death, he lent him
through a friend, without his own name appearing in the transaction, 10,000 *livres* for the purpose of rebuilding a house which was tumbling
down[2].

Molière's liberality with his money is all the
more praiseworthy, because it was that of a man
who was orderly and careful about details in
every department of life. He insisted on ex-
actitude and precision in his domestic life. A
window opened or shut at the wrong moment
made him furious, and the misplacement of a
book was enough to prevent him from working
for a fortnight. So says Grimarest, with evident
exaggeration, but we find the same love of precision and the same irritability in Molière's relations with his troop. At rehearsals he spared
no pains to bring his actors up to his own high
standard of perfection. Of his manner and method
we get an excellent idea from *L'Impromptu de
Versailles*. At the very outset he depicts his
own irritability, "La peste soit des gens!" "Je
crois que je deviendrai fou avec tous ces gens-ci."
"Ah! les étranges animaux à conduire que des
comédiens!" And then we see how cleverly he
indicates to each actor the idea underlying his
part, and how in some cases he enforces his

[1] Soulié, pp. 64–5.   [2] *Ib.* pp. 65, 218–20.

advice with a stroke of irony or criticism. When Mlle Du Parc protests that no one in the world is less affected than she is, he replies, "Quite true, and so you can shew all the better what an excellent actress you are by representing a part which is so contrary to your nature." Then he advises Brécourt "to gesticulate as little as he possibly can," and to Mlle Du Croisy he says: "Your part is that of one of those women who always give a passing dig at their neighbours, and who are loath to leave them with a good reputation. *It is a part in which you will acquit yourself fairly well, I think.*" But actors and actresses alike forgave him his irritability and his little *coups de langue* because they recognised his goodness of heart, and his unswerving loyalty to his comrades.

As regards Molière's own powers as an actor contemporary testimony is fairly unanimous. In tragedy he was not regarded as a success. In the first place his physical appearance was not suited to the part of a tragic hero.

> Les mains sur les côtés d'un air peu négligé,
> La tête sur le dos comme un mulet chargé,
> Les yeux fort égarés, puis débitant ses rôles
> D'un hoquet éternel sépare ses paroles.

This portrait of Molière as Caesar in Corneille's *Pompée*, which occurs in the younger Montfleury's *L'Impromptu de l'Hôtel de Condé*, represents the ill-natured criticism of a rival company, but it contains, no doubt, a certain element of truth[1]. Secondly, Molière's elocution in tragedy was too natural to please the public of his day, accustomed as it was to the declamatory methods of the Hôtel de Bourgogne. "Il faut dire tes choses avec emphase," he says, in the *Impromptu de Versailles* just before he begins his imitation of Montfleury *père*. "Là, appuyez comme il faut le dernier vers. Voilà ce qui attire l'approbation et fait faire le brouhaha."

But as a comic actor he was supreme. His expressive countenance, his large mouth and eloquent eyes, all lent themselves to that power of impersonation of which he was so great a master. "Il était tout comédien," says *Le Mercure galant* just after his death, "depuis les pieds jusqu'à la tête. Il semblait qu'il eût plusieurs voix; tout parlait en lui; et, d'un pas, d'un sourire, d'un clin d'œil et d'un remuement de tête il faisait plus concevoir de choses que le plus grand parleur n'aurait pu dire en une heure." Fastidious critics, indeed, said that he was *un peu grimacier*, that he made too much play with his features. But Grimarest, who reports this, adds that Molière would probably have replied that the ordinary public liked exaggeration. The criticism, however, is interesting, because it bears out what is evident from a study of Molière's plays that he had learnt from the Italian comedians the great value of gesture and movement. Grimarest, like Montfleury, notes the hiccough

---

[1] Compare Mignard's portrait of Molière in the same part at the Comédie Française.

or spasm of the throat from which he suffered, and explains it by saying that when he first began to act he noticed that his utterance was too rapid, and that the hiccough resulted from his efforts to counteract this defect[1].

The hiccough is also mentioned by Mlle Poisson[2] and the same cause is given for it. She also tells us that nature had refused him the physical gifts necessary for the stage, and especially for tragic parts, for he had naturally a voice without resonance, with metallic inflexions. But he conquered these difficulties by study and force of will, and became a great comic actor. "Not only did he please in the parts of Mascarille, Sganarelle, Hali, &c.; he was also excellent in characters of high comedy, such as those of Arnolphe, Orgon, Harpagon. It was in these parts that by the truth of his sentiments, by the intelligence of his expression, and by every refinement of art, he fascinated his audience so completely that they did not distinguish the person represented from the actor who represented him."

But there was another and deeper reason than the careful study of his art which made Molière so admirable an actor of comic, and especially of humorous parts, and that was his innate simplicity. He was always thinking of his characters and never of himself. He did not mind appearing ridiculous on the stage, or even of appear-

---

[1] Grimarest, pp. 109–14. His authority is doubtless Baron.
[2] See above, p. 40.

ing in the character of a downright fool. Quick
though he was to detect folly, he observed it
with a sympathetic eye. This is the essence of
humour, and without humour he could neither
have conceived nor have interpreted many of his
characters.

Thus Molière's company adored their chief as
a staunch friend and an incomparable actor.
"Tous les acteurs aimaient le sieur Molière, leur
chef, qui joignait à un mérite et à une capacité
extraordinaire une honnêteté et une manière
engageante qui les obligea tous à lui présenter
qu'ils voulaient courir sa fortune, et qu'ils ne le
quitteraient jamais, quelque proposition qu'on
leur fît et quelque avantage qu'ils pussent trouver
ailleurs[1]." So wrote La Grange in his Register
at that critical stage in the company's fortunes
when the Petit-Bourbon was being pulled down
and the Palais-Royal was under repair, and when
the rival actors of the Hôtel de Bourgogne and
the Marais were trying to sow dissension among
them and to attract them to their own theatres.
To La Grange, as of right, may be left the last
word in praise of his chief. The thirteen years
which followed only cemented more closely the
ties between Molière and his company.

[1] *Registre*, p. 26.

NOTE ON THE AUTHORITIES FOR MOLIÈRE'S LIFE

The only biography of Molière that can in any sense be called contemporary is the short life (*Vie de Molière en abrégé*) which serves as a preface to the edition of his works published by La Grange and Vivot in 1682[1]. We may assume that La Grange was mainly responsible for this life. At any rate it comes to us with the authority of this loyal, honourable, and business-like member of Molière's company. It is, however, very short, and it confines itself almost entirely to a bare narrative of facts. In 1705 a Paris teacher of languages named Grimarest[2], who also acted as a *cicerone*, ignoring or ignorant of this modest preface, published what he claimed to be the first life of Molière. As he was born, according to Jal, in 1658 or 1659, he was only thirteen at Molière's death, and his chief authority was the actor Baron, who was very intimate with Molière during the last three years of his life. Boileau's severe criticism of Grimarest is, on the whole, justified. In matters of fact he trips again and again, and he is quite uncritical. Some of his anecdotes and traits of character coming from Baron may be accepted as substantially true, but though they

---

[1] Printed in *Molière jugé par ses contemporains*, ed. A. P.-Malassis, 1877.

[2] Jean-Leonor de Gallois, Sieur de Grimarest. A reprint of his book was published in 1877 with a notice by A. P.-Malassis.

confirm what we know from other sources they add very little to our knowledge of Molière's character[1].

No further attempt was made to add to our knowledge of Molière's life till the nineteenth century, when an ex-commissioner of police, named Louis-François Beffara, who had come much into contact with actors and dramatic authors, and who held Molière in peculiar veneration, unearthed from the parish registers a fresh series of facts and dates relating to his hero. He published the fruit of his researches in 1821 under the title of *Dissertation sur J.-B. Poquelin Molière*. This was soon followed by a careful and conscientious life, *Histoire de la vie et des ouvrages de Molière*, by Jules Taschereau, editor of the *Revue rétrospective* and Director-General of the *Bibliothèque Nationale*. The first edition appeared in 1825, and the fifth, revised and enlarged, in 1863. In 1847 and 1848 Anaïs Bazin, author of a history of France under Louis XIII, published in the *Revue des deux mondes* his *Notes historiques sur la vie de Molière*. This appeared in book form in 1849, and again, revised and augmented from the author's marginal notes, in 1851. Bazin who, according to a friend, resembled Scott's Antiquary, and who was a man of *esprit* and critical precision[2], did good service by clearing away the

[1] See my article in the *Modern Language Review* for October 1918 (XIII, 439 ff.).
[2] See Sainte-Beuve, *Causeries du Lundi* IV, 464 ff.

rubbish which had collected since Grimarest's time, and by testing some of that biographer's stories in the light of historical knowledge. But he hazarded some unsound conjectures of his own, especially with regard to Molière's marriage, a question which his misanthropic and cynical pose and his dread of ridicule—in all of which he reminds one of Mérimée—made him unfitted to discuss.

The next step was taken by Eudore Soulié, who, supplementing the researches of Beffara, found in the archives of notaries and public offices various legal documents, such as wills, contracts, inventories, which add considerably to our knowledge of Molière's life. His *Recherches sur Molière et sa famille* appeared in 1863. In the same year Louis Moland published the first edition of his *Œuvres complètes de Molière* with a disjointed biography, which appeared in a more connected form in 1885 and 1892. Thoroughly trustworthy, it is on the whole the most compact and convenient life of the poet. During the decade from 1879 to 1889 *Le Moliériste*, under the editorship of Georges Monval, made many useful contributions to the elucidation of small points, and in the latter year the great edition of the *Œuvres de Molière* by the late Eugène Despois and M. Paul Mesnard was enriched by the addition of a *Notice biographique* (vol. x) from the pen of the surviving editor. It contains all the available information on the subject, thoroughly examined and discussed, but its character and method render it a book rather to consult with profit than to read with pleasure. Finally we have in English the *Life of Molière* by Henry M. Trollope, 1905, which for the thoroughness and accuracy of its information and the fairness with which it handles disputed points leaves little to be desired.

CHAPTER II

In spite of the efforts made by the Pleiad in the second half of the sixteenth century to introduce literary comedy into France, the only form of comedy that flourished at the Hôtel de Bourgogne, Paris's one regular theatre, under the management of Valleran Lecomte (1599–1622) was pure farce. His comic *répertoire* was composed chiefly of old medieval farces modified under the influence of the Italian companies which from time to time visited France. Three actors were special favourites with the public, Robert Guérin, known as Gros-Guillaume, Hugues Guérin, known as Gaultier-Garguille, and Henri Legrand, who acted under the name of Turlupin. In 1628, the year in which Valleran Lecomte, after six years' absence, returned to the Hôtel de Bourgogne, his company was joined by an actor, whose real name was Pierre Le Messier, but who was known on the stage as Bellerose. He aimed at a more refined style of acting than that of the popular favourites, and, though he sometimes played in farce, his bent was towards tragedy and serious comedy. Soon after joining

the company he succeeded Valleran Lecomte as
manager, and to some extent replaced in the
public estimation the famous trio, all of whom
died about the year 1634.

About the same time the stage began to
increase in reputation, largely owing to the
patronage of Richelieu, and several new writers
made their *début* both in tragedy and comedy.
Among these was Pierre Corneille, who in *Mélite*
(1629) produced "with surprising success" what
he rightly describes as "a new kind of comedy."
It is perfectly decent; it attempts to portray real
life and contemporary society; its only theme is
love; and it is absolutely devoid of the comic spirit.
It was followed from 1632 to 1634 by four
comedies of a similar type. The example of
Corneille and the influence of Louis XIII and
Richelieu combined to banish indecency from
the comic stage. About 1630 the younger female
parts began to be played by women, and a few
years later it became the fashion for ladies to
witness the performance of comedies.

Of the comedies other than Corneille's, produced about this time, Rotrou's *Les Sosies*
(1636) and Desmarets's *Les Visionnaires* (1637),
both of which furnished hints to Molière, were
extremely popular. Their gaiety must have
helped Corneille to realise that if comedy was to
compete successfully with farce it must employ
the element of laughter. Consequently *Le
Menteur*, which he produced in the winter of
1643–44, is, except for a single scene, comic

throughout. And some of the scenes are master-pieces of genuine comedy. Indeed, as Brunetière has pointed out, Corneille has made his play too comic, and by so doing has missed reality.

During the fifteen years which elapsed between the production of *Le Menteur* and Molière's return to Paris, the chief writers for the comic stage were Scarron and the younger Corneille. In the plays of both there was a strong element of farce and burlesque; indeed, in those of Scarron, which were for the most part written for the popular low comedian whose stage name was Jodelet[1], it largely predominated. There is a similar exaggeration of the comic spirit in Cyrano de Bergerac's *Le Pedant joué*. In only two plays of this period do we find any trace of real obser-vation of life and society, namely, in Thomas Corneille's *L'Amour à la mode* (1651 or 1652) and in the first two acts of Boisrobert's *La belle Plaideuse* (1654)[2].

Molière was indebted to his immediate pre-decessors, as will appear later, rather for hints and direct borrowings than for any real influence on the character of his art. His debt to Italian comedy was much more fundamental. Ever since the reign of Henry III, Italian companies had been in the habit of visiting France, especially the capital. It was such a company which, under the direction of Giuseppe Bianchi, shared, as

---

[1] See above, pp. 15–16.
[2] I have attempted a sketch of the comedy of this period in *From Montaigne to Molière*, 1908, chap. VIII.

we have seen, the Salle du Petit-Bourbon with Molière's troop. Their first visit to Paris was from 1645 to 1647, their next from 1653 to 1659. Then after an absence of three years they returned again in 1662. They were very popular, and were especial favourites with Louis XIV, who gave them a subvention of 15,000 *livres*. The chief fare which they provided was not the written comedy of Ariosto and his successors, but the *Commedia dell' Arte*, in which instead of a complete written dialogue there was only a rough sketch of the plot called the *scenario*. This had to be filled out by the improvisation of the actors, a task that was rendered easier by the fact that there were none but stock characters. A complete company comprised nine of these, a Pantaloon or Doctor, two buffoons or *zanni*, who varied somewhat both in type and name, a Scaramouche, who was at once a swaggerer and a coward, two male lovers, and three female characters, two serious and one comic[1]. In Bianchi's company the part of Scaramouche became identified with one Tiberio Fiurelli, who was a great favourite with Louis XIV, while that of the buffoon was represented successively by Domenico Locatelli as Trivelino, and by Giuseppe Biancolelli, called Domenico, as Arlecchino. The latter, who off the stage was a man of serious and melancholy temperament and

---

[1] In England Scaramouche was superseded by the Clown. The most recent work on the subject is Winifred Smith, *The Commedia dell' Arte*, Columbia University Press, New York, 1912.

distinguished manners, became very famous. He lived till 1688.

There was a great deal of rough horse-play in the performances of these Italian actors. They also used plenty of gesture, which was very helpful in playing to an audience that did not understand their language.

This particular Italian company had only been a short time in Paris when Molière left for the provinces, but two members of it, Scaramouche and Brigida Bianchi (who acted under the name of Aurelia) had previously paid a visit to the capital in 1639 and 1640. Moreover Molière must have had plenty of opportunities of witnessing the performances of Italian actors at Lyons and other towns in the south of France. Even after his return to Paris he seems to have had a predilection for Scaramouche, who did not retire from the stage till 1691 at the age of eighty-three. It was, indeed, made a charge against him in *Élomire hypocondre* that he carefully studied the "contorsions and postures" of this celebrated actor of farce, and beneath the portrait of the latter engraved by Vermeulen may be read the following quatrain:

> Cet illustre comédien
> Atteignit de son art l'agréable manière.
> Il fut le maître de Molière,
> Et la nature fut le sien.

Whatever exaggeration there may be in this, there is no doubt that Molière learnt from the

Italian actors the value of movement and gesture, especially in comedy, and this knowledge affected not only his acting but his writing. A capital example of this is *Le Bourgeois gentilhomme*, in which the dialogue is often reduced to a minimum.

But the Italian *Commedia dell' Arte* was not the only school of popular acting that Molière attended. As a boy he might just have seen the favourites of the Hôtel de Bourgogne, for Gros-Guillaume died in 1633, and Gaultier-Garguille in the year following. There were also the charlatans and mountebanks who performed on the Pont-Neuf and the neighbouring Place Dauphine, and there was the theatre of the famous Foire de Saint-Germain.

From 1634 the Hôtel de Bourgogne, the home of tragi-comedy and farce, had a rival in the Théâtre du Marais in the Rue Vieille du Temple, where a new company with less conservative tastes, of which the chief actor was Mondory, produced Mairet's *Sophonisbe*, Corneille's comedies, the immortal *Cid*, and Scarron's burlesques, the earliest of these latter, *Jodelet ou le Maître-Valet*, being presented in 1645, the year of Molière's departure from Paris. At the Hôtel de Bourgogne he might have seen Rotrou's *Les Sosies* (1636), which rivalled the *Cid* in popularity, and Corneille's *Cinna* (1640) and *Polyeucte* (winter of 1642–3).

Molière's first attempts at dramatic authorship were of a humble character. During the early years of his provincial wanderings he only tried his hand at simple farces, such as those which had been once so popular at the Hôtel de Bourgogne. One of these was *Le Docteur amoureux*, which was afterwards played with *Nicomède* before the king on the first appearance of Molière's company at Paris, and which so charmed the Court by its novelty. For, says La Grange, "it was a long time since there was any talk of these little comedies." And the same authority tells us that Molière composed this and other similar pieces "sur quelques idées plaisantes sans y avoir mis la dernière main; et il trouva à propos de les supprimer, lorsqu'il se fut proposé pour but dans toutes ses pièces d'obliger les hommes à se corriger de leurs défauts." Two pieces, however, of the character indicated by La Grange, have escaped destruction, and have since 1845 been included among Molière's works. These are *Le Médecin volant* and *La Jalousie du Barbouillé*. The former, which is developed from an Italian *scenario*[1], *Il medico volante*, contains the germs of *L'Amour Médecin* and *Le Médecin malgré lui*. It has a more or less complete plot, but there are gaps in the text which shew that something was left to the improvisation of the actors. *La Jalousie du Barbouillé*, the theme of which together with three whole scenes was utilised by Molière for *George Dandin*, has the well-known stock character of the pedant-doctor, which

---

[1] This *scenario* must be an earlier form of that of Domenico Biancolelli translated by Gueulette, for the famous Harlequin did not come to Paris till 1662. (See Molière, *Œuvres* I, 47–9.)

points to an Italian original, but in its loose construction—it is a series of short scenes with little attempt at a plot—and in its general tone it resembles a medieval farce. In one scene at least the comedy is of a more elevated type, and the dialogue, though for the most part rough and careless, sometimes bears the impress of Molière's riper genius.

Other similar farces, whether he composed them or not, formed part of his *répertoire*, but we know only by name *Les trois Docteurs rivaux* and *Le Docteur pédant*, both of which are possibly varieties of *Le Docteur amoureux* or even the same piece; *Le Maître d'école* which may be the same as *Gros-René écolier* and *Gros-René petit enfant*; *Gorgibus dans le sac*, the embryo perhaps of *Les Fourberies de Scapin*; and *Le Fagoteux* or *Le Fagotier*, which became *Le Médecin malgré lui*. It is noticeable, first, that the names in these farces, Gorgibus, Sganarelle, Gros-René (the stage name, it will be remembered, of the actor Du Parc) are thoroughly French and were used by Molière in later plays; and secondly, that *La Jalousie du Barbouillé*, except that it is in prose instead of verse, comes very near to the description by Gaston Paris of a typical medieval farce. It is, he says, "the representation in verse of a scene in private life; it is short and has few characters; it generally introduces us to the interior of a lower middle-class household; and it especially delights in depicting the infidelity and deceit of women."

In spite of the strong leaning towards French medieval farce which these experiments shewed, Molière's first regular comedy was thoroughly Italian in character. This is not surprising when we remember that it was produced at Lyons, where, in consonance with its strong Italian traditions and proclivities, various Italian companies had popularised their *répertoire*. The particular Italian play upon which Molière founded his comedy of *L'Étourdi* was entitled *L'Inavvertito*. Its author, Nicolò Barbieri, called Beltrame, had been a member of a company, known as *I Comici Fedeli*, which had paid three visits to Paris in the reign of Louis XIII, the last being in 1624–1625. Later Beltrame, having left the troop, formed one of his own, and came with it to Paris, where he received a very favourable welcome, about 1630. His *L'Inavvertito* was printed at Turin in 1629[1]. In Molière's version of it there are only two characters of any importance, Lélie, the lover, and Mascarille, the valet. As Sarcey has pointed out, Lélie is a blunderer rather than an *étourdi*; he is thoughtless, stupid, and unlucky. There are certain contradictions in his character which make for humour, but it cannot be said that he is a complete character any more than Dorante in *Le Menteur*. Mascarille, though more or less conventional, and closely modelled on the Scappino of the Italian play, is very much alive. The

[1] For an analysis see Moland, *Molière et la comédie italienne*, 2nd ed. 1867, pp. 146–59.

character which he gives himself of *Fourbum imperator* is thoroughly deserved. He has few scruples and infinite resources. He is a descendant of Panurge and an ancestor of Figaro. As for the play, which has for an alternative title *Les Contretemps*, it consists wholly in variations on the same theme, the ruin of Mascarille's brilliant schemes through his master's stupidity. It has no real plot and it only comes to an end because it has been long enough. But thanks to Molière's inexhaustible verve and comic power, it never drags and though it stands low in the list of Molière's plays as regards the number of performances, yet when it was revived in recent times, with Coquelin in the part of Mascarille and Delaunay in that of Lélie, it met with a notable success. In style and versification *L'Étourdi* stands very high among Molière's plays. Nowhere is that faculty of rhyming without apparent effort, which called forth Boileau's admiring

Enseigne-moi, Molière, où tu trouves la rime,

more brilliantly displayed. The language is remarkable not only for its energy and comic force, but for its expressive imagery. It was this which commended it to Victor Hugo, and caused him to regret that Molière had gradually abandoned "this luminous style" for the more prosaic and more abstract style of his later plays. But, as M. Rigal points out, the more prosaic style is better suited to the comedy of truth and ob-

servation, which was Molière's real business.
Those who claim for Racine a highly poetical
style forget that the psychological analysis of
the passions of ordinary men and women requires
a style *"qui rase la prose."* But to return to
L'Étourdi, note the expressive vigour of the
following:

> D'un chêne grand et fort,
> Dont près de deux cent ans ont fait déjà le sort,
> Je viens de détacher une branche admirable,
> Choisi expressément de grosseur raisonnable,
> Dont j'ai fait sur le champ avec beaucoup d'ardeur
> Un bâton à peu près; oui, de cette grandeur;
> Moins gros par l'un des bouts, mais plus que trente gaules,
> Propre, comme je pense, à rosser les épaules;
> Car il est bien en main, vert, noueux et massif[1].

Note, too, the picturesque force of the following
metaphor:

> Attaché dessus vous comme un joueur de boule
> Après le mouvement de la sienne qui roule,
> Je pensais retenir toutes vos actions
> En faisant de mon corps mille contorsions[2].

Once we touch a graver note, namely in the
fine speech by Anselme—a father worthy of
Géronte in *Le Menteur*—in which he sets before
Léandre the dangers of a rash and uncontrolled
passion[3].

But if *L'Étourdi* is even more brilliant than
Le Menteur, it is in a still less degree a national
comedy. The reference to Parisian localities
and buildings, and the description of Parisian
manners and customs, which give a certain local

[1] Act IV, Sc. 5.   [1] Act IV, Sc. 4.   [3] Act IV, Sc. 3.

colour to Corneille's play, are here entirely absent. The scene is laid at Messina—in the Italian original it is Naples—but it might just as well have been laid at Baghdad for all the connexion that the characters have with the real world. It is the world of conventional Italian comedy, and the pure Italianism of the play is shewn among other things by the very subordinate part played by the two female characters.

For his next production, *Le Dépit amoureux*, Molière again turned to Italy, selecting this time a play with a complicated plot, *L'Interesse* or Cupidity, by Nicolò Secchi[1]. But he tacked on to it an addition of his own, which is far superior to the part that he borrowed[2]. From this was constructed in the eighteenth century a two-act comedy, which forms part of the present *répertoire* of the *Théâtre français*. In the scenes of which it is composed Molière has abandoned the traditional comedy of intrigue for the portrayal of the natural sentiments of ordinary men and women. They include the famous double lover's quarrel from which the piece takes its title. The same theme was utilised again in *Le Tartuffe* and *Le Bourgeois gentilhomme*, but the first version is the best. The contrast between the two parts of the play is well represented by the difference in character between the two valets, Mascarille and Gros-René. Mascarille is the brilliant and resourceful rascal with his ready flow of wit and reason that we already

[1] Printed at Venice, 1581.   [2] Act I; II, Sc. 4; III, Sc. 2–4.

know; Gros-René is a more homely personage, but he is more sympathetic and more human. If he has less wit than his rival, he has more humour. Mascarille is a pure Italian type, Gros-René represents the *esprit gaulois*, the spirit of the *fabliau* and the farce.

Whatever the shortcomings of *L'Étourdi* and *Le Dépit amoureux*, their favourable acceptance, when they were presented at the Petit-Bourbon, after the unsuccessful performances of several of Corneille's tragedies, made it evident to Molière that the Parisian public preferred to see him and his company in comedy. Not that he abandoned tragedy altogether, but when he produced *Cinna* on November 18, 1659, he gave as an after-piece a new comedy of his own composition. That *Les Précieuses ridicules* was new there can be no doubt. Grimarest's statement that it had been played in the provinces several years before is worth nothing in the face of the positive declaration of La Grange and Vivot that "en 1659 M. de Molière fit la comédie des *Précieuses*." It will be seen that they call it a *comedy*, and so it is called in the printed edition. But Mlle Des Jardins (Mme de Villedieu), in an interesting account of the first performance which she printed in 1660, calls it a *farce*, and, whatever name Molière gave to it in the original *affiche*, a farce it undoubtedly is; for "it arouses laughter by an exaggerated representation of the ridiculous." This is especially true of Molière's costume in the part of Mascarille, which is thus described by Mlle Des Jardins:

His wig was so large that it swept the ground every time he made a bow, and his hat was so small that it was easy to see that he carried it more often in his hand than on his head. His collar (*rabat*) might pass for a smart *peignoir*, and the ruffles at his knee seemed made for children to hide in when playing hide and seek....His shoes were so covered with ribbons that I cannot say whether they were made of Russian leather, or English calf, or morocco; all I know is that they were half a foot high, and that I was puzzled to understand how heels so high and slender could support the Marquis's body, ribbons, ruffles, and powder.

Not only does *Les Précieuses ridicules* answer to the general definition of a farce, but it is a direct descendant of the French medieval farce, inasmuch as it is a scene rather than a complete play and it represents the interior of a middle-class household[1]. Moreover, in accordance with the traditions of the national comedy two-thirds of the characters are named after the actors who played the parts. The two lovers are called La Grange and Du Croisy, the two *précieuses* are Madelon, after Madeleine Béjart, and Cathos, after Catherine de Brie. Marotte, the servant, is the theatrical name of Marie Ragueneau, daughter of the celebrated Cyprien Ragueneau, pastry-cook, poet, and actor, and Jodelet we know already. Of the other three characters, Almanzor is the high-flown appellation which the *précieuses* gave to their lackey, borrowing it from Gomberville's heroic romance of *Alexandre*.

[1] See above, p. 59.

Gorgibus is a name—it is a real and not an invented name—which Molière had already used for an elderly *bourgeois* in his two early farces, and Mascarille is already familiar to us from *L'Étourdi* and *Le Dépit amoureux*. We are told that the name is derived from the Spanish *mascarilla*, a mask covering the upper part of the face, and that Molière played the part in a mask. But a reference has been found to "a little book entitled *Les Œuvres du marquis de Mascarille*," Lyons, 1620, though unfortunately the book itself cannot be traced. Apart from this, it is difficult to believe that Molière wore a mask, and in fact Brissart's illustration of this play in the 1682 edition of Molière's works represents him as without a mask.

In another and more important sense the new play is a descendant of the medieval farce. The latter sometimes took the form of an embryo comedy of manners, and even contained the germ of social satire. This side of it is developed in the first Renaissance comedy, Jodelle's *Eugène*, at least in the first scene, and still more in Belleau's *La Reconnue* and Odet de Turnèbe's *Les Contents*. Thus Molière in inaugurating the true comedy of manners was going back to the path from which French comedy had been diverted by the influence of her Italian sister.

But *Les Précieuses ridicules* is not only a descendant of the medieval farce; it is also a farce in the ordinary modern acceptation of the term, that is to say, it employs exaggeration in order to arouse laughter. One has only to compare the language of the two *précieuses* and the two valets with that of Mlle de Scudéry in her novels and letters, or, better, with that of the *précieux* salon depicted by Furetière in *Le Roman bourgeois* (1666) to see this plainly enough. Except when she is deliberately imitating the language of gallantry, Mlle de Scudéry makes sparing use of *précieux* words or phrases and in Furetière's salon the only one of the company whose speech bears any decided trace of *préciosité* is Charroselles, who stands for Charles Sorel. The exaggerated language of *Les Précieuses ridicules* may be partly ascribed to the fact that the ladies are *pecques provinciales* and that the valets are purposely burlesquing their parts. But it is chiefly due to Molière's extraordinarily skilful use of accumulation, repetition, and the other methods of comedy. A *précieux* phrase used here and there, as it would have been in real life, would have passed almost unnoticed on the stage, but the abundance with which the speakers scatter their gems of speech produces a result which is supremely and delightfully ridiculous[1]. It is this success in creating amusement for all time out of a transient social folly which makes *Les Précieuses ridicules* so wonderful, and which stamps Molière as a master of comic effect. The idea of the two valets counterfeiting their masters was a real in-

---

[1] See E. Roy, *La vie et les œuvres de Charles Sorel*, 1891, for an excellent and highly suggestive study of the language of *Les Précieuses ridicules*.

spiration, for it at once gives an underlying comic basis to the two immortal scenes (IX and XI) which constitute half the play, and it enables Molière to make legitimate use of exaggeration. Mascarille is wholly admirable in the ninth scene, but with the entry of Jodelet in the eleventh scene—"Ah! Vicomte!—Ah! Marquis!"—the fun becomes furious. Wisely Molière does not trust entirely to *préciosité* for his comic effects. When the pair recount their exploits in the wars, backing one another up with easy effrontery, and when they make the ladies feel their scars, and when Mascarille finally says,

> Je vais vous montrer une furieuse plaie,

and Madelon replies,

> Il n'est pas nécessaire: nous le croyons sans y regarder,

we are on the broad ground of human nature, and we laugh as heartily to-day as the audience did when the play was first produced nearly two hundred and fifty years ago.

The story of the old man who called out after the first performance, "Courage! Molière, voilà la bonne comédie," which has no better authority than that of Grimarest, is probably apocryphal. But it may serve to point out that it is as an embodiment of the true spirit of comedy even more than as a social satire that *Les Précieuses ridicules* is so important in the history of the French stage. More than twenty years earlier Desmarets de Saint-Sorlin had ridiculed certain social types in *Les Visionnaires*, but while his play, which is more of a caricature than Molière's, is almost unreadable to-day, *Les Précieuses ridicules* remains a perennial source of laughter.

There has been much discussion as to the real target of Molière's satire. According to some critics it is aimed in the first place at the salon of Mme de Rambouillet. But, apart from other objections, this famous salon had ceased to have any importance since the outbreak of the Fronde, eleven years before the production of the play. It is clear, however, from the fact that the performances were suspended for a fortnight and from the curious 'prediction' in Somaize's *Dictionnaire des Précieuses*—"Un alcôviste de qualité interdira ce spectacle pour quelques jours"— that certain *précieuses* of some social importance were offended by the satire. In his preface to the printed edition of the play Molière by way of defence declares that "the most excellent things are liable to be copied by silly apes," and that "the true *précieuses* were wrong to take offence at satire which was aimed at their ridiculous imitators." There is nothing in this inconsistent with the supposition that, while Molière was ostensibly laughing at third-rate provincial *précieuses*, he had in his mind Mlle de Scudéry and her friends, who were the *fons et origo mali*. He is careful, it will be noticed, not to say who the true *précieuses* are, but he advises those who claim this distinction not to put on a cap which was two sizes too large for them.

For some reason or other, perhaps on account of the temporary interdict imposed on *Les Pré-*

cieuses ridicules, Molière in his next play, *Sga-narelle, ou le Cocu imaginaire*, steered clear of social satire. The play has been described as a relapse into Italian farce. But its whole tone is much more French than Italian. Written in verse, in one act, with the merest pretence at a plot, it has all the air of a French medieval farce. It is, at any rate, comedy in an initial stage. Three of the characters are unnamed; the valet is called Gros-René, because the part was played by Du Parc who had returned to Molière's company, which he had temporarily deserted, to take the place of Jodelet; and all the rest—Lélie, Célie, Gorgibus, Villebrequin[1], and Sga-narelle—bear traditional names. The scene, which is vaguely indicated as Paris, was prob-ably outside the house of Gorgibus. But in one respect, and that not an unimportant one, the play marks an advance in Molière's art. Sgana-relle is an attempt to portray a humorous cha-racter. For the contrast between Sganarelle's jealousy and his cowardice is really humorous. His famous soliloquy in Scene XVII must surely have given Sheridan a hint for the scene between Bob Acres and his servant in *The Rivals*[2].

> Quand j'aurai fait le brave et qu'un fer, pour ma peine,
> M'aura d'un vilain coup transpercé la bedaine,
> Que par la ville ira le bruit de mon trépas,
> Dites-moi, mon honneur, en serez-vous plus gras !

[1] Villebrequin is a character in *La Jalousie du Barbouillé* and the name occurs in *Le Médecin volant*.
[2] It has been said that Molière owes something to Scarron's *Jodelet duelliste* (III, 1 ; IV, 7 ; V, 1), but the resemblances are very slight.

The part of Sganarelle was played by Molière himself with great success. From this time it is always the ridiculous and half-humorous character that he chooses for his own part; and this character frequently bears the name of Sganarelle. Sganarelle, says Sainte-Beuve in a well-known passage, personifies the ugly side of human nature, the side that is old, crabbed, morose, self-interested, ignoble, cowardly...the bad side, the side which provokes laughter." In this play, in *L'École des Maris*, in *Le Mariage forcé*, in *L'Amour Médecin* he represents a morose and self-interested *bourgeois*, in *Le Médecin malgré lui* a drunken and amusing wood-cutter, in *Don Juan* a simple and cowardly valet. But of all the Sganarelles the last is the only one who arouses any feeling of sympathy. The character of the nameless *suivante* also calls for notice. Standing for common sense, especially in Scene XXII, she is the forerunner of the admirable Dorines, Nicoles, Martines, and Toinettes of the later plays. Finally, in this play Molière makes his first appearance as a moralist, by attacking, as he was never weary of attacking, the practice of fathers marrying their daughters without consulting them. This is how Gorgibus treats Célie's remonstrances:

> Vous pourriez éprouver, sans beaucoup de longueur,
> Si mon bras sait encor montrer quelque vigueur;
> Votre plus court sera, Madame la mutine,
> D'accepter sans façons l'époux qu'on vous destine[1].

[1] Scene I.

Molière's next comedy, *L'École des Maris*, which was separated from its predecessors by more than a year and by his unsuccessful tragi-comedy of *Don Garcie*, marks a more decided advance towards his goal, that is to say, towards social comedy, based on observation and having a moral purpose. The guiding idea—the contrast between two opposite systems of education, the severe and the indulgent—is borrowed from the *Adelphi* of Terence, who, according to La Grange, was a favourite author with Molière. But, except for two or three short passages, the debt to Terence ends here. While the Latin author's examples of the two systems are young men, in Molière they are young women, and the two brothers, instead of being their father and uncle, are their guardians and intended husbands. Thus the subject of the play is well suited to such comedy as Molière had in view. And the charac-ters are conceived in a similar spirit. One of these —Sganarelle—is a real creation, the creation, in Nisard's words, of "the first man in French comedy." Instead of being portrayed by a single humour, like Dorante in *Le Menteur* or Lélie in *L'Étourdi*, or by the contrast of two conflicting humours, like the Sganarelle of the last play, he is a complete man. At his first entry on the stage he reveals himself as rude, over-bearing, and narrow-minded. He calls his brother a fool, and flings his age, which is under sixty[1], in his teeth.

[1] In Moratin's Spanish version of the play the elder brother is forty-five and the younger forty-three.

In the second scene, in which they are joined by their wards, he begins by interrupting everybody before they can finish a sentence. Yet, thoroughly disagreeable and unattractive though he is, he has a soft spot, for he is really in love with Isabelle.

J'aurais pour elle au feu mis la main que voilà.

The other characters are slightly drawn. Ariste, gentle, courteous, and tolerant, chiefly serves as a foil to his brother. Isabelle is a first sketch of Agnès, as Valère is of Horace. Léonor, the other sister, makes only a few, short appearances, but she leaves the impression of dignity and good sense. It is a further sign of true comedy that the working out of the plot is in accordance with the main idea of the play, and appears as the natural result of the respective systems of education. Léonor marries the elderly and indulgent Ariste, and Isabelle escapes from the tyrannical Sganarelle. But she escapes, not, as she would have done in a conventional Italian comedy, through the schemes of her lover and his valet, but solely by her own ingenuity. In this, as M. Rigal has pointed out, the play retains an element of farce; for in both Isabelle's ingenuity and her guardian's credulity there is a strong element of exaggeration. But the action throughout is lively and amusing, and the outwitting of the positive and self-opinionated Sganarelle by his repressed and seemingly innocent ward is of the essence of comedy.

M. Martinenche in his careful investigation of

Molière's indebtedness to the Spanish drama[1] has suggested other sources for *L'École des Maris* besides Terence. It is doubtful whether Molière owes anything either to Boisrobert's *La folle gageure ou les divertissements de la comtesse de Pembroc*, which is a translation of Lope de Vega's *El Mayor imposible*, or to Dorimond's *La Femme industrieuse*. But there is considerable probability that the extremely clever scene between Isabelle, Sganarelle, and Valère in the Second Act (Scene 9) was inspired by a similar scene between Fenisa, the Captain (to whom she is engaged) and Lucindo, his son (with whom she is in love) in Lope's *La discreta enamorada* (Act II, Scene 15)[2]. There is a more fundamental resemblance to Antonio Hurtado de Mendoza's *El marido hace mujer* (1643), in which there are two brothers, not dissimilar in character to Ariste and Sganarelle, who are married to two sisters, and whose opposite ideas on the subject of female liberty produce much the same results as in Molière's play. The fact, however, that one of the sisters in the Spanish play is called Leonor is an argument that tells as much against as for Molière's in-

[1] *Molière et le Théâtre Espagnol*, 1906.
[2] In some of the copies of the original edition of *L'École des Maris* there is an engraving which represents Isabelle pretending to embrace Sganarelle and at the same time giving her hand to Valère to kiss (*Œuvres* II, 350–1, Martinenche, pp. 97–9). There is an illustration of the same incident in the Amsterdam edition of 1725. *La discreta enamorada*, as well as *El acero de Madrid* and *La dama boba* (which will be referred to later), will be found in vol. I of Lope's *Comedias escogidas* (*Bibliotheca de autores españoles*, XXIV).

debtedness[1]. But M. Martinenche acknowledges that there is nothing Spanish in the treatment of *L'École des Maris*, and this is the important point. If the Spanish drama had had any real share in shaping Molière's art, it would have been at this period of his career when he was feeling his way towards his conception of true comedy that we should detect its influence. But though, as we shall see later, there are almost certain traces of Lope de Vega—that inexhaustible quarry— in other plays, notably in *L'École des Femmes*, and though *La Princesse d Élide* is an avowed adaptation of Moreto's *El desdén con el desdén*, it is difficult to accept M. Martinenche's contention that to the other influences which guided Molière to his true goal we must add Spanish comedy[2]. It was his own unaided genius which taught him that the basis of true comedy is the observation of life and human nature.

Molière's contribution to *Les Fâcheux*, a *comédie-ballet*, which was composed for the great entertainment given by Fouquet to the king at Vaux in August 1661, took the form of what the French call a *pièce à tiroirs*, that is to say, a succession of organically disconnected scenes strung together by a slender thread. In this case the connecting link is a Marquis named Éraste, who while on his way to a rendezvous with the lady to whom he is paying his addresses is continually interrupted by a succession of troublesome

---

[1] Martinenche, pp. 97–106. I have not read Mendoza's play.
[2] See Martinenche, pp. 84–5.

persons who insist on talking to him about themselves and their pursuits. With the exception of *l'homme à grands canons*, the encounter with whom is narrated by Éraste in his first speech, and who recalls Regnier's Eighth Satire and Horace's *Ibam forte via sacra*, they are not true bores. They are not bores under all circumstances, but they bore Éraste because he has an engagement elsewhere. He encounters in turn a *petit-maître* (Lysandre), a duellist (Alcandre), a gambler (Alcippe), two *précieuses* (Orante and Climène), a *chasseur* (Dorante), a needy pedant (Caritidès), an equally needy projector (Ormin)[1], and an officious busybody (Filinte). Each is a Parisian type of Molière's day. Thus he returns to that social satire with which he had begun his Paris career, the social satire which deals with manners and passing fashions rather than with character. As was pointed out in the last chapter, its freedom and boldness indicate Molière's growing confidence in himself and in the favour of the king. There is no question here of *pecques provinciales*; he no longer draws his characters solely from *bourgeois* life; the types that he satirises are nearly all taken from the Court, and in the person of *l'homme à grands canons* the Marquis, in whom he was to find so inexhaustible a source of ridicule, makes his first appearance, though not as an actual character of the play.

[1] There is a similar projector in Cervantes's *Coloquio de los Perros*, one of the *Novelas Exemplares*.

CHAPTER III

THE four new comedies which Molière had produced since his return to Paris were in the nature of experiments. They were all short, the first two in one act, and the others in three. In *Les Précieuses ridicules* he turned his back on Italian comedy and opened up the fruitful but almost unworked field of social satire, thus laying the foundations of a true national comedy. While adhering in some respects to the traditions of French farce, he abandoned the old methods of arousing laughter and trusted for comic effect partly to the permanent element of ridicule that underlies a transitory fashion, partly to the still more permanent element that exists in all human nature. In his second attempt he quitted the field of social satire, probably from motives of prudence, and approached more closely to the medieval farce. *Sganarelle* is far less brilliant than *Les Précieuses ridicules*, but it depends less upon exaggeration, and it contains in the character of Sganarelle an element of true humour. Moreover in his protest against parent-made marriages Molière strikes for the first time the note of social and moral reform.

This note is strengthened in *L'École des Maris*, which is in design a true social comedy, based on observation of life and manners. It contains too, for the first time in the history of French comedy, a complete character—a man and not merely a humour. On the other hand, the working out of the plot, though it is based on the characters themselves and not on arbitrary incidents, shews more of the spirit of farce than of true comedy. In *Les Fâcheux*, written at too short a notice—it is said fifteen days—to admit of the construction of a true drama, Molière returns to social satire, and portrays for the first time the society of the Court and the fashionable world of Paris. Besides these four comedies he had also produced a play which is often spoken of as a tragedy, but which he himself properly entitled a heroic comedy. The complete failure of *Don Garcie*, contrasted with the brilliant success of his comedies, determined him to keep for the future to the path which nature had marked out for him.

He had now at the age of forty reached the end of the experimental stage. He had become an assured favourite with the public, that is to say with the public of fairly well-to-do and well-educated *bourgeois* who filled the *parterre* of his theatre, and he had found favour with the king. Master of his art and sure of his position he at last ventured to produce a social comedy in five acts. He gave considerable time to it, and it was not till sixteen months after the production of *Les Fâcheux* that on December 26, 1662 he presented *L'École des Femmes* at the Palais-Royal.

The subject of his new play is identically the same with that of *L'École des Maris*, that is to say the failure of a middle-aged lover to win the affections of his ward, whom he has brought up on a deliberate system of repression and seclusion. It will be seen that it is in part Molière's own story. When he wrote *L'École des Maris*, he, a man of thirty-nine, was contemplating marriage with a young girl. When he produced *L'École des Femmes*, he had been married to her for ten months, but he had not succeeded in winning her affections. It is natural to suppose that his own situation gave the subject a sort of fascination for him, and it is interesting to notice that he is careful to tell us the ages of both Sganarelle and Arnolphe, and that they closely correspond with his own. He was thirty-nine when he wrote *L'École des Maris*, and Sganarelle is nearly forty[1]. He was very nearly forty-two when he produced *L'École des Femmes*, and Arnolphe is forty-two. In spite of the difference in the titles of the two plays, in both alike the psychological problem which arises out of the subject is regarded from more or less the same angle, that is to say from the man's point of view. In both cases the question is whether a liberal and indulgent plan of education or a narrow and repressive one is likely to make the best wife.

[1] He is twenty years younger than his brother Ariste, who is "presque sexagénaire."

The First Act of *L'École des Femmes* is constructed on similar lines to that of *L'École des Maris*. In the First Scene of the earlier play the two brothers are introduced to us, and their characters are clearly brought out; in the Second they are joined by their two wards and a *suivante*, and in the course of conversation the theme of the play, the contrast between the two systems of female education, is rapidly developed. In *L'École des Femmes* the opening is even simpler, for the First Scene not only portrays the characters of Arnolphe and his friend Chrysalde, but it states the psychological problem.

Arnolphe, Molière's own part, has some points in common with his predecessor, Sganarelle. He is rude, arrogant, self-opinionated, and self-confident. But his manners are better than Sganarelle's, for his social status is superior. He is not a noble, nor even a landed proprietor, though in a spirit of vanity which seems to have been common in his day he calls himself, after the name of his house, M. de La Souche[1]. He is a well-to-do *bourgeois*—possibly of a legal family, or holding some post under government—with the manners and *savoir-faire* of a man of the world. Like so many of Molière's characters, he is obsessed by a fixed idea; he is convinced that the great majority of wives are unfaithful. In order therefore to escape from what he believes to be the general lot of husbands, he has adopted a young girl, and has had her brought up—one cannot

[1] From the stump of an old tree in his garden.

say, educated—in a small convent with express
injunctions that every pains should be taken,

Pour la rendre idiote autant qu'il se pourrait[1].

When the play opens, she has been removed
from the convent and is living in a separate
house under the charge of an ignorant peasant
and his wife. She herself is equally ignorant,
the sum of her knowledge being, in Arnolphe's
words,

De savoir prier Dieu, m'aimer, coudre et filer.

That is Arnolphe's system. As his friend says,
he is a *fou* whose *marotte* is *une femme stupide*.
But his friend cannot shake him, for he has
absolute confidence in his system and in himself, and he has nothing but contempt and ridicule
for the conjugal misfortunes of his neighbours.

Qui rit d'autrui
Doit craindre qu'en revanche on rie aussi de lui

is Chrysalde's warning, and it might serve as a
motto to the play.

Chrysalde has sometimes been regarded as
the mouthpiece of Molière's own views, as the

---

[1] This idea of a man marrying his ward, whom he has had educated in a convent, in the belief that ignorance will ensure innocence, is taken from Scarron's *La Précaution inutile*, but it is very
doubtful whether, as M. Martinenche suggests, Molière consulted
the Spanish original, *El prevenido engañado*. On the other hand,
there is much to be said for M. Martinenche's view (*op. cit.* pp.
116–18) that Molière was indebted to Lope de Vega's *La dama
boba* for the idea of Agnès's intelligence expanding under the
influence of love. But Molière has greatly improved upon his
original, for while Finea's sudden awakening from a state border-
ing on idiocy is a psychological impossibility, the development of
Agnès is perfectly natural.

embodiment of good sense. This is not so. He is too easy-going, as his friend is too suspicious. He would leave these matters to chance and bear any misfortune that might happen to him like a philosopher. No better than Arnolphe does he realise that the true way to avoid such misfortunes is to win and keep your wife's affections. His point of view is developed at some length—indeed at too great length—on his next appearance, which is not till the Eighth Scene of the Fourth Act, and it resembles that of some of Labiche's husbands, especially of Marjavel in *Le plus heureux des trois*[1].

In the remaining three scenes (II–IV) of the First Act, the first two of which are very short, we are introduced to all the other characters of the play except Enrique and Oronte, who do not appear till the *dénouement*. Even these, in accordance with the established rules of French drama, are referred to by name. The Second Scene is one of broad comedy, displaying itself in action and gesture but based on human character, between Arnolphe and his two servants, Alain and Georgette, who are a welcome change from the conventional valet and *soubrette*. Brécourt was greatly admired in the part of Alain, in which he doubtless used plenty of gesture, for in *L'Impromptu de Versailles* Molière tells him to gesticulate as little as he possibly can. In the Third Scene Agnès (Mlle

[1] Weiss notes that in 1847 the public took exception to Chrysalde's speech. (*Molière*, 1900, p. 88.)

de Brie) makes her appearance, her needlework in her hand, and in three and a half lines
reveals her extreme innocence and simplicity.
Arnolphe is enchanted.

> Héroïnes du temps, Mesdames les savantes,
> Pousseuses de tendresses et de beaux sentiments,
> Je défie à la fois tous vos vers, vos romans,
> Vos lettres, billets doux, toute votre science,
> De valoir cette honnête et pudique ignorance.

He is soon disillusioned, for he has no sooner
uttered these words than Horace, the *beau
blondin*, appears, and with the *étourderie* of
youth recounts to his father's old friend the beginning of his adventure with Agnès, in whose
guardian—*C'est un fou, n'est-ce pas?*—owing
to his change of name, he does not recognise Arnolphe. Horace is not a strongly drawn character, but he serves admirably the purpose of the
play. His *étourderie* and vanity—the *étourderie*
of youth and the vanity of a Frenchman—

> Voilà de nos Français l'ordinaire défaut:[1]

make it quite natural that he should relate his love-
adventure to the first friend he meets. Moreover,
as interpreted by La Grange with his unfailing
grace and charm, the *beau blondin* must have won
the immediate sympathy of the spectators.

Thus, when the curtain drops on the First
Act, we have been introduced to all the real
characters—Enrique and Oronte are only puppets—the theme of the play has been stated,
and the plot has been set in action. In this

---

[1] Act III, Scene 3.

extremely skilful handling of the *exposition*, as the French call it, which is on the same lines as that of *L'École des Maris*, but which is more masterly, because more simple, Molière is carrying out the principles established by Corneille in his *Cid* and succeeding plays.

The working out of the plot takes the form of a duel between Arnolphe and Horace. The combatants are evenly matched. If Horace has the supreme advantage of youth and charm, he is handicapped by the *étourderie* with which he makes his rival the confidant of all his plans[1]. If Arnolphe has on his side possession, experience, and the information so freely imparted to him both by his opponent and by the innocent Agnès, he throws away the game from overweening self-confidence. Instead of profiting by his knowledge and removing Agnès to a safer retreat, he perseveres in his plan, and at each stage of the contest expresses his complete satisfaction with himself and it.

> Oui tout a bien été, ma joie est sans pareille[2].
> ....
> Enfin j'ai vu le monde, et j'en sais les finesses[3].

He quite fails to realise that it is Agnès's very ignorance and simplicity that expose her to the visits of Horace and his emissary. It is Arnolphe's system and his confidence in his own cleverness that bring him to final disaster. He is punished where he has sinned, which is the

---

[1] The idea of Horace's confidences to his rival is found in Straparola and Ser Giovanni (see Molière, *Œuvres* III, 115–16).
[2] Act III, Scene I.   [3] Act IV, Scene 5.

true dramatic form of punishment. Meanwhile the education of Agnès proceeds on lines which he had not contemplated. "Le cœur a ses raisons que la raison ne connaît point." Under the tuition of her heart she develops a capacity for deception and intrigue that is a little alarming. But her progress is much more gradual and is far more subtly delineated than that of Isabelle in *L'École des Maris*, and nothing is more natural, and at the same time more dramatic, than the way in which each misfortune that befalls Horace brings him nearer to her heart.

The critics objected that the play lacked action and consisted of mere narratives of what befell Agnès or Horace[1]. They would have liked to see Horace climb up the ladder to Agnès's window, miss his footing, and tumble to the ground. Yet the comedy of the play depends chiefly on these narratives of Horace's successes and misfortunes, which alternately depress and elate his rival. Uranie is perfectly right when she says in *La Critique* :

Pour moi, je trouve que la beauté du sujet de *l'École des Femmes* consiste dans cette confidence perpétuelle ; et ce qui me paraît assez plaisant, c'est qu'un homme qui a de l'esprit et qui est averti de tout par une innocente, qui est sa maîtresse, et par un étourdi, qui est son rival, ne puisse avec cela éviter ce qui lui arrive.

This treatment of the plot as a duel between two evenly matched antagonists, in which the advantage passes alternately from one to the other, has been followed by Molière's successors.

[1] *La Critique de l'École des Femmes*, Scene 6.

It is adopted by Beaumarchais with great effect in *Le Barbier de Séville* and *Le Mariage de Figaro*, and it is the saving merit of Scribe's *Un verre d'eau*.

In the great scene (Fourth) of the Fifth Act between Arnolphe and Agnès the tone deepens into seriousness and pathos. Arnolphe begins on a note of anger rising almost to fury. But Agnès, strong in the awakening of her soul, faces him boldly and confesses her love for Horace. Then she adds,

> Que ne vous êtes-vous comme lui fait aimer ?

and Arnolphe at last recognises that his system has broken down.

> Ma foi, là-dessus
> Une sotte en sait plus que le plus habile homme.

At last his anger gives way, disarmed by the gentle submissiveness which follows her avowal. After his fashion he is now thoroughly in love, and there is real pathos in the following lines, which must have come straight from Molière's heart.

> Ce mot, et ce regard, désarme ma colère,
> Et produit un retour de tendresse de cœur
> Qui de son action m'efface la noirceur.
> Chose étrange d'aimer, et que pour ces traîtresses
> Les hommes soient sujets à de telles faiblesses !
> Tout le monde connaît leur imperfection :
> Ce n'est qu'extravagance et qu'indiscrétion ;
> Leur esprit est méchant, et leur âme fragile ;
> Il n'est rien de plus faible et de plus imbécile,
> Rien de plus infidèle ; et, malgré tout cela,
> Dans le monde on fait tout pour ces animaux-là[1].

[1] Act v, Scene 5.

But Molière recollects that this is a comedy, and that Arnolphe is a character of comedy. So he quickly changes the note of pathos to one of ridicule. Arnolphe now protests his love in extravagant terms " with rolling eyes, ridiculous sighs, and childish tears[1]." Agnès is not in the least moved by this display.

> Tenez, tous vos discours ne me touchent point l'âme.
> Horace avec deux mots en ferait plus que vous.

At this point, so far as the psychological problem is concerned, the drama might have ended. Arnolphe's attempt to hoodwink and drug human nature has signally failed. He has not been able to touch Agnès's heart, or even to prevent her giving it to another. But Molière's audience demanded a more romantic and a more definite conclusion. Arnolphe therefore announces his intention of putting Agnès in a convent, and in order to prevent this, Molière, having nothing better to offer, gives us a *dénouement* of the conventional Italian type. A father from America appears on the scene and we learn that a marriage between Agnès and Horace has already been arranged by him and Oronte. Arnolphe, ignorant that it is Agnès who is Enrique's daughter, treacherously breaks his promise to help Horace, and urges Oronte to insist on his parental authority. So that

---

[1] "Avec ces roulements d'yeux extravagants, ces soupirs ridicules, et ces larmes niaises qui font rire tout le monde." Lysidas finds fault with what he calls the exaggerated comedy of this, but it is defended by Dorante as the natural behaviour of a lover. (*La Critique de l'École des Femmes*, Scene 6.)

when the parentage of Agnès is revealed and
he quits the stage with a comic exclamation of
defeat, he has lost whatever sympathy he may
have attracted by the real feeling which he ex-
hibited in the Fourth Scene.

In modern times the desire to find a tragic
element in Molière's comedies has extended
even to Arnolphe, and he has been represented as a tragic rather than a comic figure.
But it is evident from the remarks made in *La
Critique de l'École* that Molière did not represent him in that light and that the audience of
his day did not so regard him. In the original
text the exclamation with which he quits the
stage is *Oh!* which has a more or less pathetic
import. But though the comic *Ouf!* was not substituted for it in the text till 1734, we know from
Boursault's *Portrait du Peintre*, which was produced in October 1663, that the substitution
was made on the stage at quite an early date[1].
There is no doubt a real pathos in Arnolphe's
situation, and thus a tragic element may be said
to underlie the visible and external comedy.
But it is as a comic character that Molière meant
to portray him. The point is important, and
we shall have to consider it again when we come
to Tartuffe and Alceste. Another point to bear
in mind is that Molière's greatest characters
are always delineated with remarkable breadth
and sympathy. He does not label them as good
or bad, pleasant or unpleasant; he creates a

---

[1] See C. Coquelin, *L'Arnolphe de Molière* (reprinted from the
Rev. des deux mondes for April 15, 1882).

man, and leaves it to us to admire or despise
him, to love or hate him. So it is with Arnolphe.
We are at liberty to sympathise with his misfortunes, to shed tears over him, if we please.
But the play is a comedy, and from the point
of view of art he is a comic and not a tragic
figure.

L'École des Femmes was an even greater success than its predecessors. But this very success
provoked Molière's rivals and opponents to angry
criticism. It was attacked by the *précieuses* as
indecent, by the *dévots* as irreligious, and by the
critics, chiefly rival dramatists, and the *marquis*
as violating the rules and especially as wanting
in action. We have seen that by way of reply to
these attacks Molière produced on June 1, 1663
La Critique de l'École des Femmes, which George
Meredith has justly characterised as "one of the
wisest as well as the playfullest of studies in criticism." It is Molière's *Art poétique*. The scheme
of the play is a very simple one. It opens in the
salon of Uranie, with whom her cousin Élise is
staying. Presently visitors appear, first a *précieuse* (Climène), then a *marquis*, then Dorante,
then a dramatic poet, named Lysidas, and each
in turn has something to say about the new
comedy. It is severely criticised by the *précieuse*, the *marquis*, and the poet, while it is
warmly defended by Dorante, who represents
good sense as well as good breeding. The *précieuse* is scandalised by two or three touches
which shock her delicate sense of propriety, while

the *marquis* can give no reasons for his dislike except that the *parterre* was in a perpetual state of laughter. The criticisms of Lysidas are more precise and more fundamental. He objects to the play, first because it violates all the rules of Aristotle and Horace, secondly because it is wanting in action, thirdly because it descends at times to low farce; and to these general criticisms he adds others on particular points. Each criticism is taken up and discussed in order by Dorante, and it will be noticed that the order is a strictly logical one.

He begins by defending the judgment of the *parterre* as against that of the spectators in the boxes, who think themselves qualified by their rank to judge of things of which they have no knowledge.

Apprends, Marquis, je te prie, et les autres aussi, que le bon sens n'a point de place déterminée à la comédie; que la différence du demi-louis d'or et de la pièce de quinze sols ne fait rien du tout au bon goût; que, debout et assis, on peut donner un mauvais jugement, et qu'enfin, à le prendre en général, je me fierais assez à l'approbation du parterre, par la raison qu'entre ceux qui le composent il y en a plusieurs qui sont capables de juger d'une pièce selon les règles, et que les autres en jugent par la bonne façon d'en juger, et qui est de se laisser prendre aux choses, et de n'avoir ni prévention aveugle, ni complaisance affectée, ni délicatesse ridicule.

It must be remembered that the price of a seat in the *parterre*, 15 *sous*, was a fairly high one and that the spectators who occupied these seats must have been eminently respectable, and have included, as Dorante says, many persons who were quite capable of judging of a piece according to the rules. The *bourgeois* Molière is in fact appealing to his fellow-*bourgeois*. As for Lysidas's complaint that the play "sins against the rules," Dorante answers it by saying that the great rule of all is to please. A similar criticism had been passed on the *Cid* and a similar answer had been made by Jean Guez de Balzac, "To know the art of pleasing is not so valuable as to know how to please without art." It may be said, indeed, on behalf of Lysidas's contention, that the few have always been better judges of art and letters than the many, and that popular reputations not seldom vanish under the test of time. But drama, or at any rate comedy, stands upon rather a special footing. Its basis is common sense—"the first-born of common sense," George Meredith calls it—and common sense is just what you expect from an audience of plain *bourgeois*. For the plain *bourgeois* is the average man, and common sense is the general sense of the community. "Comedy," to quote Meredith again, "is an interpretation of the general mind." Moreover, as a matter of fact, professed dramatic critics have been just as often wrong in their verdict as the *parterre*. In our own day we have seen the decline of the reputations of Augier and Dumas *fils*, who were once as popular with the critics as with the public.

It is a broad rule of drama that it must have action. But if Lysidas is right in saying that "the nature of a drama consists in action," he is wrong in saying that there is no action in *L'École des Femmes* and that it consists entirely of narratives by Agnès and Horace. "There is plenty of action," answers Dorante, "and the narratives themselves are actions." He might have added that actions are of two kinds, external and internal, or bodily and mental. The actual meetings between Agnès and Horace, the climbing up to the window and so forth, are not represented on the stage, as they are, for instance, in *Romeo and Juliet*, but the narratives of these events are true actions *suivant la constitution du sujet*, because they have a direct effect upon Arnolphe. They not only help to reveal his character, but they bring about the final collapse of his system, which is the subject of the play. On the other hand, it may be admitted that some of Arnolphe's speeches are too long, and that one of Chrysalde's in the Eighth Scene of the Fourth Act is not only too long, but does not contribute to the action of the play.

Lysidas is wrong again when he criticises Arnolphe's readiness to lend money to Horace. "Seeing that he is the ridiculous character of the play, ought he to be made to act like a well-bred man of the world (*faire l'action d'un honnête homme*)?" "Yes," replies Dorante, "for there is nothing incompatible in a person being ridiculous in some matters and a well-bred man of the world in others." This is the teaching of nature and in this as in so many other features of his comedy Molière was nature's pupil.

Dorante makes yet another point when, in answer to the *marquis's* remark that Lysandre, a man of *esprit*, disapproved of the play, he says that, "there are many persons whose judgment is spoilt by a superabundance of *esprit*." There are not a few modern critics to whom this saying would apply.

Molière was being constantly told by his critics that 'farce,' as they called his comedy, was very inferior to tragedy, and he was a little sore on the subject. He therefore puts into the mouth of Dorante a defence of comedy as compared with "serious pieces." The writer of comedy, says Dorante, has a more difficult task before him than the writer of tragedy. "When you portray heroes, you may treat them as you please: they are imaginary portraits (*à plaisir*) in which one does not look for a likeness, and you have only to follow the promptings of a soaring imagination, which often abandons the truth in order to attain the miraculous. But when you portray men (i.e. ordinary men, not supermen) you must paint from nature." This attack on the tragedy of Corneille and his school helps us to understand the failure of *Don Garcie*. In the character of Don Garcie Molière wished to portray an ordinary man under the influence of jealousy, but he has failed, partly because he has portrayed not a man but merely a humour— for Don Garcie has no character apart from his jealousy—partly because he has placed this realistic study in a romantic setting. Now jealousy may be treated either as a violent passion, in which case it is a fit subject for tragedy, or as a ridiculous foible, when it falls within the province of comedy, but the study of it as an ordinary commonplace failing cannot be made romantic, or even, except with great difficulty, dramatic. The task becomes impossible when, as in *Don Garcie*, jealousy is treated, like Lélie's *étourderie*, as a recurrent disease, which is only cured by the need of ending the play. Whether this is a correct view of Molière's failure or not, at any rate it was not given to him to produce a successful tragedy on realistic lines. It was left for Racine to write tragedies which portrayed "after nature" the passions of ordinary mortals. Moreover, in the one play in which Racine has portrayed the passion of jealousy, namely *Mithridate*, he has not made it the only theme, while the scene in which Mithridate discovers Monime's love for Xipharès has been criticised as a "stratagème de *comédie*."

Finally, Dorante points out that while in serious plays it is enough to say things which are sensible and well-written, in comedy you must also be amusing (*il faut plaisanter*), and "it is a novel and arduous task to make well-bred people laugh (*c'est une étrange entreprise de faire rire les honnêtes gens*)." In the old days before the theatres were reformed laughter had been raised by the broad jokes and boisterous antics of the popular low comedians. Then Corneille in *Le Menteur* had produced a play at

which well-bred people might laugh without
loss of dignity. But in the hands of Scarron
comedy had descended again to the tone of
burlesque. Molière recognised to the full the
claims of the comic spirit, and in some of his
shorter plays he catered for those who were not
ashamed of laughing at simple but honest fun.
But in his great plays he courted Comedy in her
higher moods, and he based his appeal to laughter
on the firm and sure ground of human nature,
with its backslidings and contradictions, its
strange mixture of wise and foolish, noble and
base, lofty and ridiculous. *L'École des Femmes* was
his first essay in this highest region of comedy.
It is, as M. Rigal says, his *Cid*. Like the *Cid*,
it has some obvious imperfections, which are absent from *Le Tartuffe* and *Le Misanthrope*, but
on the whole it is an admirable example of high
comedy. Molière has at last found himself.
Henceforth he has only to pass from peak to
peak, resting sometimes on the lower slopes, but
always sure of himself, even when experimenting
on new ground.

The other little play (*L'Impromptu de Versailles*) which sprang out of the quarrel between
Molière and his critics, and which was an answer
to Edme Boursault's *Le Portrait du Peintre*, is
as simple in its construction as *La Critique*, and
even more ingenious. It represents the rehearsal
by Molière's company of an impromptu play
which he has been commanded to produce before
the king at two hours' notice. I have already

referred to it as throwing light on the characters of the various members of the company and on the combination of irritability, kindliness, tact, and irony which characterised his treatment of them as stage-manager. But the play is designed mainly as a counter-attack on his enemies. The actors of the Hôtel de Bourgogne, who had commissioned Boursault to write *Le Portrait du Peintre*, the *marquis*, and the *précieuses*, all come in for their share of ridicule. The rival actors, with the exception of Floridor, who was a favourite with Louis XIV, are taken off in turn, while the characters of the supposed *impromptu*, which include two *marquis ridicules*, a *précieuse* (the Climène of the *Critique*), and the dramatic poet, Lysidas, furnish occasion for some excellent satire.

MOLIÈRE

Dis-moi, Chevalier[1], crois-tu pas que ton Molière est épuisé maintenant, et qu'il ne trouvera plus de matière pour...

BRÉCOURT

Plus de matière? Eh! mon pauvre marquis, nous lui en fournirons toujours assez.

Molière's tone in *L'Impromptu* is bold and aggressive, the tone of one who counts on success. As far as the king was concerned he was fully justified in this confidence, for after the representation Louis assigned, as we have seen, a yearly pension of 1000 *livres* to his company.

---

[1] The Chevalier is apparently meant to be the same person as Dorante in the *Critique*.

Another feature of *L'Impromptu* and *La Critique*, besides the confident note and the boldness of the social satire, is the combination of vigour, ease, and urbanity with which they are written. They must have helped to convince Molière, as well as his audience, of the merits of prose for certain kinds of comedy. This was shewn even more forcibly in the one-act comedy, *Le Mariage forcé*, which was Molière's share in a *comédie-ballet* presented at the Louvre in January 1664. Molière here appears as a master of comic dialogue. For first to last there is hardly a line which does not tell, and which does not more or less reveal character. Two scenes, the First, between Sganarelle and his friend Géronimo, and the Ninth, between Sganarelle and Alcidas, the brother of his *fiancée*, stand out as admirable examples of humorous comedy. The best-known are those with Pancrace, the Aristotelian philosopher (Fourth), and with Marphurius, the Pyrrhonist or sceptic philosopher (Fifth). They are infinitely amusing, but being of the nature of farce are of a lower order of merit than the other two.

CHAPTER IV

TARTUFFE

L'ÉCOLE DES FEMMES involved Molière in a ten months' war, which ended in the triumphant victory of *L'Impromptu de Versailles.* Less than seven months later he was plunged into a fresh contest, which lasted for nearly five years. On May 12, 1664 he presented at Versailles the first three Acts of *Tartuffe.* On February 5, 1669 he received permission to produce the completed play in public. The story of the long struggle has often been told[1], and its incidents need only to be briefly capitulated here. Though the king, as he said to Molière, had no fault to find with the first three Acts, they provoked strong disapproval from Anne of Austria, and she was supported by the clergy, and especially by the secret society known officially as *La Compagnie du Saint-Sacrement* and in common parlance as *La Cabale des dévots.* There had been a meeting of the society on April 17, at which "there was much talk of procuring the suppression of the wicked comedy of *Tartuffe.*" In this, indeed, the society failed, but as a result of remonstrances by individual members, and es-

[1] See especially Ch. Revillout, *Louis XIV, Molière et Le Tartuffe* in *Mémoires de l'Académie des Sciences et Lettres de Montpellier, section des Lettres*, VIII, Fasc. II, pp. 261–342 (1888).

pecially by M. de Péréfixe, Archbishop of Paris, Louis XIV—probably before he left Versailles for Fontainebleau, which he did on May 14—sent for Molière and told him in kind words that he must forbid the production of his play in public.

In spite of this prohibition, and of various attacks that were made on Molière and his comedy, including a violent pamphlet by Pierre Roullé, one of the Paris clergy, the three Acts of *Tartuffe* enjoyed considerable favour in private.

> Molière avec *Tartuffe* y doit jouer son rôle

wrote Boileau in his Third Satire (1665) and in the edition of 1701 he added a note that " *Tartuffe* at that time was prohibited, and everybody wanted to hear Molière read it."

Among the persons thus favoured was the Papal Legate, Cardinal Chigi, who at Molière's request consented to hear the piece, and signified his approval of it (August 1664). More than this, a private performance was given on September 25 at Villers-Cotterets, the seat of Monsieur, the king's brother, at which their Majesties and the whole Court were present. The play was still only in three Acts, but Molière now added the other two, and on November 29 the complete play was presented at Raincy, the seat of the Princesse Palatine, in honour of the

---

[1] M. Revillout quotes D'Ormesson's Journal to the effect that Louis communicated at Easter 1664 but not at Pentecost (May 29). "Il ne ferait pas l'hypocrite" to please his mother (*op. cit.* p. 289).

great Condé, with whom since her return to Court in the previous year she had struck up a close alliance. The favour of these two great persons, deeply tinged as they were at this time with free-thought, must have tended to prejudice Molière in the minds of the orthodox.

It was not till August 1667 that he made an attempt to produce the now completed play in public. The times seemed more favourable, for the *Cabale des dévots* no longer existed, having been dispersed in March 1666. The king was in Flanders with his army, but before he had left Paris in the preceding May, he had given Molière a verbal permission to produce his play, coupled with the condition—this seems evident—that some changes should be made. Accordingly on Friday, August 5, 1667 Molière presented his comedy at the Palais-Royal under the new title of *L'Imposteur*, and promised to repeat it on the following Sunday. But M. de Lamoignon, the first President of the *Parlement*, who had been a member of the defunct Company of the Sacrament, forbade the representation, and when Sunday came the doors of the theatre were closed by his orders. On Monday the 8th Molière sent two members of his company, La Grange and La Thorillière, to Flanders to appeal to the king. They found him engaged in the siege of Lille[1], and they obtained from him a promise that on his return to Paris he would have the play examined and that it should be produced.

[1] *Second Placet au Roi.*

On August 11 M. de Péréfixe, the Archbishop of Paris, issued a decree forbidding under pain of excommunication all persons in his diocese "to represent or read or hear read, either in public or in private, the dangerous comedy of *The Impostor*." However, in spite of this anathema the piece was played before Condé at Paris on March 4, 1668 and again at Chantilly, which was in the diocese of Senlis, on September 20. Still there was no public performance, and it was not till February 5, 1669 that Louis XIV at last gave the required permission, and *Tartuffe*, with its original title restored, was presented to a curious and long expectant public[1].

In the course of the long contest certain changes were made in the text and structure of the play. We learn from Molière's *Second Placet au Roi* that for the performance of 1667 he "disguised Tartuffe in the dress of a man of fashion," that "he softened several passages," and that "he carefully cut out everything which he judged capable of furnishing the shadow of a pretext to the celebrated originals of his portrait." Further changes were made between 1667 and 1669, and of these we have more precise information. It is derived from a letter of August 20, 1667— evidently written by some friend of the author's —which gives a full and detailed account of the first public performance[2]. It appears from this

[1] Bazin conjectured that this belated permission was due to the so-called "Peace of the Church," or "Peace of Clement IX," but it is difficult to see the connexion.

[2] *Lettre sur la comédie de l'Imposteur*, 1667 ; reprinted 1668 and 1670. It is printed in *Œuvres* IV, 529–66.

that Dorine's speech in the first scene in which
she criticises Orante—"prude à son corps défen-
dant"—and people generally who blame sins in
others which they are too old to commit themselves, was in 1667 given in part to Cléante, to
whom the language is much more suited. It
also appears that in 1667 it was in this scene, and
not in the later one with Orgon (Act i, Scene 5),
that Cléante opposed to the *faux dévots*, of whom
Tartuffe was a type, certain persons whom
everyone recognised as truly religious, but who
made no display of their religion. Further, in
the first scene between Tartuffe and Elmire
(Act iii, Scene 3) some lines have been suppressed
at the end of Tartuffe's last speech, which now
ends with

Que l'on n'est pas aveugle, et qu'un homme est de chair,

and in the second great scene the "longue dé-
duction des adresses des directeurs modernes"
has been cut down to seventeen lines. Finally
in the last scene of all a passage from the speech
of the *Exempt* (or officer of the Guards), in
which he refers to the prevalence of hypocrisy,
has been omitted[1].

It will be seen that of the five changes above
noticed the three latter are simply *retranchements*, while the other two affect to some extent
the character of Cléante. It is unfortunate that
we have no similar information about the *adou-
cissements* and *retranchements* which Molière in-

[1] Nous vivons sous un règne où rien ne peut échapper à la
lumière du Prince...où l'hypocrisie est autant en horreur dans son
esprit qu'elle est accréditée parmi ses sujets.

troduced before the performance of 1667[1]. But these words seem to preclude any important alteration either in the structure of the play or in the treatment of the characters, and the ingenious conjectures made by Coquelin as to the nature of the original play of 1664 must be regarded as extremely hazardous[2]. It is possible that the changes to which Molière refers concerned only the first three Acts, which were all that the king knew, and that he may have made more radical concessions to his opponents in the two latter Acts, either while they were still in an unfinished condition[3], or even after the performance at Raincy, when he would have had the advantage of Condé's advice. In particular it has been suggested that the present *dénouement* did not form part of his original plan. It is difficult, however, to believe that Tartuffe's character, as it is now presented to us, was not inherent in the original conception of the play.

And this brings us to the question, what was Molière's original conception, or in other words, what was the genesis of the play? We know that he was sensitive to attacks, especially when he regarded them as unfair, and that he was ready to meet them with counter-attacks. It

---

[1] He speaks, however, in the preface of having "retranché les termes consacrés."

[2] *Tartuffe*, 1884.

[3] Neither the supposition that when the play was performed at Versailles the last two Acts were already written, nor Michelet's conjecture that the original play was complete in three Acts, seems the least probable.

is therefore natural to connect *Tartuffe* with *L'École des Femmes*. In the *Critique* and the *Impromptu* Molière had repaid the majority of his opponents—the *précieuses*, the *marquis*, the pedantic critics—with interest, but with one class he had not yet dealt—the *dévots*. We know both from Donneau de Visé's *Zélinde* and from Boursault's *Le Portrait du Peintre* that they had exclaimed against the scene in which Arnolphe preaches a sermon to Agnès on the duties of a wife and makes her read *The Maxims of Marriage*. They had even declared that these maxims, which Molière had borrowed through Desmarets de Saint-Sorlin from S. Gregory Nazianzen, were meant to be a parody of the Ten Commandments, though, as a matter of fact, Agnès is beginning to read an eleventh maxim, when she is stopped by Arnolphe. This charge of ridiculing religion had evidently rankled, and Molière refers to it twice in the *Impromptu*, "Pour l'endroit" (referring to *Le Portrait du Peintre*) "où on s'efforce de le noircir, je suis le plus trompé du monde si cela est approuvé de personne," and "Mais, en leur abandonnant tout cela, ils me doivent faire la grâce de me laisser le reste, et de ne point toucher à des matières de la nature de celles sur lesquelles on m'a dit qu'ils m'attaquaient dans leurs comédies[1]." Visé, however, repeated his accusation in *La Vengeance des Marquis*, which was his answer to *L'Impromptu*.

[1] Scene 5.

Boursault and Visé were young men trying to make their way in the world, and Molière knew that in their perfidious attacks on him they were only the mouthpiece of others. Behind them he saw the austere party of the Court, and the Company of the Holy Sacrament. Founded in 1680, this powerful secret society had wielded a great influence throughout France. It promoted works of charity and missionary enterprise; it took measures for the enforcement of ecclesiastical discipline and the repression of heresy; and it even attempted the difficult task of supervising morals. In the pursuance of this latter object, its members undertook crusades against the fashionable vices of the upper classes, swearing, gambling, and duelling, and they organised an elaborate system of spiritual police with its attendant evils of *espionnage* and interference with family life. In the words of M. Allier, "they had for their agents fanatics who to save souls recoiled from nothing, 'sanctifying by the purity of their intentions' what simple folk would call dirty actions." The society was all the more oppressive because it was secret, but many of the members were well-known. They included besides ecclesiastics, lawyers, officers of the royal household, ambassadors, marshals, great nobles, and even a Prince of the blood, the Prince de Conti. After the Fronde the increasing activity of the Company began to provoke violent opposition. Mazarin was strongly opposed to it, and his enmity was inherited by Colbert. The fall of Fouquet, who was favourably disposed to the society, fore-shadowed its end; but so long as Anne of Austria lived it was difficult to suppress it altogether[1]. At the close of the year 1663, in spite of perse-cution, the members were working with the feverish activity of those who, hoping against hope, are trying to stave off the inevitable end.

Against one of the members, the Prince de Conti, Molière bore a particular grudge. In his unregenerate days Conti had, as we have seen, been the patron and protector of his company, and had allowed them to bear his name. But after his conversion in 1656 he had dismissed them from his service. Later, he had declared that nothing could be more scandalous than the Fifth Scene of the Second Act of *L'École des Femmes*, and in his *Traité de la comédie et des spectacles*, which, though not printed till 1667, had been circulated in manuscript some years earlier, he had violently attacked Molière's art and pro-fession. There is no reason to doubt Conti's sincerity, and Mme de La Fayette, an excellent judge of character, who did not love bigots, declared that religion had made him one of the best men (*un des plus honnêtes hommes*) in France. But seeing what manner of life he had led before his conversion, Molière may be pardoned if he took a different view and regarded him as a hypocrite. As for the Cabal in general he pro-bably believed that there were a good many

[1] See R. Allier, *La Cabale des dévots*, 1627–1666, 1902, and, for a brief summary, my *From Montaigne to Molière*, pp. 69–73.

hypocrites in the ranks of these unscrupulous
fanatics whose methods he cordially disliked.
When we remember too that he was a devoted
member of a profession which the Church had
placed under its ban, that he was averse to excess
in every shape, and that he heartily disliked any
assumption of superiority whether intellectual or
moral or spiritual, it cannot be thought strange if
he viewed with suspicion all excessive display of
piety, and that he confounded hypocrites and
well-meaning religious busybodies in a common
condemnation. We may compare his attitude
to that of the diarist Pierre de L'Estoile, an
honest man and a sincere Christian, who regarded
the outburst of religious fervour which shewed
itself in Paris at the beginning of the seventeenth century as a sign of bigotry and hypocrisy.

Especially, Molière saw a real danger in the
growing influence of the spiritual director. It
seemed to him not only an interference with the
liberty of the individual, but an intrusion upon
the privacy of family life. Even if the director
were an honest and really religious man, it was a
post which required great knowledge of human
nature and infinite tact, a post for which according
to St François de Sales only one man in a thousand,
or even in ten thousand, was fitted[1]. But what if
he were a hypocrite, a scoundrel who assumed
the mask of religion in order to prey upon his
dupes? So the character of Tartuffe arose and
took shape in Molière's brain. Certain touches

[1] See Fénelon, *Lettre sur la direction* (*Œuvres* VII, 535 ff.).

are evidently borrowed from Scarron's *Les Hypo-crites*[1]. For instance, in that novel, which is translated with slight alteration from the Spanish, Montufar "lowers· his eyes when he meets a woman," "and preaches to the prisoners." When a gentleman, who had recognised him and tried to expose him, is beaten by the populace, he assumes an attitude of Christian humility and forgiveness, just as Tartuffe does when he is accused by Damis, and he embraces his antagonist with the words "Je suis le méchant, je suis le pécheur, je suis celui qui n'a jamais fait d'agréable aux yeux de Dieu[2]." But Montufar only turns hypocrite towards the close of the story, which, like *La Précaution inutile*, is barely redeemed from cynicism and immorality by the improbability of its incidents and the absence of all psychological analysis. In Tartuffe Molière has created a living man, and like most of Molière's greatest characters he has been variously interpreted. Some critics have dwelt exclusively upon his sinister aspect, others, like Coquelin, have regarded him as a creation of pure comedy. The truth lies between these two extremes. "Tartuffe is at once sinister and

---

[1] First printed in 1655. The evidence for the suggestion that Molière consulted the original—*La Ingeniosa Helena, Hija de Celestina*, by Alonso de Salas Barbadillo—is very slight. (See Martinenche, *op. cit.* p. 164.)

[2] Cp.

> Oui, mon frère, je suis un méchant, un coupable,
> Un malheureux pécheur, tout plein d'iniquité,
> Le plus grand scélérat qui jamais ait été.
>
> *Tartuffe*, Act III, Sc. 6.

comic[1]." But it is the comic side that is first presented to us. Before he appears on the stage, the comic Muse, in the person of Dorine, is busy with him. He is

> Gros et gras, le teint frais et la bouche vermeille.

He is a large eater,

> Et fort dévotement il mangea deux perdrix
> Avec une moitié de gigot en hachis.

In the Second Act Dorine completes the portrait,

> Il est noble chez lui, bien fait de sa personne ;
> Il a l'oreille rouge et le teint bien fleuri.

The part was played by Du Croisy, who, as has been said, was stout and good-looking. There is therefore no reason to regard Dorine's expression, "bien fait de sa personne," as ironical. Tartuffe is evidently not bad-looking in a vulgar sort of way. He is, as Dorine contemptuously says, "un beau museau." But the contrast between his florid appearance and his profession of saintliness, between his gluttony and his ostentatious piety, is of the essence of comedy. Therefore when he makes his first appearance, which is not till the Second Scene of the Third Act, and, seeing Dorine, delivers the immortal lines :

> Laurent, serrez ma haire avec ma discipline,
> Et priez que toujours le Ciel vous illumine.
> Si l'on vient pour me voir, je vais aux prisonniers
> Des aumônes que j'ai partager les deniers,

he is greeted with laughter and not with a shudder.

[1] Rigal.

And the laughter continues when he takes out
his handkerchief and begs Dorine to cover her
bosom, and when he receives Elmire's request
for an interview with a fatuous " Hélas ! très-
volontiers." So throughout the scene with Elmire
the incongruity of this stout red-faced saint making
love to his benefactor's wife in language which is a
strange compound of gallantry and mysticism
provokes as much ridicule as disgust.   Even in
the scene with Orgon, when Tartuffe's hypocrisy
begins to be more apparent, the note of comedy,
even of farce, is reintroduced by Tartuffe and
Orgon simultaneously plumping down on their
knees. " Aujourd'hui," says M. Donnay, " nous
ne rions pas de Tartuffe ni même d'Orgon." This
is the view of an over-sentimental age. We may
be sure that Molière's contemporaries laughed
at both Orgon and Tartuffe.   How could they
help it with Molière in the part of Orgon and
the stout Du Croisy in that of Tartuffe ?

Even in the second scene with Elmire the
comic element is sustained by the presence of
Orgon under the table. Scoundrel though Tartuffe
now proves himself to be, we are reassured by
Orgon's presence, and ridicule more than terror
is the predominant sentiment. So too in the
Fourth Scene of the Fifth Act, when M. Loyal
arrives with the order for Orgon and his family
to turn out of their house, the situation is saved
from becoming too tragic partly by the comic
figure of M. Loyal himself, and partly by the
intervention of the irrepressible Dorine.   It is

not till the last verse of all that Tartuffe becomes
terrible and then only for a brief moment, for he
has no sooner called upon the officer to arrest
Orgon, than he is himself arrested, and his power
for evil is crushed for ever. But if Tartuffe is a
character of comedy, if on the whole he inspires
ridicule rather than terror, we must not forget
that beneath his mask he is a sinister scoundrel.
Molière makes this perfectly clear in his Preface.

J'ai employé...deux actes entiers à préparer la venue de
mon scélérat. Il ne tient pas un seul moment l'auditeur en
balance; on le connoît d'abord aux marques que je lui donne;
et d'un bout à l'autre il ne dit pas un mot, il ne fait pas une
action qui ne peigne aux spectateurs le caractère d'un méchant
homme.

According to Sarcey the object of the long
preparation during two entire acts for Tartuffe's
appearance is to familiarise the audience with the
idea of Orgon's strange infatuation[1]. Sarcey
supports this view with much ingenuity, but it
rests upon an exaggerated idea of Tartuffe's un-
attractiveness, and it also presupposes in Molière
the technique of a modern playwright. It is
better to accept Molière's own explanation as
sufficient. In any case, one cannot sufficiently
admire the marvellous skill with which he works
up his audience to the tip-toe of expectation.
We picture to ourselves Tartuffe's outward appearance; we breathe the air of mistrust and
suspicion with which the whole family, except
the infatuated Orgon, regard him; and we feel

[1] *Quarante ans de théâtre* III, 136–47.

a vague apprehension that something sinister lurks behind his sensuality and his love of material comfort.

In his chapter *De la Mode* La Bruyère has introduced the portrait of a hypocrite which is in part a criticism of Tartuffe. La Bruyère says in effect that Tartuffe overdoes his part, and that his aims are unnaturally rash—in other words, that he is exaggerated. As has often been pointed out, this criticism shews that La Bruyère had no knowledge of the stage, the conditions of which imperatively demand a certain amount of exaggeration, or rather, of over-emphasis of salient features. But there is more than this. La Bruyère's portrait of Onuphre, like the generality of his portraits, is drawn from the outside, and does not penetrate to the inner man. It is a carefully-finished and faithful representation of a religious hypocrite, as he appears in public, but of the man himself we only get a glimpse. It is Molière's glory that we see both mask and man. The mask is comic—as it is not in La Bruyère's portrait—but the man is sinister. The mask may be exaggerated, but the man is terribly real. He is sensual, covetous, and vindictive, and it is his sensuality that, with true dramatic justice, brings about his downfall.

It has been discussed by more than one critic, whether Tartuffe is a hypocrite in the strict sense of the word, like Onuphre, that is to say, whether he is consciously playing a part, or, whether, as Rigal maintains, "his piety, though monstrous, is sincere." But in the face of Molière's express declaration that Tartuffe is a *scélérat*, this view seems untenable. A somewhat different view is taken by M. Bergson, who, in conformity with his theory that automatism lies at the basis of comedy and that comic characters act unconsciously[1], contends that Tartuffe "has entered so thoroughly into his part that he plays it, so to speak, with sincerity[2]." According to M. Bergson he would have said *Laurent, serrez ma haire*, even if he had not been aware of Dorine's presence. This is hardly consistent with the stage direction of *apercevant Dorine*, but M. Bergson is no doubt right in holding that this sort of unconscious hypocrisy helps to emphasise the comic element in the presentation of the character. The same view was expressed half-a-century earlier by Vinet, who says that "ce jargon mystique, dont il s'est fait un vêtement, est devenu pour lui une seconde nature[3]."

It was a current rumour in the seventeenth century that Tartuffe was a portrait of a certain Abbé Gabriel de Roquette who was appointed Bishop of Autun in 1666[4], and who in his earlier

---

[1] Le comique est inconscient (*Le Rire*, p. 17).

[2] *Ibid.* pp. 147–8.

[3] *Poètes du siècle de Louis XIV*, 1866, p. 440. There is an admirable characterisation of Tartuffe in Guillaume Guizot's *Ménandre*, 1855, pp. 234–6. He says, "Il est hypocrite de religion, précisément, parce qu'il a des passions grossières : il fallait ce voile à ses vices."

[4] Saint-Simon says, "C'est sur lui que Molière prit son Tartuffe, et personne ne s'y méprit." The same rumour is repeated in the Memoirs of Lenet and the Abbé de Choisy.

days had been attached to the household of the
Prince de Conti, when he had professed austere
Jansenist principles. But later, when Jansenism
was in disfavour, he had allied himself to the
Jesuits and it was said that he owed his advance-
ment to his talent for intrigue and paying court
to the great. He was generally recognised as
the original of La Bruyère's Théophile[1]. But
there is no reason for supposing that Molière
modelled Tartuffe either on him, or on the Abbé
de Pons, on whose behalf Tallemant des Réaux
makes the same claim, or on Charpy, Sieur de
Sainte-Croix, whose hypocrisy furnishes the
same chronicler with another story. It is equally
wide of the mark to regard Tartuffe either as a
Jansenist[2] on account of his austere practices, or
as a Jesuit because in the scene with Elmire he
borrows a remark from "the good Father" of
Les Provinciales. M. Allier, as we have seen,
has more justification for his view that the play
is directed against the Company of the Holy
Sacrament. He points out distinct references to
it in Tartuffe's announcement of his intention to
distribute alms to the prisoners, and in Cléante's
tirade on the contrast between the *vrais* and the
faux dévots, in which the word *cabale* occurs, as

---

[1] In the chapter, *Des grands*. Roquette died in 1707; there is
a modern life of him by J.-Henri Pignot, 2 vols. 1876, written to
rehabilitate his memory. He seems to have reformed his diocese
with wisdom and diligence.

[2] This search for originals is carried to excess by Louis Lacour
in his *Tartuffe par ordre de Louis XIV*, 1877. For him Roquette
is Tartuffe, Conti is Orgon, and the play was written against the
Jansenists by order of Louis XIV.

it does again in the Third Scene of the Fifth Act and also in Molière's second *placet*. But it does not follow from this that Tartuffe is meant to be a member of the Cabal, any more than a Jansenist or a Jesuit. To suppose this would be to limit the scope of Molière to a particular time and country. Tartuffe is simply a religious hypocrite and he is for all countries and for all time.

One other point must be insisted on. Tartuffe is a layman. When Molière says in his second *placet* that in *L'Imposteur* he has given his personage the dress of *un homme du monde*, he means by the term a man of fashion, and not a layman. The large hat, the short hair, the small collar, the absence of lace and a sword, which marked Tartuffe's original costume, denoted that he was a man of simple and austere habits; but not that he was an ecclesiastic, who would have worn a *soutane*. Molière would never have ventured to put on the stage an ecclesiastic who was at once criminal and comic. Tartuffe, in short, is a lay director, a personage not uncommon in Molière's day.

As for his dupe, he had chosen him well. Orgon is a rich *bourgeois*, with a son and daughter, both of marriageable age, by his first wife. During the troubles of the Fronde he had served the king with courage and wisdom. But like Sganarelle and Arnolphe, he is obsessed by a fixed idea,

> Mais il est devenu comme un homme hébété,
> Depuis que de Tartuffe on le voit entêté.

His belief in Tartuffe knows no limits, and
nothing is too good for him.

> Enfin il en est fou ; c'est son tout, son héros ;
> Il l'admire à tous corps, le cite à tout propos ;
> Ses moindres actions lui semblent des miracles,
> Et tous les mots qu'il dit sont pour lui des oracles.

Under Tartuffe's guidance "he tastes the delights of perfect peace, and looks on the whole
world as a dunghill." He abandons all human
affections and is wrapped up in the contemplation
of heaven. Yet this change has not improved
his character. He is rude to his brother-in-law,
tyrannical to his daughter, insolent to his wife.
He turns his son out of doors, and finally disinherits his whole family in favour of Tartuffe.
His character, no doubt, lends itself to that
worthy's manœuvres. He is credulous and hasty,
rushing from one extreme to the other.

> Eh bien, ne voilà pas de vos emportements !
> Vous ne gardez en rien les doux tempéraments ;
> Dans la droite raison jamais n'entre la vôtre ;
> Et toujours d'un excès vous vous jetez dans l'autre.

Moreover, he is one of those people who, once
they get an idea into their head, embrace it to
the exclusion of everything else. Opposition and
criticism only irritate them and make them all the
more obstinate. Nothing is more natural or more
skilfully drawn than the deterioration in Orgon's
character, till it culminates in the scene (Act IV,
Scene 3) in which he brings the contract for
Tartuffe's marriage with Mariane. He repels with
brutality his daughter's entreaties, cuts his brother-

in-law short before he can complete a sentence, and finally insults his wife by roundly disbelieving her story of Tartuffe's advances. Yet throughout Orgon is a comic character. This is partly because he is at once explosive and inarticulate;

C'est un homme...qui...ha !...un homme...un homme enfin

and

En ce cas, je dirois que...Je ne dirois rien,
Car cela ne se peut.

But it is also owing to the extreme unreasonableness of his infatuation for so manifest an impostor as Tartuffe.

Cléante, Orgon's brother-in-law, belongs to that class of Molière's characters, whose principal function is to reason with the ridiculous personage and to combat the fixed idea by which he is obsessed. We have already had two examples in Ariste of *L'École des Maris* and Chrysalde of *L'École des Femmes*, and we shall have others in Philinte of *Le Misanthrope*, Ariste of *Les Femmes savantes*, and Béralde of *Le Malade imaginaire*. Now Molière knew human nature far too well not to be aware that when a man has once got a fixed idea firmly in his head, to reason with him has no other effect but that of irritating him, and confirming him in his delusion. Ariste has this effect on Sganarelle, and Chrysalde on Arnolphe. The purpose therefore of these critics, as we may call them, is to throw into relief the character of the friend or relation, who is represented as the *fou* of the piece and whom they generally stigmatise to his face by this uncomplimentary term. "Vous êtes fou, mon frère!" says Cléante to Orgon, and Béralde apostrophises Argan in identical terms. Opposed as they thus are to the *fous*, one is tempted to regard them as the *sages* of the piece. This is not necessarily the case. It is certainly not so, either with Chrysalde or with Philinte. Cléante, however, fully deserves this appellation, which is in fact applied to him by the writer of the *Lettre sur l'Imposteur*.

Like Ariste and Chrysalde in the two earlier plays, Cléante takes little or no direct part in the action, and it is only in three scenes (I, 5 ; IV, I ; V, I) that he is at all prominent. Now we know that some alterations were made in his part between 1667 and 1669, and that one of these at any rate had the effect of accentuating his character as a true Christian. This is the transference to Dorine of the satirical attack on coquettes who have become prudes. It naturally suggests that other changes, with a similar object, may have been made in his part both before and after the performance of 1667. For instance his long speech in Act I, Scene 5, of which the latter part was spoken by him in the First Scene in 1667, may have been developed after the original performance of 1664 for the purpose of "clearly distinguishing between the character of the hypocrite and that of the truly religious man[1]." It is further possible that his speech at the close

[1] Molière's preface.

of Act v, Scene 1, which is an exhortation to
Orgon not to "renounce all good men" because
he has fallen into the toils of a scoundrel, or to
insult true piety because he has been deceived
by its counterfeit, was considerably expanded in
1667. If these conjectures are correct, they point
to a distinct change in Molière's conception of
Cléante's character, a change deliberately made for
the purpose of conciliating his opponents. The
character, as it now stands, is that of a *vrai dévot*,
but it is possible that in the original play Orgon's
words,

> Mon frère, ce discours sent le libertinage

may have been applicable to Cléante's whole
attitude towards religion. It will be recollected
that Mme Pernelle in her very first speech to
him says:

> Sans cesse vous prêchez des maximes de vivre
> Qui par d'honnêtes gens ne se doivent point suivre.

This, however, is mere conjecture. All one
can say is that, if Cléante had been less orthodox, he might have been more alive. As it is,
though, *pace* Émile Faguet, his tirade in the First
Act is a noble exposition of true Christian principles[1], and though he maintains unimpaired
throughout the play his character of *un homme
sage*, he is not so sympathetic a figure as he

---

[1] Faguet (*Rousseau contre Molière*, p. 226) in citing part of
this speech omits two characteristically Christian lines:
> L'apparence du mal a chez eux peu d'appui,
> Et leur âme est portée à juger bien d'autrui.

ought to be. One cannot get rid of the feeling that he is less the offspring of Molière's dramatic genius than a puppet shaped and patched to meet the criticisms of his adversaries.

" Voilà une femme qui n'aime pas son mari," said some critic of Elmire, and it is evident that her marriage with a rich widower who had two children was dictated by reason rather than by love. But she is a thoroughly virtuous woman ; she is a good wife and step-mother, and she is even respectful and conciliatory to her disagreeable mother-in-law. In character, she is gentle and easy-tempered, kind and compassionate, averse to family jars and disturbances. According to her mother-in-law she is fond of spending money, especially on her clothes, and though she does not court admiration, she smiles at it indulgently when it comes her way. It is the only possible character that could have fitted in with the part she has to play. Had she been in love with her husband, Tartuffe would never have made his declaration. Had she not been of a placid temperament she would never have proposed, much less have carried out, the stratagem which at last opens her husband's eyes.

Of her step-children, Damis and Mariane, there is little to be said. Of all Molière's young girls who are threatened with undesirable husbands by tyrannical fathers Mariane is the most submissive. Damis has to the full the impulsive thoughtlessness which Molière regarded as characteristic of very young men, and which we have already seen exemplified in Lélie and Horace.

This family group is completed by Orgon's mother, Mme Pernelle, who does not however live with him, and by the servant Dorine. Mme Pernelle is an excellent example as much of Molière's faculty of creating a character with one stroke of his magician's wand as of the value of movement in drama. From her first words, which are the opening words of the play,

> Allons, Flipote, allons, que d'eux je me délivre,

to the box on the ear administered to the same Flipote with which she makes her exit,

> Allons, vous ! vous rêvez et bayez aux corneilles.
> Jour de Dieu ! je saurai vous frotter les oreilles.
> Marchons, gaupe, marchons !

she dominates the scene with her perpetual fault-finding and her perpetual movement[1].

Finally, there is the irrepressible Dorine, with her shrewd common sense, her devotion to the family, and her out-spoken tongue. There was an interesting discussion between Sarcey and Coquelin, some thirty years ago, as to her age and condition[2]. The critic had called her a *vieille nourrice*[3], and this drew forth an indignant protest from the actor, who declared that the immortal Dorine was thirty-five at the most,

---

[1] She is an illustration of Bourdaloue's remarks in *La sévérité évangélique* (*Avent.* II).

[2] See *Quarante ans de théâtre* I, 158–61.

[3] Fourteen years earlier he had called her a *vieille gouvernante*; *ib.* p. 137.

and that she was a companion and not a servant.
Sarcey gave way on the first point, though he
thought she might be as much as forty, but as
regards the second he insisted that her position
of authority in the family came from long service and not from education. Here most critics
will agree with him. It is quite true, as Coquelin points out, that in Corneille's comedies—
La Galerie du Palais, La Suivante, Le Menteur—
the *suivante* is a real companion, but in Molière's
time the distinction between a *suivante* and a
servante had disappeared. The unnamed *suivante* in *Sganarelle*, Lisette in *L'École des
Maris* and *L'Amour Médecin*, though, like
Dorine, they are called *suivantes*, have nothing
to distinguish them from Nicole and Toinette,
who are called *servantes*. In fact Dorine's relations to her young mistress are exactly the same
as those of Nicole and Toinette. With regard
to the question of age it may be noted that the
part of Dorine was played by Madeleine Béjart,
who was forty-six when the play was first produced, and fifty when it was finally allowed to
be played in public, and that Molière in creating
a part always had its impersonator in his eye.
It is true that Mlle de Brie retained the part of
Agnès till she was past fifty, but then she had
the gift of eternal youth.

This well-filled picture of a well-to-do *bourgeois* family has a double significance. In the
first place it marks the importance which Molière
attached to the family in the structure of the

social fabric. We shall see other instances of this in his later plays—in *L'Avare*, *Le Bourgeois gentilhomme*, *Les Femmes savantes*, *Le Malade imaginaire*. But the family is also important from the dramatic point of view. In Molière's earlier comedies—in *Sganarelle*, in *L'École des Maris*, in *L'École des Femmes*—the scene, in accordance with the Italian practice, itself a heritage from classical comedy, had been the street or some other public place. Thus for *L'École des Femmes* the note in the *Mémoire* of Mahelot is, "Le théâtre est de deux maisons et le reste est une place de ville," one of the two houses being evidently Chrysalde's. But, in spite of the well-understood convention, there was a palpable absurdity, for instance, in Arnolphe's delivery in the street of his long lecture to Agnès on the duties of a wife. And the whole practice was all the more absurd, now that Molière had given his comedy a national setting. For though long open-air conversations might be common in Italy, they were unusual in France. It was therefore a happy inspiration which led Molière to adopt the family as the framework for his play, for it enabled him to conform to the unity of place by the simple expedient of making the whole action take place in the room of a single house.

The solidity and compactness which this expedient gives to his comedy is at once revealed by the masterly 'exposition' of the first scene, which has always been the admiration of dramatists and critics[1]. From the clash of conversation which is sustained by Mme Pernelle on one side, and by Damis and Dorine on the other —the placid Elmire and Cléante are cut short by the irascible old lady before they have barely opened their lips—we learn of the intrusion of Tartuffe into the family, and how Damis resents his supervision of their pleasures, and how Dorine suspects him of being a hypocrite. The 'exposition' is completed in the remaining scenes of the First Act. Orgon's infatuation and Tartuffe's appearance and behaviour are graphically depicted, and it appears that under Tartuffe's influence Orgon is unwilling to fulfil his promise of giving his daughter to Valère. From this point the action is developed with admirable simplicity. Orgon's determination to marry his daughter to Tartuffe, Elmire's interview with the latter, Tartuffe's declaration, Damis's complaint to his father, Orgon's conveyance of his property to Tartuffe, Elmire's stratagem, Tartuffe's exposure, Orgon's dismissal of him, Tartuffe's betrayal of his benefactor to the king, and finally the king's discovery that he is a well-known impostor are all linked together in a strictly logical chain, each act of which is the natural outcome of character. Thus the plot is worked out in true dramatic fashion, through and by the characters.

[1] Especially of Goethe. "From the very first word everything is highly significant, and points to something even more important that is to come" (Eckermann, *Gespräche mit Goethe*, 4th ed. I, 174).

The *dénouement* has been criticised as a mechanical cutting of the knot, in which the king
plays the part of a *deus ex machina*. But Brunetière is, it seems to me, right in defending it
as essential to the play as Molière originally
conceived it[1]. Had the play ended, as Boileau
suggested, with Tartuffe being merely driven
from the house, the sinister side of his character
would not have been fully revealed. To make
that clear it was necessary that he should turn
his benefactor out of his home, and then crown
his iniquity by betraying the secret of the *cassette*. After that the only possible *dénouement*
for a comedy was the swift intervention of justice
in the person of the Monarch. This is effected
in a thoroughly dramatic fashion by the arrest
of Tartuffe just at the moment when he calls on
the officer to arrest Orgon.

L'Exempt

Oui, c'est trop demeurer, sans doute, à l'accomplir :
Votre bouche à propos m'invite à le remplir ;
Et, pour l'exécuter, suivez-moi tout à l'heure
Dans la prison qu'on doit vous donner pour demeure.

Tartuffe

Qui, moi, Monsieur ?

L'Exempt

Oui, vous.

It is perhaps difficult to-day to sympathise
with the outcry which assailed *Tartuffe* on its
first appearance, and which delayed its produc-

---

[1] According to Legouvé it was warmly defended by Scribe, that
all accomplished exponent of the *pièce bien faite*. (*Soixante ans
de souvenirs*, 4th ed. II, 189.)

tion in public for nearly five years. But it must be remembered in the first place that in the reign of Louis XIV the whole stage was under the ban of the Church, and in the second, that, in spite of Molière's careful preparation, Tartuffe's absolute villainy is not so apparent at the end of the Third Act as it becomes afterwards. When the play was first presented in its incomplete shape, it might easily have seemed, at least to prejudiced and ill-disposed spectators, that it was an attack on excessive piety as much as on hypocrisy, on the whole system of spiritual direction as much as on its abuse. Even Tartuffe may have seemed to them, as he does now to M. Rigal, an instance of a religious man who has yielded to temptation, rather than of a consummate scoundrel who is deliberately playing the hypocrite. And they would have had some justification for this view. The play is undoubtedly directed against excessive piety as well as against false piety, and against the dangers of the spiritual director, even when he is honest and sincere.

But criticism of this sort was, in the eyes of the Church, not permissible to a writer of comedy. M. de Lamoignon put it to Molière with perfect courtesy and simplicity :

Je suis persuadé que votre comédie est fort belle et fort instructive ; mais il ne convient pas aux comédiens d'instruire les hommes sur les matières de la morale chrétienne et de la religion : ce n'est pas au théâtre à se mêler de prêcher l'Évangile.

This was the official view, and Molière bore

no grudge against the first President for his statement of it. On the other hand, his indignation was thoroughly roused by the Archbishop's edict which characterised his play as

Une comédie très dangereuse, et qui est d'autant plus capable de nuire à la religion, que, sous prétexte de condamner l'hypocrisie ou la fausse dévotion, elle donne lieu d'en accuser indifféremment tous ceux qui font profession de la plus solide piété, et les expose par ce moyen aux railleries et aux calomnies continuelles des libertins.

This fulmination of M. de Péréfixe is especially interesting because he takes exactly the same line as Bourdaloue in the First Part of his famous sermon *On Hypocrisy*, in which he attacked *Tartuffe*, though not by name, with all the force of his reasoned eloquence[1].

Voilà ce qu'ils ont prétendu, exposant sur le théâtre et à la risée publique un hypocrite imaginaire, ou même, si vous voulez, un hypocrite réel, et tournant dans sa personne les choses les plus saintes en ridicule, la crainte des jugements de Dieu, l'horreur du péché, les pratiques les plus louables en elles-mêmes et les plus chrétiennes.

The unfairness of this attack makes it evident that the preacher had not read the play. Had he done so he could not have spoken of Tartuffe, even in a tentative way, as an "imaginary hypocrite," nor could he have accused Molière of "turning the most sacred things to

---

[1] Bourdaloue preached a sermon on Hypocrisy on Dec. 16, 1691 before the king. But the sermon that has come down to us (*Dom.* II, 307) was preached on the seventh Sunday after Pentecost, and apparently not before the king. Probably he preached more than one sermon on the subject. (See E. Griselle, *Bourdaloue*, 2 vols. 1901, II, 777.)

ridicule in his person." But the whole argument of his First Part, which is that hypocrisy gives occasion to free-thinkers to regard with suspicion all manifestations of piety, whether true or false, is inapplicable to Molière's play on a fair interpretation of it. For in that play, as Molière points out in his preface, the contrast between Tartuffe and the truly good and religious man is made so plain that the most malicious freethinker could find no handle in it.

The Third Part of Bourdaloue's sermon is directed against simpletons, like Orgon, who allow themselves to be duped by hypocrites, and in his reprobation of them he shews less indulgence—shall we say less Christian charity?— than Molière. He says in effect to Orgon, that, when he appears before the tribunal of the Sovereign Judge, he must not expect to be pardoned for unjustly disinheriting his children, on the ground that he had been deceived by a hypocrite. That excuse is "one of the most frivolous that a Christian can offer[1]." Thus the censure of the preacher is more severe than the ridicule of the comic writer. Finally, it is at once a justification of Molière's play and a sign of his premonitory vision that Bourdaloue, the most sincere of men, and himself a director of wide experience, was deeply conscious of the evil of hypocrisy. It had no doubt greatly increased since Molière's day—" Le monde est

---

[1] Cp. P. Janet, *Les passions et les caractères dans la littérature du XVII*^e *siècle*, pp. 79–88.

rempli de faux guides," says the preacher—but it is to Molière's credit that he foresaw the danger.

What the Archbishop of Paris said in 1667 one of his clergy had said in far more violent terms in 1664[1], and Pierre Roullé's pamphlet may be taken as a sample of the attacks that were made on Molière after the first production of his piece. His only direct reply was his first *placet* to the king, but he took occasion of a new comedy on an old subject, which he was writing in the winter of 1664–65, to present the portrait of a genuine free-thinker. Pierre Roullé had called Molière "un démon vêtu de chair et habillé en homme, un libertin, un impie digne d'un supplice exemplaire[2]." Well! his enemies should see what such a character was really like. So he gave them Don Juan[3].

---

[1] See above, p. 99.

[2] From Molière's preface, which reproduces the words of the pamphlet.

[3] For *Le Tartuffe* generally see Sainte-Beuve, *Port-Royal* III, 259–311, and Faguet, *Propos de Théâtre*, 1903, pp. 178–206.

CHAPTER V

DON JUAN

THE interdict laid on *Tartuffe* was a serious blow to Molière's company. The only new play available for the winter of 1664–65 was *La Princesse d'Élide*, and this was more suited to the Court than to the Palais-Royal. So by the end of the year 1664, the receipts, which had never reached four figures, dropped to 268 *livres*, leaving very little margin for profit[1]. It was therefore necessary to take some step to repair the finances of the company, and it was suggested by Molière's comrades—so runs tradition, though the idea may well have been Molière's own—that they should produce a play on the popular subject of Don Juan. It was presented on February 15, 1665.

The old legend, the divers elements of which, found in other countries, were united in Spain, first assumed a dramatic form in Tirso de Molina's[2] celebrated play of *El Burlador de Sevilla*

[1] The 'ordinary' expenses of Molière's theatre came to about 50 *livres* a performance, but the music and dancing of *La Princesse d'Élide* added another 150 *livres*. Consequently an actor's share on this occasion (December 30) only came to 3 *livres* 60 *sous*. On December 9 when the receipts only amounted to 233 *livres*, it had vanished altogether. *Part néant—payé des frais* notes La Grange in his Register.

[2] His real name was Fray Gabriel Tellez (1571–1648).

y Convidado de Piedra. The date of its production is unknown, but it was printed in 1630[1].
It is a fine romantic play, serious in tone throughout except for the half-comic character of the
valet, Catalinón, who, well-drawn without the
exaggeration of some of his copies, is represented
as a coward dominated by fear of his master.
Don Juan himself is a thoroughly romantic figure.
Though his courage is his only good quality,
there is a certain glamour about him which accounts for the readiness with which his victims
allow themselves to be deceived. In spite of his
infernal wickedness he is not an atheist; he is
not even a free-thinker. Though he braves God,
he believes in Him and the Church. At the last
moment he asks for a confessor, but the Statue
tells him it is too late, and he dies unshriven.

This characteristically Spanish play was represented by two Italian prose versions, one by
Giacinta Andrea Cicognini and the other by
Onofrio Giliberto. Cicognini's *Il convitato di
pietra*[2] is a popular, not to say vulgar, parody
of the original. As is implied by its title, the
earlier scenes, which deal with Don Juan's ini-
quities, are much shortened, while the later ones,
those in which the Statue appears, are greatly

---

[1] The best text is that of A. Castro in *Clasicos castellanos* (Tirso
de Molina, *Obras* I, 1910). For the legend see A. Farinelli, *Don
Giovanni*, Turin, 1896 (reprinted from *Giornale storico di lettera-
tura ital.* vol. XXVII), and G. Gendarme de Bévotte, *La Légende
de Don Juan*, 1906.

[2] For the text see *Le Festin de Pierre avant Molière*, ed. G.
Gendarme de Bévotte (*Soc. des textes français modernes*), 1907,
pp. 357 ff.

developed. Thus the moral element of the Spanish comedy is effaced by the miraculous, and
machinery takes the place of psychology. In accordance with Italian custom there is a Doctor
who uses the Bolognese dialect, and a Pantaloon
who uses the Venetian, while Passarino, Don
Juan's valet, who has become a more important
and an entirely comic character, talks in a com-
posite patois in which Lombard forms predomi-
nate. It is in Cicognini's play that we find the
original of Sganarelle's *Mes gages!* and here, for
the first time, appears Don Juan's famous list
of his victims, with which we are familiar from
Mozart's opera. The exact date of the play is unknown, but it was probably produced before 1650.
It was introduced to Paris in 1658 by the company
of Giuseppe Bianchi in the form of a *scenario*,
which has come down to us through an eighteenth century translation of notes made by the
actor Biancolelli for the part of the valet—a
part in which he succeeded Locatelli in 1671 [1].

The other Italian version of Tirso's masterpiece, that of Giliberto, was printed at Naples
in 1652, but no copy of it is known to exist. It
is, however, almost certainly represented by two
French pieces on the subject, which clearly point
to another source than Cicognini [2]. The earlier
by Dorimond was produced at Lyons in 1658,

---

[1] See *Le Festin de Pierre avant Molière*, pp. 333 ff. and Moland,
Molière et la comédie italienne, pp. 191–208. See also above, p. 55.
Biancolelli had played the part as an under-study since 1662.

[2] The only alternative is to suppose the existence of a third and
quite unknown Italian version.

and at Paris, by the short-lived company of Mademoiselle, of which he was a member, in 1661. The later, which was written by de Villiers, an actor of the Hôtel de Bourgogne, was produced at that theatre in 1659. Both plays are in verse, both are called *tragi-comédies*, and both have for their title *Le Festin de Pierre*[1] *ou le Fils criminel*, the second part denoting the emphasis that is laid on the more sinister side of Don Juan's character. Dorimond's play, which owes something to Cicognini as well as to Giliberto, has a certain tragic gravity, and the comic side of the valet, who is called Briquelle, and who is represented as a glutton as well as a coward, is not exaggerated. Don Juan is a corrupt debauchee, a "grand seigneur méchant." He is also a philosopher and an inquirer. It is from speculative curiosity that he invites the Statue to supper, and it is on the plea that "Nature is his mother," that he justifies his conduct to his father; but he is not an atheist. It is in this play that we find the germ of his hypocrisy. But it is only adopted as a ruse, to protect himself, in the absence of his sword, from his enemy, Don Philippe. Here too we first meet with the curious character of the Pilgrim, of which there is no trace in Tirso or Cicognini, and which we therefore presume to have come from Giliberto. If the language of de Villiers's

---

[1] This was originally an abbreviation for *Le Festin de l'homme de pierre*, but in both plays Pierre has become the name of the Commander. Molière keeps the title, which had become familiar, but his Commander has no name.

play is more correct than Dorimond's, his verse is equally flat and commonplace. We gather from his letter of dedication to Corneille, that he and his fellow-actors counted more on the spectacular effect of the piece than on its language and construction for its success, and in conformity with this idea the scenes between Don Juan and the Statue are more numerous and of greater length than they are in the Spanish play. De Villiers claims, with apparent justice, that he has followed his original more closely than Dorimond, but similarities of expression shew that he has also used his rival's play. If he is less romantic than Dorimond, he has more verve and brutality. With an actor's love of emphasis and exaggeration he has accentuated the characters of both Don Juan and the valet.

Don Juan, as in Dorimond's play, has one moment of temporary but real repentance, but at the sight of the first woman he meets he relapses into the hardened and impenitent libertine. As in Dorimond's play, he acts the hypocrite in order to possess himself of his rival's sword, but, whereas in the earlier play he spares his rival's life, in that of de Villiers he brutally murders him. Thus his vices are unredeemed by a single virtue, unless it be the courage with which he defies the Statue. Again, as in Dorimond's play, he justifies himself on the ground that he is following Nature, and his last words are an expression of fatalistic determinism.

There is no proof that Molière was acquainted

with the Spanish *Don Juan,* but Cicognini's Italian version with the *scenario* founded on it, possibly also Giliberto's, and the two French tragi-comedies were all at his disposal, and as was the custom in those days he helped himself at his pleasure. But, though he naturally was obliged to follow the main lines of the legend, his specific debts to his predecessors are few and slight, and when he borrows, he invariably betters. It was practically impossible to treat so romantic a theme on purely classical lines. Accordingly he wholly abandoned the least important of the unities, the unity of place, and the scene, which is nominally in Sicily—as it is in *Much Ado about Nothing*—changes with each act. Such vague indications of scenery as are given in the *Mémoire* of Mahelot—a palace, a place by the sea, a wood, a wood and a tomb, a room, the tomb—remind one of the comedies of Alfred de Musset. The rule of the twenty-four hours is also violated, but not seriously. At the end of the Fourth Act only twelve hours, as we learn from a speech of Elvire's (Act IV, Scene 6), have elapsed since the opening of the play, but there is an interval of a whole day between the Fourth Act and the Fifth. On the other hand the first day is almost as well filled as the twenty-four hours of the *Cid.*

It was necessary to point out how slightly Molière has deviated from the rule of the twenty-four hours, because some critics have laid too much stress on the romantic handling of the

play. Lemaître indeed, followed by Faguet, has
by a strange oversight of Elvire's speech, boldly
suggested that the action lasts over many years,
and that Don Juan is an example, unique in
French classical drama, of the gradual development of character from early manhood to the
verge of old age. But the truth is that, though
Don Juan may seem a romantic play in comparison with Molière's other comedies, it is far
less romantic than the earlier versions of the
legend. This is especially so as regards the treatment of the principal character. In place of the
characteristically Spanish figure of the original
Don Juan with his insolent defiance of God's
laws and his submissive belief in the ordinances
of His Church, in place of the more rational-
istic and more brutal, but less intelligible and
convincing Don Juan of de Villiers, Molière has
drawn with astonishing firmness, completeness,
and consistency the portrait of a French *grand
seigneur méchant* of his own day. The scene
opens with a conversation between Sganarelle,
Don Juan's valet, and Gusman, the confidential
servant of Elvire, in which Sganarelle in the
most natural way in the world gives a sketch of
his master's character, a sketch only, as he says,
"for to complete the portrait many more strokes
of the brush would be needed." We learn that
he is "the greatest criminal that the world has
ever produced,"..."that he fears neither heaven
nor hell,"..."that he leads the life of a brute
beast"..."that he is an *épouseur à toutes mains.*"

And all this is said in order to convince Gusman that his master intends to desert Donna
Elvire whom he has just carried off from a convent and made his wife, a *lâcheté* which to
Gusman seems incomprehensible in a man of
quality. In the next scene Don Juan himself
appears, and develops in conversation with Sganarelle the cynical theory which is associated
with his name, the theory that "the whole pleasure of love consists in change," in the perpetual
alternation of conquest and abandonment. When
in the Third Scene Donna Elvire, whom he has
conquered and abandoned, demands an explanation, he pretends with an hypocrisy which
makes no effort to simulate truth that his desertion of her is due to religious scruples, to his
repentance at having persuaded her to break
her religious vows. Thus at the end of the First
Act, Don Juan, first by the report of his servant,
then by his own words, and finally by his own
deeds, is revealed to us as an odious figure, debauched, arrogant, treacherous, and cruel, and
without a single quality to relieve the blackness
of the picture. The Second Act comprises the
scenes with the peasants, admirable examples
alike of dramatic skill and fidelity to nature.
Although the scene is nominally in Sicily, these
peasants speak the dialect of the neighbourhood
of Paris, and Don Juan's dress, as described in
detail by Pierrot, is that of a French nobleman
of Molière's day. Nothing can be more natural
than the scene in which Don Juan makes love

to Charlotte, nothing more dramatically effective than that in which he pretends to Charlotte and Mathurine alternately that he is ready to marry her. This idea of a double seduction is taken from de Villiers, who possibly found it in Giliberto, but whereas in de Villiers, Don Juan with brutal cynicism makes love to both peasant-girls at once, in Molière he has at any rate the decency to pretend to each that she is his only love. Sarcey is full of admiration for this scene, which he calls a *scène-type*, because it represents the general idea of a man placed between two women both of whom he is trying to seduce[1]. But it should also be noticed that Don Juan with all his cleverness cannot help cutting a ridiculous figure between these rival beauties. The mere fact of his falling in love with both of them at once is Donjuanism reduced to absurdity. Thus Molière has succeeded, as he had succeeded in *Tartuffe*, in the difficult task of making his villain ridiculous. In Don Juan's case the task was far more difficult than in that of Tartuffe, and the ridicule which he incurs is only slight. But the ridicule exists and Comedy maintains her rights.

So far Don Juan has been portrayed chiefly as a heartless libertine, and we have only had a hint of his impiety and scepticism (Act 1, Scene 2). In the Third Act he appears as a complete disbeliever in everything supernatural. Catechised by Sganarelle as to his religious beliefs he at first refuses to answer, but at last, when the

[1] *Quarante ans*, pp. 87–91.

valet presses him, he replies, "I believe that two and two make four, and that four and four make eight." Then follows the much discussed scene with the Poor Man—a character which was probably suggested to Molière by the Pilgrim of Dorimond and de Villiers—whom Don Juan compels by threats of violence to change clothes with him. As is well known, at the first performance of the play Don Juan was represented as offering a *louis* to the man if he would blaspheme, and then on his saying that he would rather die of hunger, giving it him "for the sake of humanity (*pour l'amour de l'humanité*)." But Don Juan's proposal scandalised the audience, and at the second performance, and in the text of the original edition of 1682, the lines which contain it were struck out[1]. Even this omission was not considered sufficient, for in the expurgated copies of the 1682 edition the whole dialogue with the Poor Man is reduced to a mere question and answer as to the way to the town. In the next two scenes Don Juan at last displays some nobility of character. He has at any rate the physical courage and the sentiment of honour— where men are concerned—without which he would not have been a true picture of his class, and which contrast so forcibly with the incomparable *lâcheté* of his conduct to Elvire. In the Fifth Scene, Don Juan and Sganarelle come upon the Commander's tomb, and Don Juan's

[1] They appear in the Amsterdam edition of the separate play (1683) and in the Brussels reproduction of 1694 (see *Œuvres* v, 146).

complete disbelief in the supernatural is symbolised by his refusal to credit the evidence of his senses, when the Statue lowers its head in acceptation of the invitation to supper. "Nous pouvons avoir été trompés par un faux jour," he says, "ou surpris de quelque vapeur qui nous ait troublé la vue."

In the Fourth Act are three scenes which serve to throw further light on Don Juan's character. First there is the well-known scene (Second) with his creditor, M. Dimanche, a delightful scene of admirable comedy. Here again Don Juan appears in a somewhat contemptible and ridiculous aspect, that of a haughty nobleman cajoling in terms of almost servile civility the honest tradesman to whom he owes money. But the scene helps to complete the truth of the picture, for the non-payment of their just debts was a common vice among the nobles of Molière's day. Bourdaloue refers to it in his sermon *On Almsgiving*, preached before the Court probably about 1682.

On traite ce marchand, cet artisan, qui fait quelque instance, de fâcheux et d'importun. On le fait languir des années entières, et après bien des remises, qui l'ont peut-être à demi ruiné, on lui donne à regret ce qui lui est le plus légitimement acquis, comme si c'était une grâce, qu'on lui accordait, et non une dette dont on s'acquittât.

Bossuet too, at a date much nearer to *Don Juan* (Palm Sunday, 1666), speaks in equally plain terms of the same failing[1]. If in this scene Don

[1] *Sermon sur la Justice* (*Œuvres* XIII, 381).

Juan, with all his amusing cleverness, is slightly ridiculous, in the other two he exhibits the more odious and sinister side of his character. The scene (Fourth) with his father Don Louis is evidently modelled on that between Dorante and his father in Corneille's *Le Menteur*, the theme of Don Louis's tirade being the same as that of Géronte, that "La naissance n'est rien où la vertu n'est pas[1]." Don Juan treats his father's reproaches with insolent contempt, and on his departure utters the impious imprecation "Mourez le plutôt que vous pourrez, c'est le mieux que vous puissiez faire." The hardness of his heart is even more clearly revealed in the Sixth Scene, when his deserted wife, Donna Elvire, reappears, and after declaring that her earthly passion for him, and her anger at his desertion have given place to a pure and disinterested tenderness, warns him that the wrath of Heaven is about to fall on his head, and implores him to repent before it is too late. Don Juan with his tiger's heart, to use Sganarelle's expression, is not in the least moved by this pathetic appeal. After his wife's departure, all that he finds to say is that her tears and her languishing air have rekindled in him a few sparks of his extinct passion.

There is one trait left to complete the odiousness of Don Juan's character and that is hypocrisy, of which we have already had a hint in the first scene with Elvire. It now becomes the key-note of the first three scenes of the Fifth Act. In the

[1] Note that this is a perfect Alexandrine line.

first he plays the hypocrite with his father and in the second he expounds the advantages of hypocrisy to Sganarelle. His speech is Molière's answer to the attacks of his opponents, and is so important for the understanding of Molière's position that it must be given in full.

Il n'y a plus de honte maintenant à cela : l'hypocrisie est un vice à la mode, et tous les vices à la mode passent pour vertus. Le personnage d'homme de bien est le meilleur de tous les personnages qu'on puisse jouer aujourd'hui, et la profession d'hypocrite a de merveilleux avantages. C'est un art de qui l'imposture est toujours respectée ; et, quoiqu'on la découvre, on n'ose rien dire contre elle. Tous les autres vices des hommes sont exposés à la censure, et chacun a la liberté de les attaquer hautement ; mais l'hypocrisie est un vice privilégié, qui, de sa main, ferme la bouche à tout le monde, et jouit en repos d'une impunité souveraine. On lie, à force de grimaces, une société étroite avec tous les gens du parti. Qui en choque un se les attire tous sur les bras ; et ceux que l'on sait même agir de bonne foi là-dessus, et que chacun connaît pour être véritablement touchés, ceux-là, dis-je, sont toujours les dupes des autres ; ils donnent hautement dans le panneau des grimaciers, et appuient aveuglément les singes de leurs actions. Combien crois-tu que j'en connaisse qui, par ce stratagème, ont rhabillé adroitement les désordres de leur jeunesse, qui se sont fait un bouclier du manteau de la religion, et, sous cet habit respecté, ont la permission d'être les plus méchants hommes du monde ? On a beau savoir leurs intrigues et les connaître pour ce qu'ils sont, ils ne laissent pas pour cela d'être en crédit parmi les gens ; et quelque baissement de tête, un soupir mortifié, et deux roulements d'yeux rajustent dans le monde tout ce qu'ils peuvent faire. C'est sous cet abri favorable que je veux me sauver, et mettre en sûreté mes affaires. Je ne quitterai point mes douces habitudes ; mais j'aurai soin de me cacher, et me divertirai à petit bruit. Que si je viens à être découvert, je verrai sans me remuer prendre mes intérêts à toute la cabale, et je serai défendu par elle envers et contre tous. Enfin c'est là le vrai moyen de faire impunément tout ce que je voudrai.

Je m'érigerai en censeur des actions d'autrui, jugerai mal de tout le monde et n'aurai bonne opinion que de moi. Dès qu'une fois on m'aura choqué tant soit peu, je ne pardonnerai jamais et garderai tout doucement une haine irréconciliable. Je ferai le vengeur des intérêts du Ciel, et, sous ce prétexte commode, je pousserai mes ennemis, je les accuserai d'impiété, et saurai déchaîner contre eux des zélés indiscrets, qui, sans connaissance de cause, crieront en public contre eux, qui les accableront d'injures, et les damneront hautement de leur autorité privée. C'est ainsi qu'il faut profiter des faiblesses des hommes, et qu'un sage esprit s'accommode aux vices de son siècle.

It is clear that throughout this tirade Molière has the *Cabale des dévots*, which was not yet dispersed, in view. He believed—wrongly, as we have seen—that the Cabal was composed largely of hypocrites, of men who adopted the cloak of religion in order to cover the disorders of their youth, who took up the position of moral censors, and, under the convenient pretext of avenging the cause of Heaven, accused their enemies of impiety.

In the next scene Don Juan, putting his plan into immediate execution, plays the hypocrite with Don Carlos, and refuses to acknowledge Elvire as his wife on the pretence that it is against the will of Heaven. But he is still a man of courage, and he tells his opponent, that though he has no wish to fight—Heaven forbids the thought of it—he will presently take a walk in a certain secluded lane, and if Don Carlos attacks him—well, he will see what will happen. This is borrowed, of course, from the Seventh of the *Provincial Letters*, in which the *bon père* cites an exactly similar instance of "direction of intention," from a Jesuit casuist.

The cup of Don Juan's iniquity is now full, but he receives another supernatural warning in the shape of a spectre. Again he rejects it. " If Heaven gives me a warning, it must speak a little more clearly, if it wishes me to understand the warning." Yet if the warning had been written in letters of fire across the sky Don Juan would have rejected it. "Il ne sera pas dit, quoiqu'il arrive, que je sois capable de me repentir." So the Statue finds him unrepentant and undaunted, and as Sganarelle had foreshadowed in the opening scene, the doom of Heaven descends upon him. But the last word is with the valet. His cry of *Mes gages! mes gages!* which Molière took from Cicognini[1], and which was another cause of scandal to the devout, has the effect of relieving the tension, and of reminding the audience that the play is a comedy[2].

It will be seen that the dominant interest in *Don Juan,* the one upon which Molière has concentrated all the resources of his art, is the character of the hero. Like Hamlet and Falstaff, he is idealised, in the sense that all the features of his character are heightened and thrown into relief. But reduce them to ordinary dimensions and he becomes the type of a *grand seigneur méchant,* a type that is found in all aristocratic

[1] O pover al me Patron, al me salari.
[2] The words were omitted in the original text (*Œuvres,* 1682) and only appear in the Amsterdam and Brussels editions of the separate play.

societies, a type that was not uncommon in Molière's day. He is debauched, insolent, brutal, with no aim in life but his own pleasures; physically brave, but with a bravery which springs from social pride and lack of imagination; not devoid of intelligence, but employing it solely for the furtherance of his own ignoble aims; a disbeliever in the supernatural, but finding a childish satisfaction in blasphemy and impiety. Finally, he is base enough to assume the mask of religion in order to pursue his immoral course with greater security. Whatever impression he may have made on the stage of the Palais-Royal, when he was interpreted by an actor of so much grace and charm as La Grange, it is difficult for a reader of the play to find in him any glamour or fascination. It is true that even modern readers have been so affected, but they must surely have come to the play with romantic memories of other Don Juans, especially of the hero of Mozart's opera[1]. No, Molière's Don Juan is, like Tartuffe, an unromantic and sinister figure, *le plus grand scélérat que la terre ait jamais porté*. Nor, as we have seen, does he altogether escape from the ridicule that is comedy's true weapon. In the scene with the two peasant-girls, as in that with M. Dimanche, the laughter is not altogether on his side.

There was no lack of material to assist Molière in constructing his portrait. Retz, who had just

[1] Bazin, for instance, says of him that "il met le spectateur de son parti."

returned to Paris after his long exile, prided himself, Churchman though he was, on his numerous successes with women. Hugues de Lionne, the great foreign minister, had ruined his estate by gambling, and his health by dissipation. Among the younger men, Vardes, Lauzun, Guiche, Vivonne (brother of Mme de Montespan), the Duc de Guise, that fantastic paladin who died less than nine months before the production of Molière's play, all walked in the footsteps of Don Juan, and more or less shared his cynical views on the subject of love. Moreover, they gave evidence of that growing hardness of heart, that ingrained egoism, degenerating even into cruelty and crime, which is so odious a feature in Don Juan's character, and which Bossuet in more than one sermon has stigmatised as the natural result of a voluptuary's career[1]. Guiche, Lauzun, and above all, Vardes, were dangerous men to cross in the pursuit of their pleasures. Vardes slit the nose of an unfortunate man who had maligned him, and Bussy-Rabutin, another *grand seigneur* who had a reputation for gallantry, threatened to perform the same kind office for Boileau. When Sganarelle said, "Un grand seigneur méchant homme est une terrible chose," he was expressing the same thought as Fénelon when he spoke of "the tiger that is in every libertine."

[1] C'est le génie de la volupté : elle se plaît à opprimer le juste et le pauvre, le juste qui lui est contraire, le pauvre qui doit être sa proie...et voilà cette volupté si commode, si aisée et si indulgente, devenue cruelle et insupportable (*Sermon sur l'Impénitence finale*).

Nor, in representing Don Juan as an atheist, was Molière introducing an imaginary element into his picture. It is true that free-thought in France was on the decline when Pascal began to plan his Apology for Christianity. But in the conversation that he held with Father Beurrier, early in July 1662, six weeks before his death, he could speak of "the ungodly and the atheists" as "abounding in Paris." Earlier in the same year, on the Second Sunday in Lent, Bossuet had preached at the Louvre his famous sermon *Du mauvais Riche* or *Sur l'Impénitence finale*, in which he addressed to the worldlings of his day similar warnings to those given to Don Juan, and in the same week he had refuted the arguments of the free-thinkers in the sermon *Sur la Providence*. The free-thought which prevailed at this period, especially among the dissipated nobles of the Don Juan type, chiefly took the form of childish and tasteless impiety. The affair at Roissy, in 1659, when Vivonne, at whose house it took place, Guiche, Mancini (Mazarin's nephew), Bussy-Rabutin and others celebrated Good Friday with bacchanalian orgies, was greatly exaggerated by report, but reduced to bare fact it was typical of the attitude towards religion of these free-thinking *viveurs*[1].

Don Juan's attitude is hardly more philosophical. It is a mixture of indifference and bravado.

---

[1] A. Gazier, *Mélanges de littérature et d'histoire*, 1904, pp. 1–28 (*Molière et Conti*), thinks that Don Juan is a portrait of Conti. This does not seem possible.

He scoffs at Sganarelle's attempts at philosophic argument, but he will not or cannot answer him. His own philosophy is summed up in the belief that "two and two make four." In other words, like Bossuet's free-thinker in the *Funeral Oration for the Princess Palatine*, he acknowledges no guide but reason, not even the evidence of his senses. He at first doubts the supernatural sign given by the Statue. Then when the Statue really appears he faces it with impious bravado. He rejects with equal obstinacy the sign of the Spectre, and he only gives way when the Statue has him in its cold grasp, and the fire of Heaven descends upon him. Thus Don Juan's atheism, if hardly more philosophical, is of a more stubborn quality than that of the ordinary *libertin* of Molière's day. The latter either became converted, like Condé and the Princess Palatine and Bussy-Rabutin, or he sent for a confessor on his death-bed.

It has been made a subject of reproach to Molière that the cause of atheism is identified with an intelligent and attractive *grand seigneur*, while the defence of religion is entrusted to an ignorant and foolish valet. I have tried to shew what little justification there is for this view of Don Juan's character. Even his *esprit* is merely on the surface—the well-bred impertinence of a man of the world. Molière's treatment of the valet, who in every version of the play from *El Burlador* downwards serves as a foil to Don Juan in the same way as Sancho Panza does to Don Quixote, is of great interest. In Sganarelle the comic element, which exists in the original Catalinón, and which is exaggerated in the Italian and earlier French copies, is naturally retained. But Sganarelle is not a mere buffoon. He aspires to be a man of some reading, and even something of a philosopher; his opening speech is a disquisition on tobacco. According to Préville, the distinguished comedian of the second half of the eighteenth century, the part should be played with the greatest simplicity. "Its comic effect," he says, "depends upon an air of credulity and good faith, which it is difficult to achieve[1]." His attitude towards his master inspires us with sympathy. He has the greatest abhorrence of his conduct and opinions, but he is paralysed by fear.

Un grand seigneur méchant homme est une terrible chose : il faut que je lui sois fidèle en dépit que j'en aie ; la crainte en moi fait l'office du zèle, bride mes sentiments, et me réduit d'applaudir bien souvent à ce que mon âme déteste.

And later in the play he exclaims "O complaisance maudite, à quoi me réduis-tu!"

He is in fact exactly in the position so eloquently described by Bourdaloue :

Cet homme que vous avez à votre service et qui se soucie peu de déplaire à Dieu, pourvu qu'il vous plaise, à quoi l'employez-vous ? A être l'instrument de vos débauches, le confident de vos desseins, l'exécuteur de vos injustices et de vos vengeances. C'est lui qui prépare les voies, lui qui fournit les moyens, lui qui conduit les intrigues, lui qui porte et qui rapporte les paroles, lui qui ménage les entrevues, lui qui sert de lien pour entretenir le plus honteux et le plus détestable commerce[2].

[1] *Mémoires de Préville*, ed. Barrière, p. 172.
[2] *Sermon sur le soin des Domestiques* (*Les Dimanches*, II).

It is the terror that Don Juan inspires in Sganarelle and the consequent contempt that he feels for him that enables the dramatist to develop his character so freely and so naturally. Men like Don Juan do not soliloquise, neither do they have confidants. It is in intercourse with a sub-ordinate whom they despise that the depth of their iniquity is revealed. At the same time, Sganarelle, as the minister of his master's pleasures, is in a sort of confidential position, and it is perfectly natural that, disapproving as he does, of his conduct and opinions, he should venture on some timid re-monstrances. Moreover, being a philosopher, he has his opinions on religion. His common sense, which he modestly calls his *petit sens*, his *petit jugement*, tells him that there are more things in heaven and earth than can be explained by mere arithmetic. His statement of the old argument from final causes (Act III, Scene 1) ends in his confusion, but part of it is a reminiscence of Molière's teacher, Gassendi, being more or less a translation of his *Syntagma philosophicum*, which was published in 1658[1]. In the earlier scene, however (Act I, Scene 2), in which Sganarelle undertakes the defence of religion, he is really eloquent and effective.

Il y a de certains petits impertinents dans le monde qui sont libertins sans savoir pourquoi, qui font les esprits forts parce qu'ils croient que cela leur sied bien; et, si j'avois un maître comme cela, je lui dirois fort nettement, le regardant en face: "Osez-vous bien ainsi vous jouer au Ciel, et ne tremblez-vous point de vous moquer comme vous faites des choses les plus

---

[1] See C.-J. Jeannel, *La Morale de Molière*, 1867, p. 219 n. 2.

saintes ? C'est bien à vous, petit ver de terre, petit mirmidon que vous êtes (je parle au maître que j'ai dit), c'est bien à vous à vouloir vous mêler de tourner en raillerie ce que tous les hommes révèrent. Pensez-vous que, pour être de qualité, pour avoir une perruque blonde et bien frisée, des plumes à votre chapeau, un habit bien doré, et des rubans couleur de feu (ce n'est pas à vous que je parle, c'est à l'autre), pensez-vous, dis-je, que vous en soyez plus habile homme, que tout vous soit permis, et qu'on n'ose vous dire vos vérités? Apprenez de moi, qui suis votre valet, que le Ciel punit tôt ou tard les impies, qu'une méchante vie amène une méchante mort, et que...."

Sganarelle may be an ignorant valet, but the above tirade is not unworthy of Pascal, the fragments of whose great Apology did not appear till five years later, and Don Juan's only answer is *Paix!* Faguet thinks that Molière's position would have been clearer, if the play had included a *raisonneur* among its characters. But, as he says, Molière, who is first and foremost a dramatist, does not like *raisonneurs*. But is not Molière's position sufficiently clear? On the one side, a *grand seigneur*, who recognises no law but his own pleasure, and whose atheism is the result not of honest doubt but of his own immoral and ignoble life; on the other, a valet, ignorant, if you like, in spite of his pretensions to philosophy, but possessing the quality which Molière valued above all others—common sense. It is from the lips of the simple and ignorant, the Dorines, the Nicoles, the Toinettes, and in this case Sganarelle, that we are most likely to learn Molière's own views and opinions on any subject. Don Juan might haughtily proclaim that he believed only in "two and two make four," but common sense

told Sganarelle that this does not explain everything, and Molière agreed with Sganarelle[1].

The other characters besides Don Juan and
Sganarelle, of which there are a considerable
number, play only subordinate parts, appearing
in at most a few scenes. But they are good
examples of the ease with which Molière can
create character. Charlotte and Pierrot, with
their peasant's patois, are admirable sketches;
M. Dimanche, all bows and obsequiousness, with
his " Monsieur, je suis votre serviteur," and his
"Monsieur, il n'est pas nécessaire," is a life-like
portrait. On the other hand, Don Louis, Don
Juan's father, is only represented by the tirade
above-mentioned and by a very short scene at
the beginning of the Fifth Act, while Don Carlos,
the most prominent of Donna Elvire's brothers,
is stiff and tedious, especially in the scene with
his brother. There remains the noble and pathetic
figure of Elvire, who, though she only appears
in two scenes, has a greater importance than this
seems to imply. For, as M. Rigal has well pointed
out, her story furnishes the plot, such as there is,
of the drama. It is with Don Juan's desertion
of her that the play opens, and it is she who first
threatens him with the vengeance of Heaven.

Sache que ton crime ne demeurera pas impuni, et que le
même Ciel dont tu te joues me saura venger de ta perfidie.

The twelve men, who are reported to be looking

[1] See Paul Janet's excellent remarks on *Don Juan* in *Les passions
et les caractères dans la littérature du XVIIe siècle*, 3rd ed. 1898,
pp. 101–138, to which, on re-reading them, I find that my account
owes not a little.

for Don Juan at the end of the Second Act, were doubtless acting in her interests, and it is while he is escaping through a forest from their pursuit that he meets her brothers, who are also searching for him. It is in this forest that he comes by chance upon the Statue which is to prove the instrument of Heaven's vengeance (Act III). Once more Elvire appears upon the scene (Act IV, Scene 5), and this time it is not to reproach him with his desertion of her, but to announce her return to the convent, and to implore him to repent before it is too late. Thus the final catastrophe may be regarded as a fitting punishment for that hardness of heart, that ingrained viciousness, of which Don Juan's treatment of Elvire is the climax. But the connecting thread which her story supplies is after all a loose one. The real subject of the play is Don Juan's character, and many of the scenes, which from the point of view of the plot are mere episodes, are all important for the development of that character.

The success of *Don Juan* justified the choice and treatment of the subject. At the second performance, which was on Shrove Tuesday (February 17), and on three other occasions the receipts reached over 2000 *livres*, and it was not till the tenth performance that they dropped to three figures. After the fifteenth performance the theatre closed for the Easter holidays. When it reopened on April 14, the new play, for which a considerable run might still have been anticipated, had silently disappeared from the programme. A few days later[1] there appeared a violent pamphlet, in which Molière and his play were attacked in the most unfair and offensive terms. It professed to be by B. A. S^r. D. R. *advocat en parlement,* and in a second edition, which followed soon afterwards, the name was given in full as le Sieur de Rochemont. But this was only a pseudonym, and we do not know the author's real name[2]. It has been supposed that he was a Jansenist, but the last paragraph but one of his pamphlet suggests that he was a member of the *Cabale des dévots*; for in it he congratulates Louis XIV on having purged the kingdom of heresy, duelling, and swearing, three vices against which the Cabal had waged an unceasing warfare[3]. Moreover, an avowed member of the Company, the Prince de Conti, attacked Molière's play on similar lines in his *Sentiments des Pères de l'Église sur la comédie et les spectacles*, in which he says,

Y a-t-il une école d'athéisme plus ouverte que *le Festin de Pierre*, où, après avoir fait dire toutes les impiétés les plus horribles à un athée qui a beaucoup d'esprit, l'auteur confie la cause de Dieu à un valet, à qui il fait dire, pour la soutenir, toutes les impertinences du monde[4]?

The above remarks are so violent a distortion, or rather perversion, of the truth that it is charitable to suppose that Conti had never seen the play. But he probably represents the views of the Cabal and of the great majority of the clergy.

---

[1] The privilege is dated April 18.
[2] Livet conjectures that it was Barbier d'Aucour.
[3] Molière, *Œuvres* V, 231.
[4] Cp. this with the *Observations, op. cit.* p. 226.

There was, however, another class which had a juster ground for offence. The great nobles might well have resented the disparagement to their order that was involved in the portrait of Don Juan. Here was a man, who in his dress and deportment, in his virtues—courage and sense of honour—and even in his faults—haughtiness, impertinence, indebtedness—was a typical French nobleman, but who was also a hardened and, in some ways, a contemptible villain, and who was justly punished for his crimes by a supernatural doom, a doom more impressive to a popular audience of that day than it is easy for us to realise. It was the truth of the portrait, the truth underlying its idealism, that constituted Molière's most heinous offence.

At any rate he withdrew the play and made no attempt to revise it, nor was it printed during his lifetime. Its place on the French stage was taken by the versified and slightly expurgated version of the younger Corneille (1677). It was not till 1841 that Molière's original play was revived at the Odéon, and not till 1847 that it was restored to its rights at the Comédie Française[1].

[1] See for this latter revival an article by Charles Magnin in the *Rev. des deux mondes* for February 15, 1847.

CHAPTER VI

LE MISANTHROPE

THE withdrawal of *Don Juan* left Molière's company once more unprovided with a new play by their illustrious chief. When the theatre reopened after the Easter holidays they had to be content with Mlle Des Jardins's tragi-comedy, *La Coquette ou le Favori*, and it was not till September 22 that Molière himself provided them with a new piece. This was *L'Amour Médecin*, which had been produced at Versailles just a week before at extraordinarily short notice, five days having sufficed for its composition and rehearsal. The only other important novelty of the year was Racine's tragedy of *Alexandre* which was presented on December 4. It proved successful but, as we have seen, it was transferred to the rival Hôtel de Bourgogne after four performances. The company then had to fall back on old pieces by Molière and others, with the result that at the end of the financial year, 1665–66, an actor's share was less than half of what it had been two years previously[1]. Easter was late this year, and a little more than three weeks after the reopening of the theatre

---

[1] See above, p. 24.

Molière presented to the public, on June 4, a new five-act comedy in verse, the first that he had offered them since the production of *L'École des Femmes*, three and a half years before. The comedy was *Le Misanthrope*.

According to Brossette, Molière read the First Act at a private house in 1664[1]. But Brossette, though honest and well-intentioned, is not always trustworthy, and if his story is true, one wonders why Molière, when he had to withdraw *Don Juan*, did not at once complete the play which he had already begun. If we reject the story, the most likely period for its composition is during the four months from the middle of January to the middle of May 1666. The theatre having been closed till February 21 in consequence of the Queen-Mother's death, Molière, after recovering from his serious illness, would have had a month of leisure to devote entirely to his new piece.

If this is the case, there is much in his life at this period to account for the apparent fact that the play was conceived in a pessimistic mood. In or about October 1665 his relations with his wife had become so strained that they had agreed to separate. In the following December, Racine had behaved to him with singular ingratitude, and that by an act which not only wounded him as a friend, but also inflicted financial loss on

---

[1] *Œuvres de Boileau*, Geneva, 1716, I, 21 : Molière was to have read his translation of Lucretius, but read instead the First Act of *Le Misanthrope*.

his company. Apart from this, the company had
for a considerable time been in rather low water,
chiefly owing to the interdict on *Tartuffe* and
the forced withdrawal of *Don Juan*, blows which
deeply affected their author not only as a theatrical manager but as an artist. In *Tartuffe* he
was conscious that he had written a masterpiece,
and in *Don Juan*, in spite of the difficulties imposed on him by the subject, he had created an
immortal character. Finally in January 1666 he
had a serious illness, which permanently affected
his health. Even on the alternative supposition
that Brossette's story is true, and that the genesis
of the play took place as early as the year 1664,
there was much ground for pessimism—the constant friction between himself and his wife, the
cruel and unjust attacks that followed the *École
des Femmes*, and finally the embargo on *Tartuffe*.

What wonder then if Molière was in a misanthropic mood? What wonder if, including
the bigots who had stifled his masterpiece, the
court-gallants who had encouraged his wife's
coquetry, and the actors of the Hôtel de Bourgogne who had defamed his character, in one
common anathema, he felt that he hated the
whole world? And then his humour came to his
aid, and he realised that for one man to judge
the world by the petty measure of his own experiences was in the highest degree absurd, that,
because he had enemies who were unjust and
dishonest, it did not follow that all men were

unjust and dishonest, and that of all social vices misanthropy is the most ridiculous and the most illogical. So giving the rein to his imagination he created Alceste, and, as is the manner of true creators, he lost himself in his creation. For, if Alceste has his origin in Molière's heart, Alceste is not Molière. He is a young man—a very young man—of high rank and great promise, who fancies that he is a misanthrope.

PHILINTE

Vous voulez un grand mal à la nature humaine.

ALCESTE

Oui, j'ai conçu pour elle une effroyable haine.

PHILINTE

Tous les pauvres mortels, sans nulle exception,
Seront enveloppés dans cette aversion?
Encore en est-il bien, dans le siècle où nous sommes....

ALCESTE

Non : elle est générale, et je hais tous les hommes.
Les uns, parce qu'ils sont méchants et malfaisants,
Et les autres, pour être aux méchants complaisants,
Et n'avoir pas pour eux ces haines vigoureuses
Que doit donner le vice aux âmes vertueuses.

It was the complaisance of the world, or, rather of that small section of the world formed by the social cream of a single city, that caused Alceste's misanthropy. It was the action of his friend Philinte in embracing with protestations of good will a man whose name he barely knew and to whom he was wholly indifferent that set the train to this explosion of his sentiments. He would have men perfectly sincere in their intercourse with one another.

Je veux qu'on soit sincère, et qu'en homme d'honneur,
On ne lâche aucun mot qui ne parte du cœur.

He hates the prevailing practice of paying exaggerated compliments without making any distinction between the man of merit and the fool.

Non, je ne puis souffrir cette lâche méthode
Qu'affectent la plupart de vos gens à la mode ;
Et je ne hais rien tant que les contorsions
De tous ces grands faiseurs de protestations,
Ces affables donneurs d'embrassades frivoles,
Ces obligeants diseurs d'inutiles paroles,
Qui de civilitez avec tous font combat,
Et traitent du même air l'honnête homme et le fat.

Thus Molière, while developing the character of Alceste, poses at the same time the question how far strict veracity and sincerity should be carried out in social intercourse. Alceste will hear of no compromise.

Je veux que l'on soit homme, et qu'en toute rencontre
Le fonds de notre cœur dans nos discours se montre,
Que ce soit lui qui parle, et que nos sentiments
Ne se masquent jamais sous de vains compliments.

To which Philinte objects,

Il est bien des endroits où la pleine franchise
Deviendroit ridicule et seroit peu permise ;
Et parfois, n'en déplaise à votre austère honneur,
Il est bon de cacher ce qu'on a dans le cœur.

But opposition only stirs Alceste, as it stirs Arnolphe and Orgon, to a more intemperate expression of his views, and when Philinte, now equally frank, points out to him, as Chrysalde points out to Arnolphe and Cléante to Orgon, that his attitude is ridiculous,

Et puisque la franchise a pour vous tant d'appas
Je vous dirais tout franc que cette maladie,
Partout où vous allez, donne la comédie,
Et qu'un si grand courroux contre les mœurs du temps
Vous tourne en ridicule auprès de bien des gens.

he bursts out with,

Tant mieux, morbleu ! tant mieux, c'est ce que je demande.

The paying of exaggerated and insincere compliments was part of the ordinary social currency in Molière's day, particularly in salons where the *précieux* spirit reigned. It was said of Mme de Rambouillet that she was *un peu trop complimenteuse*, and Balzac, Voiture, and Chapelain rivalled one another in the emphasis and ingenuity of their compliments. The fashion was carried on by Mlle de Scudéry in the next generation. The "portraits," which she brought into vogue in *Le Grand Cyrus*, are all modelled on the most flattering lines, and the same flattery pervades the *commerce de galanterie* which she and her *précieuses* friends carried on with their admirers. The Marquis de Mascarille is a past master in the art, and Madelon and Cathos return the ball to him with equal zest and hardly less proficiency. But in *Les Précieuses ridicules* Molière was merely laughing at a silly and passing fashion. In *Le Misanthrope* he is concerned with the whole question of social insincerity, a question which is of no less interest at the present day than it was in the days of the *Grand Monarque*.

We have seen that one of Alceste's objections
to indiscriminate compliments and professions
of friendship was that they did not distinguish
between merit and the lack of it, between close
friends and the merest acquaintances. He re-
pudiates Philinte's friendship, when he finds him
warmly protesting his good will to a man to whom
he is wholly indifferent.

> Je refuse d'un cœur la vaste complaisance,
> Qui ne fait de mérite aucune différence ;
> Je veux qu'on me distingue, et pour le trancher net,
> L'ami du genre humain n'est point du tout mon fait.

With the sentiment of the last line every one
will agree, but there is more than offended friendship in Alceste's words. There is a touch of
wounded *amour-propre*, of irritated vanity. The
sonnet-scene shews that Alceste had a certain
reputation among his friends and acquaintances
as a young man of high character and considerable intellectual promise. He feels that to this
in part is due the friendship of so accomplished
an *honnête homme* as Philinte, who is evidently
some years older than himself. But if Philinte
is equally friendly towards every man he meets,
what is the value of his friendship?

Another source of Alceste's misanthropy is a
certain lawsuit in which he is involved. He is
sublimely confident of the justice of his cause,
he roundly refuses to follow the usual practice of
visiting the judges, and he finally declares that
if they have the effrontery to decide against him,
he shall be glad to lose his case for the pleasure

of demonstrating the perversity and wickedness of the human race. Whereupon Philinte naturally replies:

> On se riroit de vous, Alceste, tout de bon,
> Si l'on vous entendoit parler de la façon.

Up to this point there is not very much in Alceste's character to attract our sympathy. His rectitude and sincerity are counter-balanced by his quiet assumption of his own merit and by his exaggerated condemnation of the whole human race except himself. He is a prig, and like all prigs he has no sense of humour. But he is in love, and in love with a young widow

> De qui l'humeur coquette, et l'esprit médisant
> Semble si fort donner dans les mœurs d'à présent.

Philinte summons him to explain his inconsistency. His answer is full of pathos and truth:

> Non, l'amour que je sens pour cette jeune veuve
> Ne ferme point mes yeux aux défauts qu'on lui treuve,
> Et je suis, quelque ardeur qu'elle m'ait pu donner,
> Le premier à les voir, comme à les condamner.
> Mais, avec tout cela, quoi je ne puisse faire,
> Je confesse mon foible, elle a l'art de me plaire :
> J'ai beau voir ses défauts, et j'ai beau l'en blâmer,
> En dépit qu'on en ait, elle se fait aimer ;
> Sa grâce est la plus forte, et sans doute ma flamme
> De ces vices du temps pourra purger son âme.

The critics are surely right here in detecting a personal note. Molière is speaking from the depths of his own heart, thinking less of Célimène than of the actress who was to play the part[1], the young wife from whom he had so recently separated.

This confession of Alceste's love, with its divine unreasonableness, at once puts us in sympathy with him. It also provides the play with a plot—a plot which, simple though it is, possesses those elements of struggle and uncertainty that are essential to dramatic interest. Thus the opening scene has introduced us to the principal character and his friend, has presented a problem of social ethics for our consideration, and has indicated the plot which is to provide the structural framework of the play. It will be seen that the method of procedure is very similar to that of *L'École des Femmes*. There, too, the play opens with a conversation between two friends who express diametrically opposite views with regard to a social problem. But there is this difference that, while in the earlier play the plot is not disclosed till the appearance of Horace in the last scene of the First Act, in *Le Misanthrope* the greater simplicity of the plot makes its indication possible at an earlier stage. Thus the opening scene is a more or less complete exposition of the play; in its simplicity and fidelity to nature it rivals the famous opening scene of *Tartuffe*.

With the Second Scene—the scene of the sonnet—the action of the play begins. For though it is easy to regard it as a mere episode, it has

[1] Robinet says three actresses, Mlle Molière, Mlle Du Parc and Mlle de Brie, played in *Le Misanthrope*, but does not assign their parts. There can be little doubt, however, that Mlle Molière took that of Célimène, and the gentle Mlle de Brie that of Éliante.

a real connexion with the plot. Oronte is one of Alceste's rivals, and it is to Célimène, under the conventional name of Philis, that his sonnet is evidently addressed. His tactlessness, not to say impertinence, in consulting Alceste as to its merits makes the courtesy with which the latter at first treats him all the more admirable, while at the same time it helps to excuse Alceste's final outburst of temper.

But no doubt Molière's chief purpose in this scene is to throw light on Alceste's character and to put his doctrine of sincerity in social intercourse to the test. At first he comes out of the ordeal exceedingly well. He is not only sincere but he gives no ground for offence. When Oronte asks for his opinion, he does not offer the plea that he is no judge of poetry, but he warns him—this with a characteristic touch of conscious rectitude—that he will perhaps find him too severe a critic. He listens with outward patience to Oronte's reading of his sonnet, though he chafes inwardly at Philinte's insincere flattery. He puts his criticisms in an indirect form in order to spare the poet's feelings, and it is not till Oronte has appealed to him over and over again for his direct opinion, that he finally gives it.

> Franchement, il est bon à mettre au cabinet.
> Vous vous êtes réglé sur de méchants modèles,
> Et vos expressions ne sont point naturelles.
> . . . .
> Ce style figuré, dont on fait vanité,
> Sort du bon caractère et de la vérité :
> Ce n'est que jeu de mots, d'affectation pure,
> Et ce n'est point ainsi que parle la nature.

His criticism, it will be observed, is expressed in perfectly courteous terms, and it is directed rather against the fashionable poetry of the day than against Oronte's sonnet in particular. It is only when Oronte, in flagrant violation of their compact, resents Alceste's sincerity that he at last allows his irritation to get the better of his politeness.

C'est qu'ils ont l'art de feindre, et moi, je ne l'ai pas.

This is his first offensive remark, and from this point the wrath of the two men rapidly rises, till it overflows in mutual insult. But Alceste's real indignation is reserved for his friend, Philinte. He cuts short every attempt at explanation, and he declares that he will have no more intercourse with him.

He is in this frame of mind when Célimène appears, and he at once opens fire upon her. She is a coquette, and he will have nothing more to do with her. In the encounter which follows he puts himself at a disadvantage. He is jealous, unreasonable, insulting, and he is not softened by her avowal that she loves him.

Mais qui m'assurera que, dans le même instant,
Vous n'en disiez peut-être aux autres tout autant?

Even while protesting his love he is uncomplimentary;

Et c'est pour mes péchés que je vous aime ainsi.

To this comical remark Célimène sarcastically replies,

Il est vrai, votre ardeur est pour moi sans seconde.

But Alceste, who, as we have seen, is entirely devoid of humour, ignores the sarcasm.

> Jamais
> Personne n'a, Madame, aimé comme je fais.

The exaggeration, the belief that in love, as in morals, he is superior to the rest of the world, is characteristic. Yet, in spite of all this, one loves him for his honesty and for the depth of his attachment to Célimène.

He is put to a further proof in the next great scene of the play, the scene of the portraits (Act II, Scene 4). We have had Célimène the coquette. Now it is the turn of Célimène *la médisante*. *La médisance*, or evil-speaking, was, as Philinte says, a common fault of that age. During Lent 1658 Bossuet preached a sermon against it, in which he says that it "consists in a certain pleasure that one has in hearing or speaking evil of others, without any other reason in particular[1]." He speaks of it as "ce vice si universel," and he adds that the evil-speaker does not spare his best friends, a remark to which *Le Misanthrope* supplies an apt commentary :

PHILINTE. On fait assez de cas de son oncle Damis ;
　　　　　Qu'en dites vous, Madame ?
CÉLIMÈNE.　　　　　　　　　　Il est de mes amis.
PHILINTE. Je le trouve honnête homme, et d'un air assez sage[2].

---

[1] See L'Abbé Lebarq, *Histoire critique de la prédication de Bossuet*, 2nd ed. 1891, p. 161.

[2] Cp. Boileau, *Satire* IX, 161 ff. (1668):
　　"Alidor !" dit un fourbe, "il est de mes amis.
　Je l'ai connu laquais avant qu'il fût commis.
　C'est un homme d'honneur, de piété profonde,
　Et qui veut rendre à Dieu ce qu'il a pris au monde."

Again, in a sermon preached in 1681 Bossuet mentions among the common vices of the day, "cette malignité dangereuse qui vous fait empoisonner si habilement et avec tant d'imperceptibles détours une conduite innocente[1]."

Ten years later Bourdaloue, attacking the same vice, asks, "why is it that evil-speaking has become so agreeable a feature of conversation in society?" and in words almost identical with Bossuet's he calls it "the most common and most universal of vices. It is the vice of the Court and the town, of the lawyer and the soldier, of the young and the old; it is the vice of the priest as well as of the layman[2]." Again, in a sermon *Sur les faux témoignages rendus contre Jésus-Christ* he makes a detailed analysis of the same vice, and finds that one of its causes is *une envie démesurée de parler, de railler, de plaisanter.* And in a long passage, which, as Feugère points out, is an admirable commentary on the scene in Célimène's salon, he describes the part which satire and scandal play in social gatherings, "Il faut que dans les assemblées le prochain soit joué et donné en spectacle par des louanges médisantes[3]."

But in spite of stage and pulpit the evil went on increasing. Sainte-Beuve in his *causerie* on D'Argenson's *Journal* (1742–1756)[4] says that

[1] Sermon *Sur les effets de la Résurrection de Jésus-Christ.*
[2] *Sur la médisance* (*Dimanches* III).
[3] *Exhortations et Instructions Chrétiennes* II. See Feugère, *Bourdaloue*, p. 335, for the whole passage.
[4] *Causeries du Lundi* XII, 93 ff.

he is struck by the writer's constant reference to the prevailing vice of his time, which was the cultivation of *esprit* at the expense of the heart, and as a result the growth of satire, evil-speaking, and ill-natured ridicule. It was the vice, truly adds Sainte-Beuve, of the whole eighteenth century, and especially of its first half. It found a congenial atmosphere in the salon, the revival of which as a social force may be said to date from the organisation of Mme de Lambert's salon in 1710. For in the salon, where every one strove to shine in conversation and to become the centre of attention, there was no readier way of achieving this desired object than to speak ill of your neighbour. And *médisance par vanité* led to *méchanceté par vanité*, so that, whereas in 1715 you have a comedy by Destouches entitled *Le Médisant*, in 1747 Gresset produces *Le Méchant*, the malicious hero of which play was immediately recognised as a common Parisian type of the day. Indeed no less than ten young nobles, none of whom greatly protested, were named as the originals[1]. Thus Molière, in fastening upon the love of evil-speaking as a dangerous canker in salon life, shewed at once insight and prescience.

But to return to Célimène's salon. In this scene Alceste shews his real nobility of character. For him to love is to understand, and to under-

---

[1] Aujourd'hui la méchanceté est réduite en art; elle tient lieu de mérite à ceux qui n'ont en point d'autre, et souvent leur donne de la considération (Duclos, *Considérations sur les mœurs*, 1750).

stand is almost to pardon. He recognises in Célimène an illustration of La Rochefoucauld's maxim—the first authorised edition of his book appeared the year before the production of *Le Misanthrope*—that "On est ordinairement plus médisant par vanité que par malice." For some time he listens in silence to Célimène's portraits, each more malicious than its predecessor, of her friends and acquaintances. At last he boils over with indignation, not so much against Célimène as against the two *marquis*, who had been encouraging her.

Non, morbleu ! c'est à vous ; et vos ris complaisants
Tirent de son esprit tous ces traits médisants.
Son humeur satirique est sans cesse nourrie
Par le coupable encens de votre flatterie ;
Et son cœur à railler trouveroit moins d'appas,
S'il avoit observé qu'on ne l'applaudît pas.

But the whole company, including Célimène herself and his friend Philinte, are against him, and he can find no one to support his view that,

Plus on aime quelqu'un, moins il faut qu'on le flatte ;
À ne rien pardonner, le pur Amour éclate.

The three principal scenes (1, 4, and 5) of the Third Act seem at first sight to be purely episodic, but this is not so. It is true that from Scene 1, which is famous for the inimitable display of fatuity given by Acaste, we merely learn that he, as well as Clitandre, is an aspirant for Célimène's hand. But Scenes 4 and 5 have a real bearing on the plot, though Molière, it must be admitted, has hardly made this clear. The passage of arms between Célimène and Arsinoé (Scene 4) is an admirable exhibition of high comedy, which serves to bring out the characters of both ladies. Arsinoé gets the worst of the encounter, and in the succeeding scenes between her and Alceste she evidently concocts a trick which she hopes will at once avenge her on Célimène and give her a claim to Alceste's gratitude. She shews Alceste a letter written by Célimène which she makes him believe was addressed to his rival, Oronte, though she does not seem to have explained to him how it came into her possession[1]. This leads to the fine scene (3) in the Fourth Act, in which Alceste, blinded by jealousy, violently reproaches his mistress, while she, justly incensed by his accusation, refuses a complete explanation, and with cold dignity puts him entirely in the wrong[2]. Yet the scene ends on what is almost a comic note, for Alceste expresses a wish that, in order to prove the ardour of his love, the lady may suffer misery and unpopularity. No wonder she replies in a tone of irony,

C'est me vouloir du bien d'une étrange manière !
Me préserve le Ciel que vous ayez matière…!

[1] If the letter was really written to Oronte, how did Arsinoé come by it?

[2] More than three-eighths (62 lines out of 160) of this scene has been taken over from the unpublished *Don Garcie*—chiefly from Act IV, Sc. 8 and Act V, Sc. 2—and for the most part without any alteration. The superiority of *Le Misanthrope* to *Don Garcie* as a study of jealousy is well worked out by Saint-Marc Girardin in his *Cours de littérature dramatique* V, clxxxiv.

In the next scene but one (Act IV, Scene 4), which is the one really comic scene of the play, Alceste hears of the loss of his lawsuit and this finally determines him to take the step which he was contemplating when the play opens, that of withdrawing from human society (Act V, Scene 1),

> Puisqu'entre humains, ainsi, vous vivez en vrais loups,
> Traîtres, vous ne m'aurez de ma vie avec vous.

He even professes, with comic fury, to be delighted at his misfortune.

> Ce sont vingt mille francs qu'il m'en pourra coûter ;
> Mais, pour vingt mille francs, j'aurai droit de pester
> Contre l'iniquité de la nature humaine,
> Et de nourrir pour elle une immortelle haine.

But he still remains the ardent irrational lover, and he designs to put Célimène's love to the test by inviting her to share his banishment. However, his love for her has first to undergo a further trial. The two *marquis* return in hot haste, each with a letter from Célimène, in which she has exercised to the full her talent for satirical portraiture. Unfortunately according to agreement they have shewn one another their letters, and each has the pleasure of reading his own portrait. The letter to Clitandre also contains portraits of Oronte ("l'homme à la veste") and Alceste.

> Pour l'homme aux rubans verts, il me divertit quelquefois avec ses brusqueries et son chagrin bourru; mais il est cent moments où je le trouve le plus fâcheux du monde.

The worst feature of Célimène's action is not

her satire but her insincerity, for in each letter
she insinuates to the recipient that he is the
favoured one. As far as the *marquis* and Oronte
are concerned she is not in the least penitent,
but it is otherwise with the man for whom in her
way she really cared. Her confession of her fault
is as pathetic as Alceste's counter-confession that
he loves her in spite of it. But he makes his forgiveness conditional on her consent to following
him to the desert, otherwise his country estates,
where he proposes to spend the rest of his days.
The prospect of being banished from Paris and
Versailles, even in company with Alceste, has no
charms for Célimène.

> Moi, renoncer au monde avant que de vieillir,
> Et dans votre désert aller m'ensevelir !

She will give up her liberty to the extent of
marrying her lover, but solitude, even *à deux*,
has too great terrors for "une âme de vingt ans."
But Alceste will have all or nothing.

> Puisque vous n'êtes point, en des liens si doux,
> Pour trouver tout en moi, comme moi tout en vous,
> Allez, je vous refuse, et ce sensible outrage
> De vos indignes fers pour jamais me dégage.

It will be seen from this brief analysis, with
some omissions, of the play that from the point
of view of construction it is not merely a succession of dramatic *tableaux*. On the contrary,
the scenes are linked together by a sufficient, if
simple, theme, namely the devotion of Alceste,
with his impassioned love of sincerity and his
hatred of social conventions, to a satirical and

insincere coquette, to whom society is the very breath of life. But, as in all Molière's greatest plays, the chief interest lies in the characters, and before all in Alceste.

He is a young man of rank and fortune, in whom his friends recognise unusual merit. He is frank, candid, and sincere and, except when he is irritated beyond control, he has the courteous bearing of a high-bred gentleman. All the three women in the play are more or less in love with him, and Éliante finds in his sincerity something noble and heroic. "Comment une femme peut-elle ne pas aimer Alceste?" said Mlle Mars, one of the best and most charming of Célimènes. But he is proud and conscious of his own merits, and he especially piques himself on his frankness and sincerity. He is brusque, irritable, and explosive; his favourite expression of *morbleu* is highly characteristic; he has all the exaggeration and impulsiveness of youth; he has no sense of humour or proportion; and, what is a grave defect in Molière's eyes, he lacks common sense. As the result of these failings, which are due partly to age and partly to temperament, he not only says and does ridiculous things, but his whole position is more or less ridiculous. Because a limited section of society is too fond of paying compliments to a man's face and laughing at him behind his back, he professes hatred for the whole human race. Further he is in love with a woman who is a finished example of those very faults for which he detests the world. The miracle is that in spite of qualities which more often than not make a man unamiable and unpopular, he has won the love of countless readers for two hundred and fifty years.

We love and admire Alceste, while we laugh at him—that probably sums up the attitude of the average reader to the *homme aux rubans verts*. But it is not the universal attitude. Setting apart the few who regard him as a gloomy and self-righteous prig, there are a considerable number, including French critics of renown, whose admiration for him is mingled with pity, but not with laughter. For them he is a wholly tragic figure, at war with an evil world, which he tries in vain to reform. This view is, of course, a permissible one. Great characters in fiction, like great characters in history, appear differently to different ages, and what in one age rouses laughter may in another provoke tears. But though a tragic Alceste may appeal to the imagination of modern readers, this is not the Alceste either of the seventeenth century or of Molière.

How Molière's contemporaries interpreted the character may be gathered from the account of the play by Donneau de Visé which was prefixed to the original edition (1667). For though it may be true that Molière was not pleased with the account, it doubtless represents, more or less, the general opinion of the day[1]. In summing up the

---

[1] Grimarest and Brossette in their different versions of the story, both of which present difficulties, agree as to Molière's dissatisfaction (Molière, *Œuvres* v, 369–370).

play Visé says, "le héros en est le plaisant sans
être trop ridicule......Le Misanthrope, malgré
sa folie, si l'on peut ainsi appeler son humeur, a
le caractère d'un honnête homme, et beaucoup
de fermeté......Bien qu'il paroisse en quelque
façon ridicule, il dit des choses fort justes." As
for Alceste's creator, though we may be sure that
he fully realised the tragic side of his character,
it was not this aspect that he wished to present
to the public. He was writing a comedy, and
for its hero he required a character of comedy.
According to unanimous tradition he made an
admirable Alceste, relieving, as we may conjecture, the simple and natural gravity appropriate
to a serious part, which had failed to please in
Don Garcie, with the whimsical touches of the
born comedian. His successor in the part was
his pupil, Baron, who first played it at the age
of nineteen, seven days after his master's death,
and who still played it at the close of his life,
when he was seventy-six, and in the opinion
of Collé, "played it divinely[1]." According to
another eye-witness, "il mettait non seulement
beaucoup de noblesse et de dignité, mais il y
joignait encore une politesse délicate et une fonds
d'humanité qui faisaient aimer le Misanthrope...
Il se permettait quelques brusqueries et de
l'humeur, mais toujours ennoblies par les tons et
par son jeu....Il ne déclamait jamais, il parlait.
Il jouait avec sentiment la scène du quatrième
acte avec Célimène; il conservait toujours, même

[1] Baron retired from the stage in 1691, but returned to it again
in 1720, when he was sixty-six.

dans sa fureur, les égards et la politesse que l'on doit aux femmes, lors même elles n'en méritent point." Grandval, who assumed the part about the year of Baron's death, and who did not retire from the stage till nearly forty years later, was also praised for his delicacy, grace, and natural dignity. Molé (1776–1802) introduced into the part an element of exaggerated energy, playing the scene with Célimène in the Fourth Act with the fury of an indignant and jealous lover. But Fleury, who succeeded to Molé's parts and retired in 1818, returned to the traditions of Baron and Grandval, and played Alceste with the same finish, reticence, and natural dignity[1].

Rousseau's well-known attack on *Le Misanthrope* in his *Lettre sur les spectacles* is of more importance as a revelation of his own character than as a criticism of Molière's play[2]. But his reading of the character of Alceste is the traditional one. "Vous ne sauriez que nier deux choses : l'une qu'Alceste est un homme droit, sincère, estimable, un véritable homme de bien ; l'autre, que l'auteur lui donne un personnage ridicule." The second proposition is true in the sense that Alceste does and says ridiculous things, or, in Rousseau's own words, that he " has some real defects which we are not wrong to laugh at." But this is not "to ridicule virtue." As Dorante says in *La Critique de l'École des Femmes*, " il n'est pas incompatible qu'une

[1] Molière, *Œuvres* V, 398–407.
[2] See Faguet, *Rousseau contre Molière*, pp. 3–84.

personne soit ridicule en de certaines choses, et
honnête homme en d'autres." "You may estimate your capacity for comic perception," truly
says George Meredith in his *Essay on Comedy*,
"by being able to detect the ridicule in them
you love, without loving them less." But Jean-
Jacques had absolutely no capacity for comic
perception, and he resented Alceste being made
ridiculous all the more, because he saw in him
a likeness of the man he loved best in the
world—himself. It was a further grievance with
him that the likeness was not sufficiently idealised.
The misanthropy of the noble misanthrope—
like Rousseau—"is a violent hatred of vice
engendered by an ardent love of virtue, and
embittered by the ever-present spectacle of the
wickedness of men." He may often be unjust
and unreasonable, but he must not be irritated
by puerilities. He must direct his anger against
the vices and disorders of his time, and bear the
evils which affect himself with calm composure.
Alceste ought not to have been surprised at the
behaviour of Oronte, or at the loss of his lawsuit. "Mais il falloit faire rire le parterre." So
Molière, he complains, makes his noble misanthrope ridiculous. But Molière was drawing,
not an abstract character, not a monster of perfection who thinks all the world except himself
imperfect, but a living man, with a man's in-
firmities—a man like Don Quixote, at once noble
and ridiculous, perverse and lovable.

It was commonly said in Molière's day that
Alceste was a portrait of the Duc de Montausier,

the husband of Julie d'Angennes, Mme de Rambouillet's daughter. Olivet in his *Histoire de l'Académie française*, Saint-Simon, Segrais in his table-talk, Ménage, all repeat the story, though with considerable variations, and several of Molière's commentators have noted the resemblance between Alceste and the portrait which Mlle de Scudéry has drawn of Montausier under the name of Mégadate in *Le Grand Cyrus*. He is of a "naturel fort violent...il est ennemi déclaré de la flatterie : il ne peut louer ce qu'il ne croit point digne de louange." It may be true that contemporaries noticed a resemblance between the noble misanthrope and the Duke who was an enemy to flattery, and that the Duke, who was fifty-two, was pleased with the supposed portrait, and that Molière, who knew that even plain-speakers are not impervious to the subtler forms of flattery, took care not to undeceive him. But that Montausier did more than furnish Molière at the most with a hint or two cannot be supposed for a moment. Another hint was furnished by Boileau, who liked to think, and was perhaps justified in thinking, that he had served as a model for Alceste in the sonnet-scene[1]. The occasion was the candidature for the *Académie française* of the Marquis de Sainte-Aulaire, whose claims as a writer of light songs seemed to the critic far from adequate. These, however, were mere hints and details.

---

[1] This does not exclude the possibility that the idea of the scene was suggested to Molière by a passage in Cervantes's *El Licenciado Vidriera.*

Alceste is the creation of Molière's brain working upon his own experiences and sympathies.

According to Rousseau, whereas Alceste is
made ridiculous, Philinte is represented as "le
sage de la pièce ; un de ces honnêtes gens du
grand monde dont les maximes ressemblent
beaucoup à celles des fripons." And then follows
a violent denunciation of these same *honnêtes
gens*, which must be regarded as an analysis,
not of Philinte, but of Rousseau's enemy, Grimm.
For the real Philinte has many good qualities.
In the first place he is a staunch friend, especially to Alceste. He is quite unaffected by his
rudeness and ill-temper ; he arranges his affair
with Oronte without taking any credit to himself ; and the play closes with an appeal to
Éliante to join him in persuading their friend
to abandon his rash project. Nor in the scene
of the portraits does he join the two *marquis*
in presenting his neighbours as targets for
Célimène's shafts. He even says a good word
for Damis, praising him in terms which might
apply to himself:

Je le trouve honnête homme, et d'un air assez sage.

But in the eyes of Alceste he has a grave
fault. He is insincere in his relations with mere
acquaintances, especially in the matter of paying
compliments. Like Mme de Rambouillet he is
un peu trop complimenteux.

La chute en est jolie, amoureuse, admirable.
. . .
Je n'ai jamais ouï de vers si bien tournés.

No wonder Alceste is inwardly furious.

In fact Philinte answers very closely to the conception of the *honnête homme* as portrayed in La Rochefoucauld's maxims on society. He fully recognises the obligation "to find his pleasure in that of others, to treat with consideration their self-love and never to wound it." But like La Rochefoucauld—indeed, like most of the moralists of his day—he takes a low view of human nature.

> Oui, je vois ces défauts dont votre âme murmure
> Comme vices unis à l'humaine nature;
> Et mon esprit enfin n'est pas plus offensé
> De voir un homme fourbe, injuste, intéressé,
> Que de voir des vautours affamés de carnage,
> Des singes malfaisants, et des loups pleins de rage.

Possibly, like La Rochefoucauld, he has formed this estimate as the result of his own experience. But it has not made him either indignant or morose. Rather it has inclined him to take a lenient view of men's vices.

> Mon Dieu, des mœurs du temps mettons-nous moins en
>   peine,
> Et faisons un peu grâce à la nature humaine;
> Ne l'examinons point dans la grande rigueur,
> Et voyons ses défauts avec quelque douceur.
> Il faut, parmi le monde, une vertu traitable;
> À force de sagesse, on peut être blâmable;
> La parfaite raison fuit toute extrémité,
> Et veut que l'on soit sage avec sobriété.

But Philinte is not *le sage de la pièce* in the sense that Cléante is in *Tartuffe*. He is not, as Donneau de Visé supposes, held up for our imitation, nor is he the spokesman of Molière's

views. As between the brusque candour of the
misanthrope and the insincere flattery of the
well-bred man of the world Molière holds the
scales with scrupulous fairness. But it is easy
to see that his heart is with Alceste.

And what of Célimène? Is she, as George
Meredith would have us believe, the principal
person of the comedy? Hardly so, though
doubtless she would have been, had he had the
telling of the story. It is enough to speak of
her, as a French critic does, as the "point lumi-
neux de la pièce." As for her character, she is,
as we have seen, a coquette and a *médisante*.
As a coquette it is easy to find excuses for her.
She is only twenty, and she has a train of admirers, whom, as Meredith says, she finds it
hard to cut off. It is greatly in her favour that
Alceste has her preference. But she is unwilling
to declare that preference, and it is only when
her other admirers have found her out that
she at last capitulates—but not on Alceste's
terms. "She will give her hand to honesty, but
she cannot quite abandon worldliness." If she
eventually marries Alceste she will remain in
the world, she will still have admirers, but in
her fashion she will be true to Alceste. It is in
her satirical tongue that lies her greatest danger.
It is true, as Alceste says, that it is stimulated by
the love of applause rather than by real ill-
nature. Moreover she has an incomparable
gift for satirical portraiture, and it is not surprising that, given encouragement, she should

love to exercise it. But one cannot help comparing her to a character in real life who had the same clear-sighted vision and the same talent for concise and satirical portraits—I mean Mme Du Deffand—and one wonders whether, if Alceste stands firm to his purpose, Célimène, whose heart, even now, is not of the warmest, will not in old age suffer from disillusion and *ennui* as much as the friend of Horace Walpole.

As for Alceste, if, as is reasonable to suppose, he is a very young man, his case is not a hopeless one. The mellowing that will come with years and with a greater knowledge of himself and the world will make him more lenient to the imperfections of human nature. He will learn that it is possible to be frank and sincere without being offensive, that one small section of society is not the whole world, and that one's own wrongs are not necessarily a measure of the injustice of mankind. Molière wisely leaves Alceste's future to the imagination of his readers, but the concluding lines of the play allow those who do not insist upon a tragic ending to hope that his decision is not irrevocable.

Molière has drawn his secondary characters in the spirit of a painter composing a great picture. They serve to throw into relief the three central figures. Thus, on the one hand, the prude Arsinoé gives emphasis to the wit and charm of Célimène, while, on the other, the sincere and sympathetic Éliante makes us more conscious of Célimène's faults. Similarly Oronte and the two *marquis* with their vanity and self-importance help to accentuate the virtues of Alceste, while their marked inferiority to Philinte prevents us from regarding that excellent specimen of an *honnête homme* with the prejudiced eyes of a Rousseau.

In accordance with the traditions of a classical play, the number of characters is small, but, as M. Rigal has pointed out, the canvas is enlarged, at any rate to our imagination, by the scene of the portraits. The seven men and one woman who are offered up as victims to Célimène's satirical talent are all no doubt *habitués* of her salon, and we can picture them all playing their part in it—Damis, the censorious *bel esprit*, Timante with his mysterious whispers[1], Damon with his endless chatter, Adraste with his vanity and self-love, Géralde with his airs of a *grand seigneur*, and Bélise with her insupportable lack of conversation. La Bruyère's portraits, which surely owe something to this scene of Molière's, are executed, for the most part, in greater detail, but they are less truly imaginative. The little sketches in *Le Misanthrope* are yet another instance of Molière's wonderful faculty for creating character by a few rapid strokes.

Judged by the receipts *Le Misanthrope* was not one of the most successful of Molière's plays. It was decidedly less successful than

---

[1] Commentators have noted the resemblance between Timante and La Bruyère's Théodote, in whom all the 'keys' recognise the Abbé de Choisy.

L'École des Femmes and *Don Juan*. Only on the first two days did the takings exceed a thousand *livres*, and after the ninth performance there was a very decided falling off. But Grimarest greatly exaggerates this comparative want of success. It is not true that the second performance was "more feeble," i.e. less successful, than the first. Far less is it true that at the fourth performance Molière coupled with it *Le Médecin malgré lui*, and that this addition brought all Paris to his theatre. As a matter of fact, Molière did not put *Le Médecin* on the stage till August 6, when, in conjunction with Donneau de Visé's *La Mère coquette*, it was moderately successful, the receipts amounting to 632 *livres*. It was not till September 3 that he gave it with *Le Misanthrope*, and the two plays together produced nearly a thousand *livres*. Evidently, however, *Le Misanthrope* was not a special favourite with the *parterre*. The want of outward action and strongly marked comedy is sufficient to account for this. But good judges from the first recognised its merits. The writers in the rhyming news-sheets, Subligny and Robinet, hailed it with an enthusiasm which reflected the views of acknowledged leaders of taste. Above all, Boileau recognised it as his friend's masterpiece, as superior even to *Tartuffe*. Molière remained for him "l'auteur du *Misanthrope*[1]."

[1] See Molière, *Œuvres* v, 362–366.

CHAPTER VII

AMPHITRYON, GEORGE DANDIN, L'AVARE

DURING the winter of 1666–1667 Molière was chiefly occupied in preparing plays for the brilliant fêtes which were held at Saint-Germain from December 2 to February 19. We have seen that his contribution consisted of *Mélicerte*, a *Pastorale comique*, and the charming little comedy of *Le Sicilien*, which was presented at the Palais-Royal in the following summer (June 10). In none of these pieces do we find any trace of the gloom which inspired the conception of *Le Misanthrope*. But the year 1667 reopened the sources of Molière's pessimism. His illness, which kept him from the theatre for two months, the defection of Mlle Du Parc, the renewed failure of his attempt to play *Tartuffe* in public, the closing of his theatre for the greater part of August and September, all these trials and vexations moved him, as we have seen, to contemplate retirement from the stage[1]. But before the end of the year he had finished writing a new play, and the year 1668 proved one of the busiest in his whole career, for it witnessed the production of *Amphitryon, George Dandin*, and *L'Avare*.

I have pointed out that in all these plays there is a certain flavour of pessimism, with an under-

[1] See above, p. 32.

lying suggestion of tragedy. A large proportion of the characters are rascals or fools, and the rascals not only go unpunished but come out triumphant. Is this merely accidental, or is it due to a recrudescence of that pessimistic mood, that sense of the power of evil, that misanthropic view of human nature, which seems to have oppressed Molière when he conceived *Le Misan-thrope?* It is an interesting speculation, but a speculation it must remain. One is on surer ground in pointing out that all three plays are based upon an earlier play on the same subject, and that in each case Molière has found a difficulty in adapting the original play to his own needs. The reason is that the subject of all three is unsuited to that form of comedy to which Molière most inclined, namely, social comedy. The mythological story of Jupiter and Alcmene is a possible theme for a quasi-religious drama like Plautus's *Amphitruo*, but strip it of its religious import and it presents insuperable difficulties to treatment as a social comedy. The plot of the same writer's *Aulularia* lends itself far better to gay comedy than to the serious study of avarice, however strongly relieved by comic scenes. *George Dandin*, treated as a mere farce, with no pretensions to a moral basis, is highly amusing, but as a transcript of life it is open to misunderstanding.

Molière's choice of Plautus's *Amphitruo* as the groundwork of a new play was, no doubt, mainly determined by the knowledge that an earlier version of it, Rotrou's *Les Sosies* (1636), had rivalled the *Cid* in popularity, and that on its revival in 1650 it had been equally successful. It is a play of some merit, gay and lively in its comic scenes, and written in an easy, if careless, style. But the chief cause of its popularity seems to have been the spectacular display occasioned by the appearance of Jupiter in the clouds. This at any rate was the special feature of the performances in 1650, *La Naissance d'Hercule*, as the play was then called, being designated as a *grande pièce de machines*.

In the interests of his theatre Molière did not neglect this feature of the entertainment. Robinet in recounting the performance at the Court on January 16—this was the third performance, the two preceding ones having been given at the Palais-Royal—speaks of

> les décorations
> Avec des machines volantes,
> Plus que les astres éclatantes.

But for us the main attraction of *Amphitryon*, apart from the brilliance of its verse, is the character of Sosie. From the monologue which ends in the delightful imaginary dialogue between himself and Alcmène in the first scene to the ironical epilogue with which he concludes the play, he is a perennial source of delight. In his unabashed cowardice and greediness he resembles the valet of Don Juan, but he is readier of speech, wittier, and, above all, more humorous. If he does not aspire to the philosophy which

Sganarelle has acquired from a smattering of book-knowledge, he has a shrewder philosophy of his own, based upon experience and knowledge of human nature. " Un grand seigneur méchant homme est une terrible chose," is what Sgana-relle has learnt from his service with Don Juan; but Sosie's reflections embrace the whole class of *les grands*.

> Notre sort est beaucoup plus rude
> Chez les grands que chez les petits.
> Ils veulent que pour eux tout soit, dans la nature,
> Obligé de s'immoler.
>   . . . .
> Parlerai-je, Monsieur, selon ma conscience,
> Ou comme auprès des grands on le voit usité?
>   Faut-il dire la vérité,
>   Ou bien user de complaisance?

And at the end of the same scene (Act II, Sc. 1), when his master, who is not *méchant* like Don Juan, declares that he is weary of listening to his *sottises*, he retorts:

> Tous les discours sont des sottises,
> Partant d'un homme sans éclat :
> Ce seroit paroles exquises
> Si c'étoit un grand qui parlât.

Sosie is a cousin of Figaro, and it is perhaps no mere chance that La Bruyère, who must greatly have appreciated his aphorisms, has borrowed his name to designate a valet who rose to wealth and rank.

The inimitable scenes between Sosie and Mercury and between Sosie and Amphitryon have their counterparts both in the original play and in Rotrou's version, but Molière is easily superior to his predecessors—to Plautus in delicacy, and to Rotrou in humour. In fact a comparison between *Les Sosies* and *Amphitryon* helps one to realise Molière's extraordinary power of seizing the comic and humorous features of a situation and of giving the fullest expression to it by action and dialogue. In this play he has added to the comedy of the situation by making Alcmène's *suivante* the wife of Sosie, and by introducing two effective and amusing scenes between her and Mercure-Sosie as pendants to those between her mistress and Jupiter-Amphitryon.

Another addition is the witty and charming prologue, which takes the form of a dialogue between Mercury seated on a cloud and Night in her car, and which thus serves as a fresh occasion for spectacular machinery. Molière no doubt got the hint for this, but no more, from Rotrou's first scene, in which Mercury addresses the Moon. On the whole, his debt to his immediate predecessor is slight. He has borrowed a couple of lines in one place, and eight lines in another, and in the famous, "Moi vous dis-je, ce moi plus robuste que moi, &c.," he has amplified and improved a similar tirade of which the idea already existed in Plautus. Further,

> Le véritable Amphitryon
> Est l'Amphitryon où l'on dîne,

was suggested by

> Point, point d'Amphitryon où l'on ne dîne point.

But while Rotrou puts the words in the mouth of one of the captains, Molière assigns them, far more appropriately, to Sosie. Finally the germs of the scathing epilogue in which the latter sums up the situation are to be found in the following lines:

> Cet honneur, ce me semble, est un triste avantage:
> On appelle cela lui sucrer le breuvage,
> Pour moi j'ai, de nature, un front capricieux,
> Qui ne peut rien souffrir, et lui vînt-il des dieux.

It is in the scenes between Alcmène and her real and supposed husbands that the difficulty of making the play acceptable to a modern audience presents itself. In spite of Mercury's irreverent remarks, the Latin play doubtless passed muster as a quasi-religious drama. Rotrou took the play as he found it, and preserved the serious character of the scenes in question. If his dialogue lacks the force and serious brevity of Plautus, in substance it closely follows the original. Nor is it till we come to Sosie's speech at the end of the play that we get the faintest suggestion that Rotrou considers Jupiter's conduct open to criticism. In fact though his play is called a comedy, it is really a tragi-comedy, the name which Plautus, in the person of Mercury, proposed for his own play, saying that it was a tragedy so far as it treated of gods, and a comedy by reason that it included a slave amongst its characters.

In Molière's play the two gods are stripped of all divinity. Jupiter is an ordinary French

gallant, a *précieux* Don Juan, one of that privi-
leged class whose privileges Sosie so keenly
resents. The subtle distinction (much admired
by some critics) that he draws between the lover
and the husband, which naturally shocks the
virtuous Alcmène, stamps him as a libertine.
Mercury is represented rather as Jupiter's confidential valet than as his son, and he is well
suited to the part. He is Sganarelle without
his conscience and his good feeling, and his
character cannot be more fitly summed up than
in Sosie's pithy remark:

> Et je ne vis, de ma vie,
> Un dieu plus diable que toi.

Sosie's comment on the whole situation has
already been noticed. It is an answer to Jupiter's

> Un partage avec Jupiter
> N'a rien du tout qui déshonore,

and it may be taken as a clear proof that Molière
did not share Jupiter's view:

> Le grand dieu Jupiter nous fait beaucoup d'honneur,
> Et sa bonté sans doute est pour nous sans seconde;
> Il nous promet l'infaillible bonheur
> D'une fortune en mille biens féconde,
> Et chez nous il doit naître un fils d'un très-grand cœur:
> Tout cela va le mieux du monde;
> Mais enfin coupons aux discours,
> Et que chacun chez soi doucement se retire.
> Sur telles affaires, toujours
> Le meilleur est de ne rien dire.

Irony can hardly be more scathing than this.
The suggestion first made by Rœderer, and
readily accepted by Michelet, that Molière in-

tended the play to be a glorification of the loves of Louis XIV and Mme de Montespan has been shewn to be highly improbable, merely as a question of dates. But the whole tone of the play, and in particular Sosie's final comment, put the matter beyond dispute.

In two soliloquies by Amphitryon a tragic note makes itself heard, the bitter cry of a husband who believes that he has suffered dishonour. On the other hand, in the scene of reconciliation between Alcmène and Jupiter (Act II, Scene 6) the tone is distinctly lyrical, the effect being produced partly by the language, which is that of passion and not of action, and partly by the *vers libres* in which the whole play is written. Molière had already used this metre in the *Remercîment au Roi*[1], written in 1663, and also for letters in *Le Dépit amoureux* and *Don Garcie* and for the *Maximes du Mariage* in *L'École des Femmes*, and La Fontaine had given some brilliant examples of it in his *Contes* (1665). But the idea of writing a play in *vers libres* was probably suggested to him by Corneille's *Agésilas*, which was produced in 1666. Now *Agésilas*, though it is called a tragedy by reason that it deals with kings and princesses, differs hardly at all, except in the more elevated tone of its language, from the comedies with which Corneille began his career. To borrow the just description of Jules Lemaître "it is the story of three couples of ill-assorted lovers, who, after four acts of mis-

[1] *Œuvres* IV, 295–300.

understandings and explanations, re-sort themselves in the *dénouement*." M. Lanson is of
opinion that the *vers libres* are "well suited to the
half unreal character of this sentimental comedy."
It seems to me, rather, that the dignified and
well-reasoned utterances of these self-controlled
and unimpassioned lovers might have been better
expressed in ordinary Alexandrine couplets.
But Molière, with his quick insight, may well
have recognised the suitability of the metre for
a play more or less lyrical, or, as we should say,
operatic in character, and he may have at the
same time realised that by giving this character
to his version of *Amphitryon*, a character which
was already indicated by the need of machinery
and spectacular display, he would be able to
some extent to get over the difficulty of the story.
It would help the spectators to forget the essential immorality of the plot, if the play took the
form of a fairy extravaganza in which comedy,
lyrical passion, and irony were blended in an
exquisite whole. As M. Romain Rolland says,
"*Amphitryon* est une musique à soi seul."

As regards the technique of Molière's *vers
libres*, it is sufficient to point out that they differ
from Corneille's in the employment of lines of
ten and seven syllables in addition to those of
twelve and eight syllables, and from La Fontaine's in their strophic character. It has been
shewn by M. Comte that the lines of seven
syllables, "light, rapid, dancing," appear, with the
exception of three lines in a speech by Naucratès,

only in the parts of Mercury, Sosie, Cléanthis, and the goddess, Night, that is to say, only in those parts which are comic in character[1]. The same writer, however, goes too far when he contends that the whole play is written in stanzas of varying length; it is better to accept the modified conclusion of Chatelain that the rhymes are grouped in such a way as to form poetic periods, which are not true stanzas, but which for the most part resemble them[2]. The difference between these views is, after all, not very great, and it is less important to decide between them than to point out that, while the greater freedom of La Fontaine's treatment is better suited to narrative, Molière's arrangement is more in keeping with the lyrical character which he wished to impress upon his work. In any case, his handling of this more or less novel experiment in versification is a striking testimony at once to his metrical genius and to his high standard of artistic achievement[3].

In July 1668 the peace of Aix-la-Chapelle (May 2) was celebrated at Versailles by magnificent fêtes. They included a *grand divertisse-*

[1] Charles Comte, *Les stances libres dans Molière*, Versailles, 1893.

[2] *Les vers libres de Molière dans Amphitryon* (*Mélanges de philologie offerts à M. F. Brunot*, 1904, pp. 41–55). Henri Chatelain, who was professor of French in the University of Birmingham, died at Paris in August 1915, of an illness which he had contracted at the front.

[3] In 1786 *Amphitryon* was produced at Versailles as an opera ; the music was by Grétry and the words by Sedaine, who closely followed the development of Molière's play (M. Pellisson, *Les comédies-ballets de Molière*, 1914, pp. 194 ff.).

ment royal, consisting of a *comédie-ballet* in which a prose comedy by Molière and a sort of pastoral opera with words by Molière and music by Lully were skilfully blended. As was usual with these royal entertainments, Molière had very short notice. So he bethought him of an old farce, *La Jalousie du Barbouillé,* which had served already, under the title of *La Jalousie de Gros-René* or *Gros-René jaloux,* with more or less refashioning, during the years 1660–1664[1]. But now Molière took it up again, and retaining the same primitive theme and the scenes in which Angélique—the name is the same in both pieces —finds herself shut out of her husband's house and then turns the tables on him, he expanded it, and partially transformed it into a social comedy. In *George Dandin ou Le Mari confondu* the social *milieu* is definitely indicated: George Dandin is a rich countryman—our word "peasant" does not adequately convey the idea of *paysan*— married to the daughter of one of those provincial nobles known as *hoberaux* whose increasing impoverishment without any diminution of their privileges was one of the prime causes of the French Revolution. Probably George Dandin owned his own land, while his father-in-law, M. de Sotenville, had little but his ancestral home and his seignorial rights. He retained, however, to the full his family pride, and in this he was even surpassed by his wife, of the noble family

[1] The idea of the husband being shut out of his own house is the theme of two stories in the *Decameron* (VII, 4, and VII, 8).

of La Prudoterie, "maison où le ventre anoblit."
M. and Mme de Sotenville are, in fact, two of
the most entertaining and humorous figures in
the whole of Molière's gallery, and the scene
which signalises their first appearance (Act I,
Scene 4) is a joy for ever.

They must have been even more entertaining
to Molière's contemporaries, who could testify
to the fidelity of the portraits and appreciate all
the little idiosyncrasies of language in which
M. de Sotenville indulges—his love of feudal
terms, such as *forfaire* and *forligner*, and of
other quaint archaisms, his favourite objurgation
of *corbleu*, his *m'amour* with which he addresses
his wife, and his love of homely metaphors. But
wholly ridiculous though this couple must have
seemed on the stage, the reader finds in them an
element of pathos, even of tragedy. For with all
their absurd pride in their family and their order,
they are honest and honourable folk. "Nous n'en-
tendons pas raillerie sur les matières d'honneur."
"L'honneur de notre famille nous est plus cher
que toute chose." Yet, by marrying their daughter,
without consulting her, to a man beneath her in
station, with whom she has nothing in common,
they have brought this honour which is so dear
to them into a highly precarious position. Even
more obviously pathetic to a reader of the play
is the figure of George Dandin. Though the
laughter is against him from first to last, we
sympathise with him while we laugh at him, and
we can feel the tragedy of his last remark,
"Lorsqu'on a, comme moi, épousé une méchante

femme, le meilleur parti qu'on puisse prendre, c'est de s'aller jeter dans l'eau la tête la première."

In 1877 the Comédie-Française was embolden-ed to give effect to this aspect of the play, and, with no less an artist than Got in the principal part, the experiment of a representation on realistic lines was made. Got's acting was masterly, but the performance was a failure. The audience found the piece *triste à mourir*, and it was with-drawn after the second night. We can imagine Molière's shade addressing the members of his old company somewhat in this fashion: "My dear friends, I am as sensible as you are of the tragedy of George Dandin's married life, and I am far from blind to the nobler elements in the charac-ters of that ridiculous but respectable couple, M. and Mme de Sotenville. But the traditional theme of the old farce, which I took as my starting-point, makes it impossible to treat the play in the serious fashion befitting a true social comedy. George Dandin must remain *Le mari confondu*. Played, as you have played it, as a transcript of real life, and as if George Dandin and M. and Mme de Sotenville were real human beings, the piece becomes no longer a comedy but an ignoble tragedy, devoid of grandeur, and unillumined by one gleam of the ultimate triumph of good. No—the only way to make *George Dandin* acceptable is to play it as a farce through-out, accentuating every element of caricature and treating the characters as grotesque puppets[1]."

From the point of view of stage representation,

---

[1] Cp. Sarcey, *Quarante ans de théâtre*, pp. 121–127.

Rousseau's censure of *George Dandin* is as futile as it is unjust. "Quel est le plus criminel," he asks, "d'un paysan assez fou pour épouser une demoiselle, ou d'une femme qui cherche à déshonorer son époux? Que penser d'une pièce où le parterre applaudit à l'infidélité, au mensonge, à l'impudence de celle-ci, et rit de la bêtise du manant puni?" But, even granting that it is a question of infidelity, which is by no means clear, the audience, though it laughs at the husband, is far from applauding the wife. They have no feelings of approval or disapproval towards either of them. They regard them as mere puppets, like Punch and Judy, and moral considerations do not enter their heads. Finally, it must be remembered that in the original representations the atmosphere of farce and unreality was accentuated by the setting of the play, by the singing and dancing which preceded and followed each act. Molière perhaps made an error of judgment in tacking a social comedy on to a medieval farce, but he might fairly have alleged as excuses, that he had to produce a play at very short notice that while the king's taste was for farce his own was for social comedy, and that it was extremely difficult to combine the two.

It is a fair supposition that Molière's attention was drawn to Plautus's *Aulularia* when he was engaged upon the *Amphitruo*, and with his wide knowledge of dramatic literature he would have remembered that his predecessor, Pierre de

Larivey, at the close of the sixteenth century, had used the same play, either at first hand or through the *Aridosio* of Lorenzino de' Medici, for his best and best-known comedy, *Les Esprits*. The *Aulularia*, which, like the *Amphitruo*, has come down to us in an incomplete state, is an amusing play, of which the main interest lies in the character of Euclio and in the situations which arise out of the plot. Euclio is not a true miser. He is only poor and stingy, stinginess being hereditary in his family. But one day he finds a treasure in a pot (*aula*) and straightway his stinginess is transformed into avarice. He hides the pot, and is for ever changing its hiding-place, for he suspects the whole world of predatory intentions. He has a daughter, who is in love with one Liconides, but whom he promises to the old and rich Megadorus on condition that the latter provides the dowry and the wedding-feast. Then Strobilus, the slave of Liconides, discovers the hiding-place and carries off the pot, and it is only restored to Euclio on his consenting to his daughter's marriage with Liconides instead of Megadorus. In the end, the old man makes his son-in-law a present of the treasure[1].

Taking this gay comedy as his starting-point, Molière has transformed it into a serious study of avarice. In place of the not unsympathetic Euclio, whose avarice is more or less of a hallu-

---

[1] The fifteenth century scholar, Urceo Codro, wrote a conclusion to this effect, based upon a single line in the earlier of the two *argumenta* or summaries, which dates from *circ.* 100–50 B.C.

cination, he has portrayed a true miser. Avarice, like some malignant germ, has poisoned his soul. It has stifled his natural affections, and made him hard-hearted, unjust, and suspicious. The result is that his children are deceitful and disobedient and his servants dishonest. It is this disintegrating effect of avarice on family life that Molière has above all things attempted to portray. With this intention he has varied the plot of the *Aulularia* by introducing a double love-story, and he has added to the poignancy of the situation by making the son the rival of his father. For Harpagon, the hard-hearted miser, is in love with a penniless girl, or, at least, he wants to marry her. Moreover, in spite of his unprepossessing figure and his untidy and unfashionable dress—"Ah! Frosine, quelle figure," exclaims his intended wife at the first sight of him—he is vain of his personal appearance. It is these peculiarities, these traits of character not usually associated with avarice, which help to give him individuality, and which disprove the criticism that he is a mere type.

But though his personality is quite distinct, it has been said that he is an enigma. It is not Molière's habit to tell us much about the social conditions of his characters, and we are generally left to piece together what information we can glean from scattered statements or inferences. In the case of Harpagon we learn that he keeps his carriage, though his horses are starved and his coachman is also his cook; that he has at least three men-servants, including the cook-coachman, and one female servant; and that his son has his own valet, though his daughter has no maid. We also know that he wears a diamond ring. Thus he is comparatively rich, but whether it is position or mere vanity which leads him to keep a carriage and a considerable staff of servants, we are not told. If it is position, he may either have inherited money or he may hold some legal or administrative post. The latter alternative seems unlikely, and, on the whole, the most probable conjecture is that he is a man of independent means, and that he belongs to the *noblesse de robe*.

In any case it is strange that he should keep a sum of ten thousand crowns, which has just been paid him, buried in his garden. He gives as an explanation that he does not trust strong-boxes, but this is a little thin. The real explanation is that Molière has borrowed the theme of the hidden treasure from the *Aulularia*, as being a fertile source of comic situation and dialogue. For, having determined to make his play a serious study of avarice, he saw that unless he relieved it with scenes of genuine comedy it must inevitably become a realistic, not to say a sordid tragedy—a kind of drama which no seventeenth century audience would have tolerated. A rapid review of the piece will make this clear. It is evident from the first two scenes—between Élise (the miser's daughter) and Valère (her lover) and between Élise and Cléante (the miser's son)—that it is the evil effect of avarice on family ties that Molière has especially in view. "L'excès de son avarice et la manière austère dont il vit avec ses enfants pourraient autoriser des choses plus étranges," says Valère, when he is combating Élise's scruples. "Enfin peut-on rien voir de plus cruel que cette rigoureuse épargne qu'on exerce sur vous, que cette sécheresse étrange où l'on vous fait languir?" says Cléante in justification of his rebellious attitude. Avarice has not only made Harpagon parsimonious, but it has stifled his natural feelings. He shews no affection towards his children, and he treats his servants with unwarrantable brutality. "Hors d'ici tout à l'heure, et qu'on ne réplique pas! Allons, que l'on détale de chez moi, maître juré filou, vrai gibier de potence!" is his salutation to La Flèche, his son's valet, at the opening of the Third Scene.

This scene, the first part of which is imitated from the first scene of the *Aulularia*—a far better opening, by the way, than Molière's—is one of broad comedy, evidently intended as a relief from the two serious scenes which precede it. Then we have another serious scene (Sc. 4), followed by one of high comedy (Sc. 5), in which comic effect of a simpler kind is also obtained by Harpagon's constant repetition of *sans dot.* The moderately comic scene between Cléante and La Flèche, which opens the Second Act, leads up to the almost terrible disclosure which reveals that the usurer into whose hands Cléante has fallen is his own father. At this point Molière seems to have felt that his play was in danger of becoming a tragedy of a sordid type. Accordingly he proceeds to strengthen the comic element, and from here to the end of the Third Act he gives us comedy and even farce (Act III, Scenes 1 and 9). So again, the next conflict between the father and son, in which Harpagon threatens to enforce obedience with a stick (Act IV, Scene 3), is immediately followed by the highly comic scene in which Maître Jacques pretends to reconcile them. Then, after another quarrel, even more violent so far as words go, in which Harpagon renounces, disinherits, and finally curses his son, comes the robbery of the chest with its hoard of gold. The alternations of tragedy and comedy in Harpagon's frenzied lamentation over his loss, which is inspired in the first place by Plautus, but which also, perhaps, owes something to Larivey, are typical of Molière's whole treatment of his miser's character. The contrast between its two aspects is too violent for perfect art. If we compare him with Tartuffe and Alceste, especially with Tartuffe who, like Harpagon, is at once terrible and ridiculous, we get the impression that the tragic and the comic elements have not been completely fused in Molière's imagination. The result is a certain lack of unity, and, seeing how rare this is in Molière's work, especially in his creation of character, we naturally infer that it is due to want of time or leisure. And this view finds confirmation in other features of the play. The *dénouement* is of that conventional Latin and Italian type to which Molière had not resorted since *L'École des Femmes*, and it is even more romantic than that of the earlier play. For Anselme, *alias* Don Thomas d'Alburcy, to whom Harpagon has promised his daughter, turns out to be the father of Valère and Mariane, who had no idea of their relationship to one another, and who were supposed by their father to have been lost at sea. Possibly this *dénouement* was suggested to Molière by the similar instances of romantic recognition in Larivey's *Les Esprits* and *La Veuve*, but the shipwreck *motif* is so common that the resemblance has little significance.

In no play, however, are Molière's debts to his predecessors so numerous. According to Riccoboni, the well-known actor and manager of the Italian company which produced so many of Marivaux's plays, "there are not four scenes which are of Molière's invention[1]." But Riccoboni was chiefly thinking of the "canvasses" or sketches of the *Commedia dell' Arte* with which he was so familiar, and the similarity between them and some of the scenes in *L'Avare* may arise from their borrowing from a common source. It is possible, too, that in some instances the Italians and not Molière were the borrowers. But there are other debts in *L'Avare* which are more

[1] *Observations sur la comédie et sur le génie de Molière*, 1736. Riccoboni was born about the time of Molière's death.

important and better substantiated. The scene between Harpagon and his son, in which the former is discovered to be the usurer from whom the latter is borrowing (Act II, Scene 2), is certainly inspired by a similar scene in Boisrobert's *La Belle plaideuse* (Act I, Scene 8). With regard to Larivey's *Les Esprits*, the instances of similarity may often be due to the two authors having worked from the same model. In nearly all the cases the resemblance is trifling, and it is only in Act I, Scenes 3 and 4 of *L'Avare* that the debt to *Les Esprits* II, 3, is obvious and considerable[1]. Another obvious case of borrowing is furnished by the scene between Harpagon and Frosine (Act II, Scene 5). Not only does it bear a general resemblance to that between Ambroise and Guillemette in *La Veuve*, which Larivey in his turn had adapted from *La Vedova* of Nicolò Buonaparte, but the first portion of the dialogue is taken, and in part literally translated, from Ariosto's well-known *I Suppositi* (Act I, Scene 2). Another debt to the last-named play is to be found in Act III, Scene 1, where Maître Jacques on his master's invitation gives him a faithful account of what his neighbours say of him, and gets a drubbing for his pains[2].

In Quinault's *La Mère coquette* (1665) there is a miser, Crémante, who is his son's rival, and Frosine's flattery of Harpagon in Act II,

[1] For a full list of resemblances see *L'Avare*, ed. E. G. W. Braunholtz, Cambridge, pp. xl–xlii.

[2] Cp. *I Suppositi* II, 4, and see Braunholtz, *op cit.* pp. xlii–xliv for other possible debts to the same play.

Scene 5, is evidently inspired by a similar scene in the earlier play (Act I, Scene 4)[1]. It is much more doubtful whether Act III, Scene 7, in which Cléante, under colour of respectful compliments to his proposed step-mother, makes love to her on his own account, owes anything to a somewhat similar scene in Lope de Vega's *La Discreta enamorada*. Finally M. Émile Roy has suggested yet another source in Doni's *L'avaro cornuto*[2].

We have seen that the character of Harpagon, powerful though it is, is a little perplexing, and especially that it lacks the unity of a perfectly artistic creation. But none of the other characters have the same individuality. The best is Maître Jacques, who combines the functions of cook and coachman, and in whom honesty, imbecility, love of his horses, loyalty to his master, and prejudice against Valère are skilfully blended. La Flèche is a typical valet of comedy, and Frosine, who is qualified as "femme d'intrigue," is interesting as the first appearance in Molière[3] of a type which he repeated in Nérine of *Monsieur de Pourceaugnac*, and which became common in the plays of Dancourt, Regnard, and Lesage, the type of Mme Thibout, the chief character of *La Femme d'intrigues*, and Mme Amelin in

[1] See Braunholtz, *op. cit.* pp. xlvi–xlvii for this and more doubtful points of resemblance to *La Mère coquette*.

[2] *Rev. d'hist. litt.* I (1894), 38 ff.

[3] In *L'École des Femmes* (Act II, Scene 5) mention is made of an old woman whom Horace employed as an emissary to Agnès.

Les Bourgeois à la mode[1] (the Mrs Amlet of Vanbrugh's *The Confederacy*), of Mme La Ressource in *Le Joueur*, and of Mme Jacob in *Turcaret*. In *L'Avare* she appears merely as an *intrigante* or *entremetteuse*, and we hear nothing of any other activities, but in the plays of Molière's successors she is generally also a money-lender and a dealer in old clothes[2]. There are similar characters in Larivey's *La Veuve* and Odet de Turnèbe's *Les Contents*, but both of these approach more nearly to the type of Regnier's Macette.

There is nothing very distinctive about any of the four lovers, though they all have sufficient spirit to sustain their part in the dialogue with dramatic effect. The opening scene, however, between Valère and Élise has, as we have seen, been criticised as lacking this quality. The style, in fact, is diffuse, involved, and languid. Moreover, Valère and Élise employ in their love-making the usual *précieux* commonplaces of the day—*bontés, feux, obligeantes assurances, témoignages ardents*, and even *Ne m'assassines point*. But, as I have pointed out elsewhere, this *langage figuré* is the ordinary style of lovers, both in Racine (*Andromaque*) and Molière (*Tartuffe, Le Misanthrope*)[3].

[1] See J. Lemaître, *Le Théâtre de Dancourt*, 2nd ed. 1903 (a reprint), pp. 170 ff. There is a Frosine in Dancourt's *La Foire de Bezons*.

[2] Dame Ursula Suddlechop in *The Fortunes of Nigel* is a similar character.

[3] *From Montaigne to Molière*, pp. 201–204.

Finally there is one passage which, more convincingly than any other feature of the play, points to hurry on the part of the author. In the First Scene of the Fourth Act Frosine improvises a plan by which some friend of hers is to play the part of a rich *marquise* or *vicomtesse* who has fallen madly in love with Harpagon and is prepared to settle all her property on him by a marriage contract. But we hear nothing more of this, though it might have furnished a scene of excellent comedy.

On the whole, then, we seem justified in inferring from these various considerations—the want of unity in Harpagon's character, the sketchiness of most of the other characters, the romantic and mechanical *dénouement*, the frequent borrowing of scenes from earlier plays, and, above all, the oversight just mentioned, which could have been rectified by the simple omission of Frosine's speech—that *L'Avare* was imperfectly conceived and hastily executed. Molière's idea of representing the evil effects of avarice on family life was admirable, but he was unable to surmount the difficulty of developing this idea as a theme of comedy. He clung to the hidden treasure of the *Aulularia* as a fertile source of comic effects, but he could not completely fuse the comic Euclio of his predecessor with his own more profound conception of a miser.

This inability to reconcile two conflicting ideas, to produce a true comedy with a back-

ground of tragedy, as he had done in *Tartuffe*
and *Le Misanthrope*, was not necessarily due to
shortness of time. It is true that he may not
have begun to work at *L'Avare* until after the
production of *George Dandin* (July 18), in which
case, allowing time for the actors to learn and
rehearse their parts, the interval would be hardly
more than a month. But it is much more likely
that the new play began to occupy his thoughts
six months earlier, as soon as he had got *Amphitryon* off his hands. That would have given
him plenty of time, if he could have completed
the working out of his design to his satisfaction.
It was because his conception had not taken
final shape in his brain that he put off the actual
writing of the play, and that, when he finally
set to work, he was glad to avail himself of help
from his predecessors in the way of suggestion,
situation, and even of dialogue.

But, as always, he greatly improved upon
what he borrowed, and whatever defects *L'Avare*
may have as a whole, there is no gainsaying the
excellence of many of its individual scenes.
Perhaps from no play of Molière's do we get a
better idea of his genius as a comic dramatist.
In some of the scenes, e.g. in Act III, Scene 1
(Harpagon and his servants), and Act IV,
Scene 4 (Valère and Maître Jacques), the
comedy borders at times almost into farce; but
others, such as that between Harpagon, Maître
Jacques and the Commissioner (Act V, Scene 2),
and that between the same persons with Valère,

which contains the famous "les beaux yeux de ma cassette" (Act v, Scene 3), preserve throughout the tone of true comedy, the former because it is founded upon human nature, the latter because it rests upon a perfectly natural misunderstanding.

It is, doubtless, the excellence of these scenes, which act almost of themselves, as well as the character of Harpagon, that have made *L'Avare* one of the most popular of Molière's comedies for stage representation[1]. But when it was first produced it had no such popularity. The receipts for the first performance only just reached four figures; for the second they dropped to 495 *livres* and for the eighth to 143 *livres*, and after the ninth the play was withdrawn for a couple of months. Six representations in the following December, when it was accompanied by another piece, *Le fin Lourdeau* (anonymous, and never printed), produced better results, but in the following year (1669), when there were eleven performances, and in 1670, when there were six, the receipts only on five occasions reached 300 *livres*, and only once—on a Sunday—surpassed this modest figure. It was much the same in the years 1671 and 1672; the play still kept the stage, but, except on Sundays, it never attracted even moderately large audiences. According to Grimarest and Voltaire, this want of success

[1] Between 1680 and 1906 the number of performances at the Comédie-Française was 1549, as against 2111 for *Tartuffe* and 1625 for the *Médecin malgré lui*.

was due to its being written in prose. As they
both make more than one erroneous statement
about the play, their information on this point
would hardly deserve credence did it not appear
to be confirmed by the following lines of the
contemporary Robinet:

> Il parle en prose, et non en vers;
> Mais, nonobstant les goûts divers,
> Cette prose est si théâtrale
> Qu'en douceur les vers elle égale[1].

Ever since Corneille had inaugurated classical
comedy with *Mélite*, it had been the practice
to use verse for comedies which aspired to the
dimensions of five acts. Even Scarron had
adhered to this custom in his burlesques; alone,
Cyrano de Bergerac had violated it in *Le Pedant
joué*. It is true that Molière himself had written
Don Juan in prose, and that it had been very
well received. But in this case the choice of
prose was certainly due to pressure of time, and
the popularity of the piece was largely due to
its subject and to the spectacular display which
that subject demanded. It is therefore natural
to suppose that it was want of time which primarily led Molière to write *L'Avare* in prose.
But there was also another reason. When
he had determined that, in order to prevent
the play from turning into sombre tragedy, he
must introduce some scenes of broad comedy,
he must have realised at the same time that
prose was the only possible medium for such

---

[1] Quoted by Rigal, II, 142.

scenes. It has been noticed that in the prose of *L'Avare* there may be detected metrical fragments, and even complete Alexandrines[1]. There is nothing remarkable in this, for doubtless verse came almost as easily to Molière as prose, and similar instances occur in *Les Précieuses ridicules, Le Médecin malgré lui, George Dandin,* and *Les Fourberies de Scapin.* But what is remarkable about *L'Avare* is, that in the first four speeches of the play there are to be found not only Alexandrines but traces of rhyme. Is it not a natural inference that Molière began to write his play in verse, but very soon abandoned verse for prose?

All these signs of hurry and improvisation forbid the supposition that Molière in blending tragedy with comedy and adopting prose as his medium was deliberately making an experiment in the direction of modern drama. But temporary expedients are often the prelude to future discoveries, and it may fairly be said that our poet's efforts to fit his conception of a miser into a framework of comedy prepared the way, to a certain extent, for the kind of drama, intermediate between tragedy and comedy, which Diderot and Mercier attempted, with no great success, and which, after Beaumarchais had reintroduced the comic element, finally took shape in the hands of Augier and Dumas *fils.* Give

---

[1] *Et vous repentez-vous de cet engagement* and *Cent choses à la fois*: *l'emportement d'un père*, both of which occur at the opening of the First Scene.

more prominence to the tragic element in
L'Avare and eliminate the more farcical scenes,
and you get something not very dissimilar from
a modern comedy. In one respect, indeed,
L'Avare shews a deliberate advance from classical comedy to a more modern type of play,
and that is in the number of characters. This
innovation has already been noticed in *Don Juan*,
the other five-act play which Molière wrote in
prose, the play in which he abandoned the unity
of place. In *L'Avare* there are fifteen characters,
only one less than in *Don Juan* (if you do not
count the Spectre, the attendants of Don Juan
and the two brothers); and in two scenes (III,
1, and V, 4) there are as many as eight characters on the stage at once, and in one (V, 5),
there are even nine[1].

There are few plays of Molière's which do
not present some special feature of artistic interest, testifying to the versatility of his genius,
and to his power of adjusting his art to the re-
quirements of his subject. But the three plays
of 1668 have certain features in common. They
are all, as we have seen, founded upon an earlier
play : *Amphitryon*, upon a quasi-religious drama,
which its author suggested should be called a
tragi-comedy, *George Dandin* upon a broad farce,
and *L'Avare* upon a gay comedy. In each
case Molière has introduced a tragic element

[1] Since this chapter was written there has appeared a scholarly
edition of *L'Avare* by Prof. A. T. Baker. (Manchester University
Press, 1918.) The critical appreciation of the play—*Introduction*,
pp. lxviii–lxxvii—is excellent.

which is foreign to the original play. In *Amphitryon* and *George Dandin* he has indicated, without dwelling upon it, this underlying aspect of the drama ; in *L'Avare* he has converted the amusing portrayal of a temporary aberration into the study—none the less serious for containing a large element of laughter—of an ingrained vice, far-reaching in its effects. In each case he has overcome the difficulties which he had thus created from the point of view of stage representation. All three are admirable acting plays, and *Amphitryon* is an artistic triumph. But the reader cannot, like the spectator, forget in the glamour of representation the underlying element of sordid tragedy. He sympathises, as Molière means him to sympathise, with the jealousy and shame of Amphitryon, and with the despair of George Dandin, and he realises, as Molière means him to realise, the baneful influence of Harpagon's avarice upon his family and household. Hence the impression that he receives from these plays is confused and blurred. He is conscious that Molière the moralist is not in complete harmony with Molière the dramatist.

CHAPTER VIII

LE BOURGEOIS GENTILHOMME AND *COMÉDIE-BALLET*

THERE is no doubt that the favour and protection of Louis XIV was of great assistance to Molière, more particularly during the years from 1662 to 1667, when his enemies were most numerous and most aggressive. Without this protection the increasing boldness of his satire from *Les Fâcheux* to *Le Misanthrope* would have been impossible. Louis never pretended to be a connoisseur of literature, but he had plenty of common sense, and it was this quality in Molière which especially appealed to him. Moreover, it must have accorded with his autocratic views of kingship as well as have caused him considerable amusement to see his courtiers held up to ridicule. His own taste, however, lay in the direction of farce and ballet, rather than of high comedy, and it was to suit this taste that a large number of Molière's plays were written.

This fact has greatly concerned some of his critics and admirers. They lament that he should have wasted his time over such trifles instead of writing more masterpieces like *Tartuffe* and *Le Misanthrope*. But if one considers the list

of twelve *comédies-ballets* which were written for
the royal pleasure—including *Les Fâcheux*,
which was ordered by Fouquet for the fête
which he gave in the king's honour—there are
only very few that we could wish unwritten. Certainly not *Le Malade imaginaire* nor *Le Bourgeois gentilhomme*, nor that other example of
the Aristophanic side of Molière's genius,
Monsieur de Pourceaugnac, nor those two admirable little comedies, *Le Mariage forcé* and
L'Amour médecin, nor *Les Fâcheux*, with its
brilliant versification and its wide and accurate
observation of social types, nor *Le Sicilien*,
which only lacks the setting of music to be the
most charming of light operas, nor *Les Amants
magnifiques*, which, though in five acts, is
hardly longer than *Le Sicilien* and hardly inferior to it, nor *George Dandin* with its inimitable characters of M. and Mme de Sotenville,
nor *La Comtesse d'Escarbagnas*, that interesting
and faithful picture of provincial life. There
only remain *La Princesse d'Élide* and *Mélicerte*,
which might be sacrificed with no great loss.
But as *Mélicerte* was left unfinished, and *La
Princesse d'Élide*, begun in verse and finished
in prose, was written in great haste, the time
spent on them would not have gone far towards
the creation of a great masterpiece.

Thus, without endorsing M. Maurice Pellisson's suggestions that all Molière's *comédies-
ballets* should be represented on the stage with
their proper accompaniment of music and danc-

ing, one may cordially agree with him that these pieces, especially those in which the music and dancing are intimately blended with the comedy proper, represent a very interesting side of Molière's genius[1], and that none of them, not even *La Princesse d'Élide* or *Mélicerte*, should be neglected by the reader.

The *comédie-ballet*,[2] as it gradually developed in Molière's hands, sprang out of the *ballet de cour*, which was already highly popular in the reigns of Henri IV and Louis XIII, and which continued to be so during the Regency of Anne of Austria. It was in the ballet of *Cassandre* (1651) that the young Louis XIV, then in his thirteenth year, who danced well and had an excellent ear for music, made his *début*. Other famous ballets were the *Ballet de la Nuit* (1653), which lasted for thirteen hours, the *Ballet de Psyché* (1656), the *Ballet des Noces de Thétis et de Pélée* (1657), and *Alcidiane* (1658), in which Louis XIV danced with Mazarin's nieces. The ballet consisted ordinarily of *Récits*, *Entrées*, and *Vers*. First, actors, who took no part in the dancing, recited or sang verses (*récits*) which bore on the subject of the *entrée*. This was followed by the *entrée* itself, composed of dancers, who performed their evolutions to the accompaniment of music. The *vers* consisted of short

---

[1] M. Pellisson, *Les Comédies-Ballets de Molière*, 1914.

[2] See V. Fournel, *Les contemporains de Molière*, 3 vols. 1866, II, 173–221 (*Histoire du Ballet de Cour*); Romain Rolland, *Histoire de l'opéra en Europe avant Lully et Scarlatti* (*Bibl. des écoles franç. d'Athènes et de Rome, fasc.* 71), 1895.

descriptions, sometimes panegyrical, sometimes satirical, of the princes and courtiers who took part in the *entrée*. They were not spoken or sung like the *récits*, but were printed on the *livre du ballet* which was distributed to the spectators. When Molière returned to Paris in 1659 the *récits* and *vers* were always written by Isaac Benserade, who after his first triumph in the great *Ballet de la Nuit* (1653) retained his supremacy for the next sixteen years. A similar monopoly for the music of the *ballet de cour* was enjoyed by the Florentine composer, Jean-Baptiste Lulli, who began his series of successes with *Alcidiane* in 1658.

Molière's first association with *comédie-ballet* arose by chance, as he himself explains in his preface to *Les Fâcheux*. It was originally intended that this comedy should be a distinct performance from the *ballet*, but as only a small number of good dancers were available, it was decided to interpolate their entries between the acts of the comedy, so as to give them time to change their costumes. Further, in order not to interrupt the thread of the piece, the entries were connected with it as far as possible, so as to fuse comedy and ballet into a single whole. "The combination," adds Molière, "is new to our stage, but one might find authority for it in antiquity; and, as everybody was pleased with it, it may serve as a suggestion for other performances which can be worked out more at leisure."

It was not, however, till nearly two and a half years later that Molière had an opportunity of carrying out the above suggestion. In *Le Mariage forcé* comedy and ballet were placed together, and the *récits*, which had been omitted in *Les Fâcheux*, took the form of songs set to Lulli's music and sung by professional singers. The dancers consisted chiefly of professionals, but they were assisted by a few distinguished amateurs, namely, the king himself, who figured as a gypsy, the Comte d'Armagnac, the *Grand Écuyer* who was generally designated as M. le Grand, the future Maréchal de Villeroy, the Duc de Saint-Aignan, an Academician to whom was often entrusted the task of organising the court festivities, and Monsieur le Duc, Condé's only son, then in his twenty-first year, who, in later life, in spite of his sordid avarice, almost rivalling that of Harpagon, gave at Chantilly some magnificent fêtes of his own devising. The composer Lulli, who was an excellent dancer, also took part in one of the *entrées*, while among the professionals the chief burden fell on Beauchamp, the most famous French dancer of the seventeenth century, to whom the treasurer of Molière's company paid fifty *louis* for arranging the ballet.

In spite of the close connexion between comedy and ballet in *Le Mariage forcé*, it cannot be said that the ballet is an essential part of the play. When *Le Mariage forcé* was played with *Amphitryon* in 1668, the ballet was omitted, and, judging by the impressions of the modern reader, the comedy suffered nothing from the omission.

In *La Princesse d'Élide*, presented little more than three months after *Le Mariage forcé*, and entitled in the first printed edition (1682) *Comédie galante, mêlée de musique et d'entrées de ballet*, the music, which is again Lulli's, and the entries, without being absolutely essential to the conduct of the piece, play a very important part, and no doubt contributed to its success at the Palais-Royal, where it ran for twenty-five days, from November 1664 to January 1665. The comedy itself, which, as we have seen, was written in great haste, is little more than an adaptation of Moreto's *El Desdén con el Desdén*, to which it is far inferior. Molière, however, has made an amusing character of Moron the court buffoon, which was his own part. The *entrées* or *intermèdes* are mostly pastoral in character, which, together with the fact that love is the principal theme of the play, brings it into line with the unfinished *Mélicerte, comédie pastorale héroïque*, the scene of which is laid in the classical valley of Tempe, with *Le Sicilien*, which, though not pastoral, is a *comédie d'amour*, and with *Les Amants magnifiques*, the scene of which is also laid in the valley of Tempe, and which, though itself a true social comedy, includes amongst its *intermèdes* a little pastoral piece in five scenes. To these must be added the *Pastorale comique*, which replaced the unfinished *Mélicerte* in the third *entrée* of the *Ballet des Muses*. Though the spoken dialogue no longer

exists, probably because it was merely improvised from a sketch by Molière, the singing
parts are preserved in the *livre du ballet*[1].

These pastoral and semi-pastoral pieces reveal a side of Molière's genius, which would
otherwise have remained hidden—a tender and
romantic side, which sometimes finds expression
in passages of really poetic sentiment and language. Thus the *Pastorale comique* furnishes
the following charming little song, which should
have a place in all anthologies of French verse,
but which, so far as I know, is to be found in none:

> Croyez-moi, hâtons-nous, ma Sylvie,
> Usons bien des moments précieux;
>   Contentons ici notre envie,
> De nos ans le feu nous y convie:
> Nous ne saurions, vous et moi, faire mieux.
> Quand l'hiver a glacé nos guérets,
> Le printemps vient reprendre sa place,
> Et ramène à nos champs leurs attraits;
>   Mais, hélas! quand l'âge nous glace,
> Nos beaux jours ne reviennent jamais.
>
> Ne cherchons tous les jours qu'à nous plaire,
> Soyons-y l'un et l'autre empressés;
>   Du plaisir faisons notre affaire,
> Des chagrins songeons à nous défaire:
> Il vient un temps où l'on en prend assez.
> Quand l'hiver a glacé nos guérets,
> Le printemps vient reprendre sa place,
> Et ramène à nos champs leurs attraits;
>   Mais, hélas! quand l'âge nous glace,
> Nos beaux jours ne reviennent jamais[2].

[1] Fournel, *op. cit.* II, 573–618.
[2] Mme de Sévigné in a letter to her daughter of April 20, 1690,
quotes the two lines of the refrain. See A. Martin in *Rev. d'hist.
litt.* XIX (1912), 32–39.

The nine-syllable line here employed is only found very rarely in the sixteenth, seventeenth, and eighteenth centuries. In the nineteenth century it began to gain ground and Verlaine used it with comparative freedom, as in his well-known *Art Poétique*[1]:

> De la musique avant toute chose,
> Et pour cela préfère l'Impair,
> Plus vague et plus soluble dans l'air,
> Sans rien en lui qui pèse ou qui pose.

Le Sicilien ou l'Amour peintre has a special charm and interest. It formed part of the fourteenth and final *entrée* of the *Ballet des Muses*, which was added in the middle of February 1667, probably on the 14th. It deals with the well-worn theme of an elderly and jealous guardian of a girl—in this case an enfranchised slave—whom he intends to marry, and a young lover who visits her in disguise and carries her off in spite of her guardian's vigilance. But the theme, hackneyed though it is, lends itself to romance, and Molière has treated it with freshness and charm. This is partly due to the songs and dances with which it is interspersed, but also to the *vers blancs* in which a considerable portion of it was written.

> Chut...N'avancez pas davantage,
> Et demeurez dans cet endroit,
> Jusqu'à ce que je vous appelle.

[1] L. E. Kastner, *A History of French Versification*, Oxford, 1903.

> Il fait noir comme dans un four:
> Le ciel s'est habillé ce soir en Scaramouche
> Et je ne vois pas une étoile
> Qui montre le bout de son nez.

The above are the opening words of the valet Hali's soliloquy in the First Scene, and it will be seen that they fall into a series of octo-syllabic lines varied by a single Alexandrine. Indeed, Anatole de Montaiglon went so far as to print the whole play as if it were written throughout in verse. This is clearly not the case ; the verse is interspersed with prose, which predominates in the dialogue. Thus the form of the play more or less resembles the libretto of an opera, in which recitation is mingled with song, and it only requires the addition of music throughout to make of *Le Sicilien* a true opera of the lighter kind. *Le Barbier de Seville*, which opens with a similar serenade, certainly owes something to it, but nearer akin to it than Beaumarchais's play is Rossini's opera[1].

Le Ballet des Muses was the last occasion on which Benserade collaborated with Molière. Two years later (1669) he composed his last ballet, the *Ballet de Flore*, and made his farewell bow. His retirement was partly due to Molière's increasing success in the field in which he had so long reigned supreme. In the *Grand Divertissement Royal*, of which *George Dandin* formed

---

[1] There is a German arrangement of it as opera, made about 1780. Molière's play with Lulli's music was presented in London on July 14, 1917, by members of the University of London French Club.

part, Molière had dispensed with his assistance, and had provided everything, except the music, himself. He did the same for *Les Amants magnifiques* (1670), for which he composed no less than six interludes, all very elaborate and of great variety. The comedy itself, though it is divided into five acts, is no longer than an ordinary one-act piece, and Molière evidently set little store by it. It was never produced at the Palais-Royal, and it was not printed in his lifetime. The subject, which was given him by the king, has little dramatic promise; it is simply that of two princes who regale the princess for whose hand they are rivals with every sort of gallant entertainment. But this is developed by Molière into a comedy which does not lack interest. Among the characters is Clitidas, the court fool, who is not a buffoon like Moron in *La Princesse d'Élide*, but a humorous and well-bred gentleman, who uses the language of high comedy. Molière played the part himself and he is surely speaking in his own person when he says to the Astrologer, " Il est bien plus facile de tromper les gens que de les faire rire," and then adds, as an aside addressed to himself, " Vous vous émancipez trop, et vous prenez de certaines libertés qui vous joueront un mauvais tour...Taisez-vous, si vous êtes sage." Astrology was more or less in fashion at this time, and two years earlier La Fontaine in his Fable of *The Astrologer who fell into a well*, had said boldly ;

Charlatans, faiseurs d'horoscope,
Quittez les cours des princes d'Europe.

Clitidas plays an important part in the action of the play. It is he who elicits from Sostrate, the distinguished general, the avowal of his love for the princess Ériphile, and from the princess the avowal of her love for this soldier of fortune. The scenes between Sostrate and Clitidas (Act I, Scene I), Ériphile and Clitidas (Act II, Scene 2), Sostrate and Ériphile (Act II, Scene 3, and Act IV, Scene 4), and Ériphile and Clitidas (Act V, Scene I) are all instinct with charm and delicacy, and reveal a knowledge of the psychology of growing love which one would hardly have suspected in Molière. The difference in rank between the princess and her lover has naturally suggested a comparison with Araminte in *Les fausses Confidences*[1], and here, for once, Molière almost rivals Marivaux on his own ground. The only criticism that suggests itself is that Ériphile's bearing and sentiments are rather those of a married woman than a young girl, but then she is a princess, accustomed to command.

If this slight but graceful and interesting comedy seemed of little account to its author without its setting, it has, like *Le Mariage forcé* and *L'Amour médecin*, an independent life of its own, and, though its lack of action, when divorced from its accompaniment of song

---

[1] Cp. particularly Act IV, Sc. 4 with Act II, Sc. 15 of *Les fausses Confidences*. M. Lafenestre also points out that Marivaux is indebted to *La Princesse d'Élide* for several scenes in *Les Surprises de l'Amour*, *Les Serments indiscrets*, and *L'heureux Stratagème*.

and dance, may make it unfitted to the stage, it can give pleasure to the reader.

Four months before *Les Amants magnifiques* Molière had produced at Chambord a *comédie-ballet, Monsieur de Pourceaugnac*, in which he had satisfactorily solved the difficulty of holding the balance even between comedy and ballet, and of fusing the two into a harmonious and inseparable whole. It is true that in *L'Amour médecin*, which he introduces to the reader in as modest a preface as that prefixed to *Les Amants magnifiques*, laying stress upon "les airs et les symphonies de l'incomparable Monsieur Lulli meslés à la beauté des voix et à l'adresse des danseurs," the interludes had been skilfully devised to suit the comedy, and that on the whole the aspirations of the prologue, in which Comedy, Music, and the Ballet join in the chorus of " Unissons-nous tous trois," are sufficiently realised. But it is a union rather than a fusion. The music and dancing are not really essential to the comedy, because they are foreign to its whole tone, and especially to the personality of the selfish and unromantic *bourgeois* who is the central character.

But in *Monsieur de Pourceaugnac* and its successors, *Le Bourgeois gentilhomme* and *Le Malade imaginaire*, Molière, with the inspiration of genius, has invented a new type of play, in which the ridiculous side of the chief character assumes such fantastic proportions that it can only find its full expression in an extravaganza of song and dance. M. de Pourceaugnac's capacity for being gulled, M. Jourdain's credulous vanity, Argan's fear of death, are all so grotesque as to be almost sublime. They transport the spectator and reader into the sphere of imagination and poetry where the grotesque and the sublime meet. As Sainte-Beuve eloquently says, we have in these plays the "poetry of the comic," the "lyricism of irony and gaiety[1]."

Monsieur de Pourceaugnac, says Voltaire, is a farce, and this is true in the sense that *Les Précieuses ridicules* is a farce, that is to say, it is a caricature of real life rather than a sober representation of it. But M. de Pourceaugnac himself is fundamentally a true type of a French provincial, especially in his attitude to Paris, a type which has often been represented in French literature, and which probably has not altogether ceased to exist. Why Molière has chosen Limoges as the native town of his butt it is impossible to say Had he, as Robinet suggests, a certain *Marquis* who came from Limoges in his mind? Or did he bear a grudge against the place? Or was it merely, as La Fontaine implies in one of his letters to his wife, and, as might be inferred from Rabelais's *écolier limousin*, that the district had a traditional reputation for dullness[2]? Modern sentiment has found

---

[1] *Portraits littéraires*, pp. 33–35, and cp. J.-J. Weiss, *Molière*, pp. 60–63.
[2] Michelet in his *Tableau de la France* says that the hills of

Molière's treatment of M. de Pourceaugnac unduly cruel, but it forgets the farcical and fantastic character of the play, which, as in *George Dandin*, prevents one from judging it by ordinary ethical standards. The first interlude, that of the doctors, is scarcely suited to modern tastes, but it is exceedingly funny, and must have proved infinitely diverting to Louis XIV and his courtiers, who delighted in horse play, and who, according to our ideas, had little sense of decency. The second interlude, that of the lawyers, with their refrain,

> La polygamie est un cas,
> Est un cas pendable,

is more decorous, and equally amusing.

The piece was composed for the royal entertainments at Chambord, being improvised apparently while the troop was at Chambord, and was produced on October 7 (1669). On November 15 it was presented, interludes and all, at the Palais-Royal, where it ran with marked success till the end of the year. Forty years ago there was a revival of it, with the songs and dances and Lulli's music, at the Gaîté[1].

The effervescing gaiety of *Monsieur de Pourceaugnac* seems inspired by the favourable turn that had taken place in Molière's theatrical fortunes. The clouds had at last lifted : the in-

---

the Limousin "nourrissent une population honnête, mais lourde, timide et gauche par indécision."

[1] April 2 and 9, 1876, under the direction of M. Weckerlin.

terdict had been removed from *Tartuffe*; and when La Grange came to balance the accounts of the company for the year 1668–1669, the sum available for division proved to be larger than it had been since 1663–1664[1]. The same gaiety pervades *Le Bourgeois gentilhomme*, which was produced about a year later (October 1670) than *Monsieur de Pourceaugnac*, and, like its predecessor, at Chambord. According to tradition, one of the landing-places of the famous spiral staircase was turned into an improvised stage, while seats for the king and his court were arranged on the staircase itself.

The play arose out of a royal command. On November 1, 1669 an ambassador from the Porte had arrived at the French court, and, though he was anything but an important personage in his own country, he had been received at Versailles with great pomp. In memory of this occasion Louis XIV expressed a wish that a Turkish ceremony should be included in the *comédie-ballet* which Molière was to produce at Chambord. Thereupon Molière, who, as we have seen, was developing his ideas of *comédie-ballet* more and more in the direction of a complete fusion of the two elements, undaunted by the difficulties of his task, determined to construct his comedy in such a way that the Turkish ceremony should not be a mere adjunct to it, but should spring naturally from it. For this purpose it was essential to create a character so

---

[1] See above, p. 32.

grotesquely vain and credulous that he could be taken in by the extravagant imposture of the Turkish episode. Probably Molière was meditating on the theme of middle class citizens who aped the manners and fashions of nobles when the royal command reached him. In *L'École des Femmes* he had already touched on the subject, and had represented Arnolphe as assuming the territorial name of M. de La Souche in virtue of a small piece of land which was attached to his house. This sort of vanity was evidently common in France in Molière's day, as indeed it is in most countries and most ages.

> Se croire un personnage est fort commun en France;
> On y fait l'homme d'importance,
> Et l'on n'est souvent qu'un bourgeois.
> C'est proprement le mal français:
> La sotte vanité nous est particulière[1].

It is this *sotte vanité* which is the dominant trait in M. Jourdain's character. Indeed, it has assumed in him such monstrous proportions that, like some malignant disease, it has vitiated his whole character, blinding his judgment and stifling his natural affections. In the series of inimitable scenes with his music-master and his dancing-master, his fencing-master, his teacher of philosophy, and his tailor, which make up the first two acts, he displays to the full his all-pervading vanity. His childish delight in his new clothes, his pride in his two lackeys with

---

[1] La Fontaine, *Le Rat et l'Éléphant* VIII, 15.

their gorgeous liveries, his naive acceptation of his teachers' compliments, his anxiety to follow every fashion of the *gens de qualité*, are all depicted in the most natural and life-like manner. After the flatterers come the critics, in the persons of his maid and his wife (Act II, Scenes 2 and 3). His maid, the delightful Nicole, laughs at him, while his wife tells him some home-truths, but neither ridicule nor censure has the slightest effect. Then we are introduced to Dorante, the noble black-leg, whose attitude towards M. Jourdain and his family with its impertinent condescension reminds one of the scene between Don Juan and M. Dimanche. Only while Don Juan merely evades the payment of M. Dimanche's account, Dorante, who has already borrowed large sums from M. Jourdain, comes to borrow more. So far there has been no suggestion of a plot, but in the next six scenes (8—13), such plot as there is begins to develop. It is nothing more intricate or novel than a love-story, the love of Cléonte for M. Jourdain's daughter, Lucile, which is favoured by Mme Jourdain but repulsed by M. Jourdain because Cléonte is not of noble birth. M. Jourdain's vanity and snobbishness are further illustrated by a subsidiary episode in which figure Dorante and a *Marquise* named Dorimène. The latter is more or less of an enigmatic character. Some critics regard her as a pure adventuress, but Sarcey is probably right in his view that she is "un peu légère mais honnête," that she is quite unaware of Dorante's character, and that she really believes that the ring and the other presents come from him and not from M. Jourdain. It must be confessed, however, that one would have expected her to shew some surprise at Dorante's entertainment being given in M. Jourdain's house. M. Rigal sees in her a resemblance to Lesage's Baroness in *Turcaret*, and, in fact, the situation *à trois* is almost identical in the two plays. Possibly Lesage borrowed it from Molière. Between Dorante and the Chevalier there is not much to choose, but the difference between Dorimène and the unscrupulous Baroness is a measure of the moral decline in French Society which took place between the years 1671 and 1709.

There is also this difference between the two plays that whereas in *Turcaret*, which is essentially a comedy of manners, the situation is used as an opportunity for portraying certain social types in the persons of the Chevalier, the Baroness, and the financier Turcaret, in *Le Bourgeois gentilhomme* it is devised partly, indeed, for the illustration of M. Jourdain's character, but mainly for the sake of the elaborate *Ballet des Nations* with which Dorante entertains his mistress. But before this takes place we have the Turkish episode which occupies the rest of the comedy. How Cléonte and his valet Covielle personate respectively the son of the Great Turk, and his ambassador, how the son of the Great Turk asks for the hand of Lucile,

and how M. Jourdain is made a Mamamouchi
or paladin, "than which there is nothing more
noble in the world," by means of an imposing
ceremony, in which figure a Mufti (played by
Lulli himself), four dervishes, and various
Turkish dancers and musicians, is too well-
known to need repetition. It should be noted
that when the comedy proper ends M. Jourdain
is still undeceived. He firmly believes that he
is going to marry his daughter to the son of the
Great Turk. Moreover, when Dorante proposes
that the notary who draws up the marriage-
contract shall also draw up one between him
and Dorimène, he is convinced that Dorante
says this merely in order to throw dust in Mme
Jourdain's eyes. "C'est pour lui faire accroire?"
he asks, and Dorante replies, "Il faut bien
l'amuser avec cette feinte." He can thus enjoy
the *Ballet des Nations* with his vanity unruffled
and without the slightest premonition of the
rude awakening that awaits him.

Thus Molière at last succeeded in constructing
a *comédie-ballet* in which comedy and ballet are
completely fused, and when *Le Bourgeois gentilhomme* was produced at the Palais-Royal
(November 25), neither the music nor the
dances, in spite of the expense which they en-
tailed, were omitted. Since Molière's day the
comedy has been more often represented without them, but one at least of the *intermèdes*, the
famous Turkish ceremony, is absolutely essential
to the *dénouement*; another, the *Ballet des*

Nations, cannot be omitted without bringing the action to an abrupt conclusion, while the three earlier ones, in which dancers, tailors, and cooks respectively play a part, all help to produce that atmosphere of fantastic gaiety which is so striking a feature of this remarkable production of Molière's genius[1]. How greatly the ballet element adds to the charm of the piece can be testified by the present writer, who had the good fortune to witness a gala performance in October 1880 with Lulli's music and the whole ballet, in which nearly every member of the Comédie-Française took part[2].

The creation of M. Jourdain to fit in with the Turkish ceremony commanded by the king was a brilliant stroke of inspiration, and in the portrayal of M. Jourdain's personality lies the chief interest of the play. The other characters are hardly more than sketches. The most individual are Mme Jourdain and Nicole. Mme Jourdain is described by Sarcey as *avenante et gaie,* but this is not the general opinion. Rather, her common sense is rendered less attractive than it otherwise would be by a certain dryness, not to say sourness, of disposition, and she would have had more influence over her husband had she been less uncompromising in her hostility to his foolish aspirations. The fact that the

---

[1] See R. Rolland, *op. cit.* pp. 270–272.

[2] The performance was one of those given in honour of the second centenary of the official foundation of the Comédie-Française. (See *Deuxième centenaire de la fondation de la Comédie-Française,* 1880.)

part was played by Hubert, who, since the retirement of Joseph Béjart at Easter of the preceding year, had replaced him in the rôle of
Mme Pernelle, lends support to this reading of
the character. Nicole's individuality is chiefly
shewn in her uncontrollable laughter at the appearance of M. Jourdain in his new clothes.
She is a frank and joyous creature, and the part,
though less important than that of Molière's
other famous servants, has always been
a favourite one both with actresses and with
the public. The most famous Nicole of the
eighteenth century was Mme Bellecour, who
retired in 1791 at the age of sixty. Seven years
later, owing to pecuniary losses, she once more
appeared in her old part of Nicole, but she was
only a shadow of her former self. Forty years
ago the part was rendered with inimitable
verve by Jeanne Samary. When *Le Bourgeois
gentilhomme* was first produced, a new actress,
Mme Beauval, made her *début* as Nicole. She
played with such success that Louis XIV, who
had not been taken with her appearance, said
to Molière after the performance, " Je reçois
votre actrice."

Nicole's lover Covielle is merely the stock
valet of Italian comedy. Cléonte and Lucile
are a charming pair, but there is nothing very
distinct about them. From Cléonte's frank confession that he is not a *gentilhomme* we learn
how easy it was in Molière's day to call yourself
noble without any real claim to the status. "On

tranche le mot aisément. Ce nom ne fait aucun
scrupule à prendre, et l'usage aujourd'hui semble
en autoriser le vol." Others in his place, he says,
would consider themselves entitled to the name,
for his family have filled honourable offices, and
he himself has served for six years in the army,
and is well enough off to maintain a certain
position in the world. "Vous n'êtes point gentilhomme, vous n'aurez pas ma fille" is all M.
Jourdain's reply.

M. Jourdain's four teachers are all admirable
examples of professional vanity and pedantry,
and, when their pride in their respective professions leads them to reciprocal insults and
even blows, the fun becomes hilarious. The
most humorous of the four is certainly the
teacher of philosophy, and the scene between
him and M. Jourdain (Act II, Scene 1) has
always been one of the most popular and effective in Molière's whole *répertoire*.

If the fact that the characters, with the exception of M. Jourdain, are sketches rather than
finished portraits points to rapidity of conception,
the extreme brevity of the dialogue in all but
a very few scenes is a sign of similar rapidity
in the execution. The fun of the first two acts
depends largely upon action and movement. So
in the double lovers' quarrel of the Third Act
(Scene 10), while the dialogue is reduced almost
to nothing, the editions of 1682 and 1734 give
stage directions which indicate a perpetual
movement on the part of the four characters.

This repetition, too, of a motive which had already served in *Le Dépit amoureux* and *Tartuffe* was probably due to the fact that Molière was pressed for time. Hurry is further shewn in the looseness and irregularity of the construction. The middle of the Third Act is reached before the action begins even to develop. Even the court which M. Jourdain is paying to his *Marquise* is merely hinted at in the first two acts. Moreover in the published editions the Third Act is two-thirds as long as all the others put together. In the libretto which was distributed to the audience at Chambord there are only three acts, the first comprising our Acts i and ii, and the third Acts iv and v. Indeed, as M. Rigal has pointed out, there is in point of fact only one act, interrupted by dancing and music.

It is significant of the success with which Molière has blended comedy and ballet in *Le Bourgeois gentilhomme* that in the original edition it alone of Molière's comedies bore the title of *comédie-ballet*. So pleased was Louis XIV with it that he charged the author to prepare a play for the inauguration of the new theatre of the Tuileries, which had been specially designed for the production of spectacular pieces. The choice of the subject being left to Molière, he chose the story of Psyche, of which his friend La Fontaine had made a romance in the previous year (1669), but not having time to write the whole play himself, he sought the collaboration of Corneille and Quinault: the latter contributing the words of the songs. Lulli furnished the music, and *Psyché* appeared as a *tragédie-ballet* with a gorgeous display of scenery and spectacular effect on January 17, 1671. After careful deliberation it was determined to produce it at the Palais-Royal. The preparations took more than three months, and cost 4359 *livres*. But the company was rewarded, for from July 24 to October 25 there were thirty-eight performances, and the receipts came to 33,011 *livres*, which, allowing 351 *livres* for the ordinary expenses of each performance, represents a net profit of over 15,300 *livres*. Part of the success was due to the charming fashion in which Mlle Molière and the youthful Baron interpreted the parts of Psyche and Cupid.

Before the end of the year Molière was again in demand at Court, and on December 2, *La Comtesse d'Escarbagnas* was produced at Saint-Germain for the fêtes in celebration of the marriage of Philippe d'Orléans, the king's brother, with the Princess Palatine. This little comedy, which consists of only nine scenes, was to serve as a pretext for a great *Ballet des ballets*, that is to say, a selection from the best ballets of recent years, but Molière has made no attempt to connect the comedy with the ballet, except in a mechanical fashion. The first seven scenes are continuous; then follows an entertainment which the Vicomte is giving in honour of his mistress Julie, consisting of a pastoral play (also written by Molière, but lost) interspersed with the usual songs and dances. After this come Scenes 8 and 9, and then the piece concludes with a final *intermède* taken from *Psyché*.

Molière was to write one more *comédie-ballet*, but that demands a chapter for itself, and before coming to it we must consider his next play, which was a pure comedy, *Les Femmes savantes*.

CHAPTER IX

LES FEMMES SAVANTES

On March 11, 1672 Molière presented *Les Femmes savantes* at the Palais-Royal. It was, says Donneau de Visé, in his notice of the play in *Le Mercure galant*, the first comedy *tout-à-fait achevée* that he had produced for four years, —that is to say, since *L'Avare*, or perhaps since *Amphitryon*, for possibly Visé would not have regarded *L'Avare*, written as it was in prose, and shewing distinct traces of hurry, as a comedy *tout-à-fait achevée*. But for a true social comedy written in verse we must go further back than *Amphitryon*, namely to *Le Misanthrope*. The well-thought-out conception and the finished execution of *Les Femmes savantes* shew that Molière must have spent a good deal of time over it. During the greater part of the year 1671 he had his hands fairly free. It is true that between *Psyché* (January), and *La Comtesse d'Escarbagnas* (December), he produced in May at the Palais-Royal a new piece, *Les Fourberies de Scapin*. But this free adaptation of the *Phormio* of Terence, which owes something to medieval farce, and considerably more to Italian comedy, cannot have taken Molière long to put together.

Thus he may have been able to devote most of his time, not only between May and November (allowing a short time for *La Comtesse d'Escarbagnas*), but also between January and May, to the planning and execution of *Les Femmes savantes*. The date of the privilege, December 31, 1670, shews that the idea of the play came to him even earlier than this.

If Molière had scotched *préciosité* by *Les Précieuses ridicules*, he certainly had not killed it. Though Mlle de Scudéry's famous Saturdays came to an end in the very year of its production, she still continued to see her friends in the Rue Vieille du Temple. In the same quarter of Paris, —the Marais—Mme de Caumartin, who was neither a *précieuse* nor a *femme savante*, and Mme Deshoulières, the Tenth Muse, who was both, held salons which were frequented by the same guests as Mlle de Scudéry's. More aristocratic in character, but still tinged with the spirit of *préciosité*, were the salons of Mlle de Montpensier, the Duchesse de Bouillon, the Duchesse de Richelieu, and Mme d'Albret. In the *bourgeois* salons of the Marais, at any rate, the same amusements were in vogue that are ridiculed in *Les Précieuses ridicules—bouts-rimés*, impromptus, portraits, *questions d'amour*. In the year before the production of *Les Femmes savantes* a volume was published under the title of *Questions d'amour ou conversations galantes*. The popularity of the *Recueils* or collections of occasional verse continued unabated till 1668.

The *Recueil des pièces choisies*, which is mentioned in *Les Précieuses ridicules*, found numerous readers down to 1666. In that year Furetière published *Le roman bourgeois*, in which he ridicules the fashionable verse-making of the day. "J'aime surtout les bouts-rimés," says Hippolyte, a *précieuse* and would-be *femme savante*, who is one of the guests in Angélique's salon, "parce que ce sont le plus souvent des impromptus, ce que j'estime la plus certaine marque de l'esprit d'un homme."

The account of this salon is no doubt a faithful picture of a second-rate Paris salon of the period. One especially notes in it the growing importance attached by women to learning. The sensible hostess is probably Angélique Petit, who is described in Somaize's *Dictionnaire des Précieuses* as a good linguist and mathematician.

Of greater importance in the literary and social world of Paris were Mlle de La Vigne and Mlle Du Pré, both of whom had a considerable reputation for learning, especially for their knowledge of Latin and the Cartesian philosophy. Mlle de La Vigne was thirty-eight in 1672, and her friend a year or two older. The younger lady, in spite of her real learning, did not aspire to be a *femme savante*, and in reply to a poem, in which the shade of Descartes is represented as urging her to write an account of his philosophy, she replied in another poem, some lines of which are happily inspired by Clitandre's speech ("Je consens qu'une femme ait des clartés de tout") in *Les Femmes savantes*. Marie Du Pré, who was a niece of Desmarets de Saint-Sorlin, was called "La Cartésienne." Like Mlle de La Vigne, she was a friend and correspondent of Conrart's, and at the time of the publication of *Les Femmes savantes* was corresponding with Bussy-Rabutin, and interchanging with him *bouts-rimés* and other kinds of occasional verse. In a letter to him dated June 22, 1671 she says, "L'amour est bien aveugle; n'ai-je pas raison de le mépriser?... A sa place j'ai rempli mon cœur d'amitié." In this professed contempt for love she was perhaps making a virtue of necessity, for Somaize, who is never sparing of his compliments, can only say of her that "he is sure that she is pretty rather than ugly." In her devotion to philosophy and her aversion to love, but not in her character, for she seems to have been an excellent and agreeable woman, she reminds us of Armande.

In 1672 *préciosité* flourished, not only in the salons, but also in the Academy. Chapelain, Segrais, Conrart, Pellisson, the two latter adepts at conducting a *correspondance galante*, the five Abbés, Charles Cotin, Jacques Cassagne, Jean Testu de Maury, François and Paul Tallemant, all belonged to the *précieux* school. The last named had been elected to the Academy in 1666, at the age of twenty-four, on the strength of his *poésies galantes*. A sixth Abbé, Jacques Testu, who immediately preceded him, had also no small share of the *précieux* spirit. He aspired to be the Voiture of the Hôtel de Richelieu. In

1670 this *précieux* group in the Academy had been reinforced by Quinault, and in the following year by Charles Perrault. It was not till ten months after the production of *Les Femmes savantes* that recognition was accorded to the new school of Nature and Reason in the person of Racine. He was accompanied by the *précieux* Fléchier.

During the interval of thirteen years that elapsed between *Les Précieuses ridicules* and *Les Femmes savantes* Molière had continued his attack. In *Les Fâcheux* we have two *précieuses*, Orante and Climène, besieging Éraste for his opinion on a subtle *question d'amour*. In *La Critique de l'École des Femmes* another *précieuse*, Climène, criticises "cette méchante rapsodie de *l'École des Femmes*" for its indecencies and violations of good taste, and in the same play there is a portrait of the Marquise Araminte, who is at once a prude and a *précieuse*.

The Comtesse d'Escarbagnas in the play of that name is represented chiefly as a foolish provincial, who is always prating about her "quality," but she has some of the tricks of a *précieuse*, while the verses which the Vicomte reads to his mistress, Julie, if superior in merit to those of Oronte, are marked by the conventional exaggerations and conceits of the love-poem of the period. It is fair to add, however, that both the Vicomte and Julie are quite aware of this weakness. Similar in character are the lines which the musician sings for M. Jourdain's benefit in *Le Bourgeois gentilhomme.*

In *Les Femmes savantes*, as in *Tartuffe*, *L'Avare*, and *Le Bourgeois gentilhomme*, Molière has studied his subject from the point of view of family life. In the First Act we are introduced to the two daughters of the family, Armande and Henriette, to their aunt Bélise, a vain old maid, who thinks every man is in love with her, and to Clitandre, who, having been rejected by Armande because she disapproves of marriage, has transferred his affections to Henriette. We also learn that the head of the family, a rich *bourgeois* named Chrysale, is entirely under the thumb of his wife, Philaminte.

> Mon père est d'une humeur à consentir à tout,
> Mais il met peu de poids aux choses qu'il résout;
> Il a reçu du Ciel certaine bonté d'âme
> Qui le soumet d'abord à ce que veut sa femme;
> C'est elle qui gouverne, et d'un ton absolu
> Elle dicte pour loi ce qu'elle à résolu.

Clitandre completes the picture of the household by expressing his aversion for *les femmes docteurs*, of which Philaminte, Armande and Bélise are all examples, and by drawing a highly unfavourable portrait of M. Trissotin, the *bel esprit* with whom these ladies are infatuated.

In the First Scene of the Second Act Chrysale makes his appearance in company with his brother Ariste, but Philaminte does not come on the stage till the Sixth Scene. She has been preceded by another and not unimportant member of the household, Martine the kitchen-maid, who has been discharged by Philaminte for violating the rules of grammar[1]. Except for a lackey, whose part is an insignificant one, the family is now complete.

Brunetière has called attention to the fact that in two only of Molière's comedies, *Les Précieuses ridicules* and *Les Femmes savantes*, he uses a plural title, whereas in the *répertoire* of Dancourt, who is essentially an observer of manners, this is more common, e.g. *Les Bourgeoises à la mode*, *Les Bourgeoises de qualité*, *Les Agioteurs*, *Les Curieux de Compiègne*, and he points out that it is natural for a dramatist, when he is satirising a passing social craze, to introduce more than one example of it. Thus in Molière's new play we have three *femmes savantes*, each representing a different phase of the character. Bélise, who resembles Hespérie in Desmarets de Saint-Sorlin's *Les Visionnaires* (1637), is perhaps slightly caricatured, but less so than her prototype, and hardly more than is required for effective presentation on the stage. Her fond belief that every man is in love with her is only made possible by her theory that they are all too respectful to give any sign of their love, a theory which has evidently been nourished on the romances of La Calprenède and Mlle de Scudéry. Philaminte,

---

[1] Martine is called *servante de cuisine*. She is evidently not the head cook; in education and social position she is inferior to Molière's other servants. In the highly amusing scene (Act II, Scene 6) in which she is called to account by the learned ladies for her lapses in grammar, Molière has borrowed some details from Larivey's *Le Fidelle* (published 1611), which is a translation of the *Fedele* of Luigi Pasqualiero (Molière, *Œuvres* IX, 98 n. 3).

whose part was played by Hubert, is a stronger character. Though she is hardly less silly than Bélise in her prudery and her pedantry, and in her affected display of knowledge that she does not possess, she has a real if unintelligent enthusiasm for learning and literature. She is, moreover, a masterful woman, who rules her family, including her husband, with an autocratic hand. When, owing to the supposed loss of her husband's and her own fortune, Trissotin withdraws his proposal for Henriette, she accepts Clitandre's offer of his person and his fortune with a graceful acknowledgement of his generosity, and when Armande complains that she is being sacrificed to her sister and Clitandre, she retorts, with a mocking allusion to Armande's words in an earlier scene,

> Ce ne sera point vous que je leur sacrifie,
> Et vous avez l'appui de la philosophie.

Armande is a more complex character. She is quite as ecstatic as the other two in her admiration for Trissotin's verses, and Vadius's Greek, but even more than Philaminte she is a pronounced feminist, and the goal of her ambition is to prove that women are as well able as men to excel in learning and science. Her affectation of prudery and of aversion to marriage ("Ah! mon Dieu, fi!") is even greater than her aunt's and her mother's, but though she has refused to marry Clitandre, she resents the idea of his marrying her sister, and rather than lose him

altogether she is willing to waive her objection
to " fleshly ties and corporeal chains " ;

> Puisque pour vous réduire à des ardeurs fidèles,
> Il faut des nœuds de chair, des chaînes corporelles,
> Si ma mère le veut, je résous mon esprit
> A consentir pour vous à ce dont il s'agit.

But she makes this proposal only after she has
tried first to work upon Henriette's feelings by
insisting that it is her duty to obey her mother,
and then to prejudice Philaminte against Clitandre by telling her of his failure to admire her
poems. In her jealousy and perversity she reminds
one of Ériphile in Racine's *Iphigénie* (1674), but
she is harder and more acrimonious than that
unhappy and extremely modern young woman.

M. Rigal points out that there is a tendency
in modern criticism to prefer the vague romanti-
cism and insincere idealism of Armande to the
good sense and charm of Henriette. It may be
true that Henriette sometimes carries her common
sense too far, as when she declines to accept
Clitandre's offer on the ground that when poverty
comes in at the door love flies out of the window;

> Rien n'use tant l'ardeur de ce nœud qui nous lie
> Que les fâcheux besoins des choses de la vie,
> El l'on en vient souvent à s'accuser tous deux
> De tous les noirs chagrins qui suivent de tels feux.

But her simplicity, her directness, and, above all,
her sense of humour, make her the most delightful
of Molière's young women. When Trissotin talks
about her *célestes appas* she cuts him short with,

> Eh ! Monsieur, laissons là ce galimatias.

And when the other ladies embrace Vadius on his introduction to them as a great Greek scholar, she declines with,

> Excusez-moi, Monsieur, je n'entends pas le grec.

Clitandre is worthy of her. He has the easy manners of a perfect *honnête homme*, such a character as La Grange excelled in portraying. He is also generous, impulsive, and outspoken. He cannot bear Trissotin :

> Son monsieur Trissotin me chagrine, m'assomme
> Et j'enrage de voir qu'elle estime un tel homme.

He says bluntly to Bélise :

> Je veux être pendu si je vous aime...

Like Dorante in *La Critique de l'École des Femmes*, he is a good example of a sensible and modest courtier, and like Dorante he defends the Court against the aspersions of third-rate authors such as Lycidas and Trissotin. In terms almost identical with those of Dorante he declares that common sense, good taste, and the spirit of society make better critics than all the obscure learning of pedants. The scene in which Clitandre makes his defence is noted by Sarcey as an admirable example of Molière's love of gradually working up to a climax a dispute between two opponents. In this instance it is a remark of Philaminte's which incites Clitandre to make an oblique attack on Trissotin, who is at first slow to take it up. Then he meets sneer with sneer, and stroke with counter-stroke, till

at last Clitandre, whose temper is far hotter than
Trissotin's, pours forth against his rival his final
outburst with the famous tirade ;

> Il semble à trois gredins, dans leur petit cerveau,

and so on for twenty lines without a single full
stop.

It has been suggested that Clitandre's character
is an *amende honorable* for Molière's numerous
attacks on courtiers, and it has been pointed out
that his name is that of one of the *Marquis* in
Le Misanthrope. But this latter circumstance is
probably a mere accident, and since *Le Misanthrope* no more *Marquis* had been held up to
ridicule. Molière, too, from the first was quite
capable of appreciating the good side of the
Court, as we see, not only from *La Critique*, but
also from *Les Fâcheux*, two years earlier in date,
in which there is nothing ridiculous about Éraste,
apart from the situation in which he is placed.

With the exception perhaps of Bélise, all these
characters are drawn with great delicacy and
considerable subtlety. But the gem of the piece
is Chrysale, the part which Molière reserved for
himself. How delightful he is in the very first
scene in which he appears, with his reminiscences
of his visit to Rome!

> ...Nous n'avions alors que vingt-huit ans,
> Et nous étions, ma foi, tous deux de verts galants.
> ...Nous donnions chez les dames romaines,
> Et tout le monde là parlait de nos fredaines.

His whole attitude towards his wife is a masterpiece of delicate humour, the contrast between his assumption of mastery in her absence and his complete submission in her presence being admirably portrayed. The emphatic "Je ne veux pas, moi," with which he comforts Martine, is immediately followed by his abject abandonment of the position on Philaminte's appearance. In the next scene (Act II, Sc. 7) he boldly declares,

> Il faut qu'enfin j'éclate,
> Que je lève le masque, et décharge ma rate.

But Philaminte's abrupt "Comment donc?" frightens him completely, and turning to Bélise, he says mildly, "C'est à vous que je parle, ma sœur."

But he has a tender heart, and he is a loving parent, if a feeble one.

> Ah ! les douces caresses !
> Tenez, mon cœur s'émeut à toutes ces tendresses ;
> Cela regaillardit tout à fait mes vieux jours,
> Et je me ressouviens de mes jeunes amours.

His brother Ariste plays a very small part in the drama, apart from the fact that he brings about the *dénouement*. His only other dramatic function is to encourage poor Chrysale, which he does in an admirable scene (9) of the Second Act. In the Third Act he has only half a line allotted to him, in the Fourth only two lines, and in the Fifth only eight. Yet he is necessary for the conduct of the play, and, though he is uninteresting, he has a larger share of the action than can be measured by the number of lines assigned to him.

Trissotin does not appear till the Third Act, while his friend and rival Vadius is only on the stage in the Third Scene of that Act. Both are types of the second-rate author of Molière's day who frequented the *précieux* salons and enjoyed a considerable reputation as a *bel esprit* and writer of occasional verse. But they represent different varieties of the type. Vadius is more learned than Trissotin.

> Il a des vieux auteurs la pleine intelligence,
> Et sait du grec, Madame, autant qu'homme de France.

He is not quite such an ass as his rival, but he is more disagreeable. He has an even better opinion of himself, and a worse opinion of others. He makes a civil, if brusque, excuse for having found fault with Trissotin's sonnet, but in his eagerness to read his own *ballade* he does not realise how deeply he has wounded his friend's *amour-propre*. It is usual to distinguish Trissotin as the *bel esprit* and Vadius as the pedant, but it must not be forgotten that Trissotin in his different way is hardly less of a pedant than Vadius, and that Vadius has equal pretensions to be a *bel esprit*.

As every reader of Molière knows, additional interest was given to these two characters when the play was first presented to the public by the knowledge that Trissotin represented the Abbé Cotin[1], and that Ménage, though less clearly indicated, was the original of Vadius. It has

---

[1] See Ch. Livet, *Précieux et précieuses*, 1859, 113–130.

been stated by two contemporaries that Trissotin was originally called Tricotin, but this seems disproved by a letter of Mme de Sévigné dated Wednesday, March 9, 1672, two days before the first performance, in which she says, " Molière lui (Retz) lisa samedi *Trissotin*, qui est une fort plaisante chose." Besides his name, thus maliciously travestied, the Abbé Cotin provided the sonnet and madrigal. Moreover we are told by D'Olivet in his history of the *Académie* that a quarrel, very similar to that between the two pedants of the play, took place between Cotin and Ménage in the salon of Mme de Montpensier, and that the subject of the quarrel was the very sonnet to the Princesse Uranie—otherwise the Duchesse de Nemours. It is true that D'Olivet was not born till ten years after the production of *Les Femmes savantes*, but in the *Menagiana* we read much the same story, though the scene is transferred to the house of Gilles Boileau.

There are also certain traits in the delineation of Vadius which point to Ménage. The speech of Trissotin,

> Nous avons vu de vous des églogues d'un style
> Qui passe en doux attraits Théocrite et Virgile,

recalls the fact that Ménage was particularly proud of his eclogues, while

> Va, va, restituer tous les honteux larcins
> Que réclament sur toi les Grecs et les Latins

is a palpable hit at a scholar who, with great erudition and a wonderful memory, was notoriously devoid of originality. While, however, Cotin recognised the allusions to himself and was much offended and distressed by them, Ménage took the wiser part of ignoring the likeness and commending the play.

For the present-day reader these personalities neither add to the interest of the play nor detract from its artistic merit. Stripped of the personal allusions Trissotin and Vadius would have been equally immortal as types of the poetaster-pedant. One may add, in palliation of Molière's descent to personalities, that Trissotin, though he is invested with some of Cotin's attributes, is not meant to be a portrait of him. Cotin was sixty-eight, while Trissotin is a man in the thirties—it is never hinted that he is too old for Henriette—and as Cotin was in Orders he could not possibly have played the rôle of fortune-hunter assigned to Trissotin. Secondly, it was Cotin who was the first aggressor. In *La Satire des Satires* (before 1666) he had attacked both Boileau and Molière and had followed this up by a still grosser attack on "Le Sieur des Vipéreaux" in *La Critique désintéressée sur les satires du temps* (1666). The same pamphlet had also contained an impertinent remark on Molière's profession. Boileau had avenged himself in his ninth Satire (1668) which has no less than four hits at Cotin, the last being the well-known lines,

> Qui méprise Cotin n'estime point son Roi,
> Et n'a, selon Cotin, ni Dieu, ni foi, ni loi.

It remained for Molière to pay his share of the score. He paid it in full, especially in the speech

in which Clitandre tells Philaminte what Trissotin is really thought of in the world of letters.

Much of the satire in the Third Act of *Les
Femmes savantes* is directed against the *bourgeois*
salons of which mention was made in the earlier
pages of this chapter. The exaggerated love of
compliment, the laborious cult of *esprit*, the
fashion of reciting verse, all of which were marked
features of salons like Mlle de Scudéry's or Mme
Deshoulières's, are portrayed faithfully and without caricature. From what has been said of Mlle
de La Vigne and Mlle Du Pré we may infer
that dabbling in Cartesianism and in Greek
philosophy was also a feature of the *précieux*
salons. But this ridicule of salon life only fills
two scenes. The whole play—at least this is the
orthodox view—is directed against the higher
education of women. If any of Molière's plays
is a *pièce à thèse*, says Faguet, it is *Les Femmes
savantes*. Now, granted that female education is
the main subject of *Les Femmes savantes*, it may
be called a problem-play in the sense that it
deals with a question to which there are, or at any
rate were in Molière's day, admittedly two sides.
But is not the scope of Molière's play much
wider than this? Is it not primarily concerned
with a question of greater moral and social
import? Is not Molière's attack directed, not
merely against women who affect a sham learning, though these are put in the foreground, but
against all women who neglect their children,
their household, and their business affairs for

work outside their home, whether it be literary,
or political, or philanthropical? Let us consider
the case of Philaminte. Regardless of the comfort
of her family, she sends away a competent kitchen-
maid because she violates the rules of grammar,
she rides rough-shod over her daughter's deepest
affections by ordering her to marry a fortune-
hunting pedant, and she totally neglects all business matters (*la grande négligence que vous avez
pour vos affaires*). That is the gravamen of the
charge against Philaminte, not that she dabbles
in learning and science, but that her interest in
her studies leads her to neglect her family and
her affairs. Henriette may be a shade too sensible, but in such a family, with a weak father,
an unbalanced sister, and a mother selfishly
absorbed in her own pursuits, common sense
was badly needed.

But one must not press this point to the exclusion of the more particular and more obvious
aim of Molière's satire, the ridicule of the *précieuses* and blue-stockings of his day. The interesting question here is how far did Molière
mean to go. Primarily, no doubt, he is laughing
at the affectation of learning in women. Philaminte and Armande and Bélise are not really
learned. They have simply picked up a few
catch-words of the learning and science of the
day[1]. Their taste in literature may be measured

---

[1] M. Bergson points out that the comic effect in Act III, Scene 2
is produced by the ladies speaking of scientific ideas in terms of
feminine sensibility (*Le Rire*, p. 184).

by their admiration for Trissotin's verses. Just
as Molière had declared in his preface to *Les Pré-*
cieuses ridicules that he was not attacking true
précieuses, so he might now have declared that he
was not attacking true *femmes savantes*; women,
for instance, like Mme de La Sablière, whom Mlle
de Montpensier, hostess of a rival salon, contemptuously called a *petite bourgeoise savante et*
précieuse. But in spite of Molière's disclaimer,
which, as was pointed out in the second chapter,
was a perfectly truthful one, it is evident that
he disliked *préciosité* in any form or shape, even
the *préciosité* of a 'true' *précieuse* like Mlle de
Scudéry. So with regard to learning in women,
it is equally clear that he abhorred a blue-stock-
ing, that is to say a woman who displayed her
learning, however genuine her learning might be.
It is always dangerous to look for Molière's own
opinions in the speeches of any of his characters,
but it is generally agreed that the well-known
speech of Clitandre in the Third Scene of the
First Act fairly represents Molière's views.

> Mon cœur n'a jamais pu, tant il est né sincère,
> Même dans votre sœur flatter leur caractère,
> Et les femmes docteurs ne sont point de mon goût.
> Je consens qu'une femme ait des clartés de tout;
> Mais je ne lui veux point la passion choquante
> De se rendre savante afin d'être savante;
> Et j'aime que souvent, aux questions qu'on fait,
> Elle sache ignorer les choses qu'elle sait;
> De son étude enfin je veux qu'elle se cache,
> Et qu'elle ait du savoir sans vouloir qu'on le sache,
> Sans citer les auteurs, sans dire de grands mots,
> Et clouer de l'esprit à ses moindres propos.

On the other hand, Faguet[1], who maintains
that Molière, during the fourteen years of his
career as a successful playwright, became, under
the influence of his public, more and more sub-
servient to the ideas and prejudices of his age,
especially to those of the Paris *bourgeoisie*, regards Chrysale as the interpreter of his attitude towards female education, and compares the
latter's long speech in Act II, Sc. 7, in which he
declares that a woman knows enough, if she has
the capacity

A connaître un pourpoint d'avec un haut-de-chausse,

that her conversation should be confined to household topics, and that her only books should be
her thimble and her needle, with the similar
remarks of Arnolphe in *L'École des Femmes*:

Et c'est assez pour elle, à vous en bien parler,
De savoir prier Dieu, m'aimer, coudre et filer.

But is there any reason for supposing that
Chrysale represents Molière's views any more
than Arnolphe? Yes, says Faguet, for Arnolphe
is a ridiculous character, while Chrysale is a
sympathetic one—or at any rate sympathetic in
comparison with Philaminte, Armande, and Bélise. The answer to this is that though it is quite
true that the *bonhomme* Chrysale is sympathetic,
it does not prevent him from being at the same
time ridiculous, not only in his character of

[1] See *Propos de théâtre*, 1903, pp. 148–177.

hen-pecked husband, but also by reason of his general ignorance and unintellectuality.

> Vos livres éternels ne me contentent pas;
> Et, hors un gros Plutarque à mettre mes rabats[1],
> Vous devriez brûler tout ce meuble inutile,
> Et laisser la science aux docteurs de la ville.

It would be just as reasonable to make Martine Molière's mouthpiece as Chrysale. But if the common opinion is right which finds in Clitandre's speech the true expression of his views, there is after all very little difference between Molière and Fénelon, who is generally regarded as a pioneer in the matter of female education in France. In his *De l'Éducation des Filles* which, though not published till 1687, was written in 1681, or nine years after the production of *Les Femmes savantes*, he begins by referring to the general view on the subject, the identical view, be it noted, which is held by Chrysale. "Pour les filles, dit-on, il ne faut pas qu'elles soient savantes, la curiosité les rend vaines et précieuses; il suffit qu'elles sachent gouverner un jour leurs ménages, et obéir à leurs maris sans raisonner." But then he goes on, "il est vrai qu'il faut craindre de faire des savantes ridicules," which is exactly Molière's point of view. More than half of Fénelon's short treatise (chapters iii–viii) is concerned with the education of children, but after two chapters (ix and x) devoted to the considera-

---

[1] This touch is borrowed from Furetière's *Le Roman bourgeois*, but Molière has improved on his source by the picturesque addition of Plutarch.

tion of certain especially female defects, including female vanity and the love of dress, he comes at last to the duties of women. Here he is in substantial agreement with Molière. First, he asks, what is woman's special work in life? and he answers, to educate the children, to look after the servants, and to control the household expenditure, including, usually, the granting of leases and the receiving of rents. Now these are just the very duties which Philaminte neglected. Moreover we are told by Charles Perrault that Molière was led to write *Les Femmes savantes* because he had remarked that women were ambitious of being learned, and that this was detrimental to the *esprit de ménage*[1].

Even as regards the intellectual training of women Fénelon hardly goes beyond Molière. Reading and writing, the four rules of arithmetic, a few legal notions, especially those connected with marriage-contracts, Greek and Roman history, together with some French history and that of the neighbouring countries. He sees no utility in learning Italian or Spanish. Latin is preferable, "for it is the language of the Church." As for the literature of their own country, he would allow them to read carefully selected prose and poetry, provided they had a real taste for literature and a sound judgment. Does this programme, limited though it appears to us, but an advanced one for Fénelon's day, go much beyond Clitandre's modest ideal?

[1] *Œuvres*, 1725, IV, 509.

Still, when all is said, it remains that while Fénelon's aim is positive, Molière's is negative. *Les Femmes savantes* is not a treatise on female education, but a satire on women who neglect their domestic duties, which Fénelon, like Molière, rightly puts in the foreground, for the sake of learning and science. For no doubt, though the three women of the play are all *savantes ridicules*, Molière would have included in his condemnation women of real learning who similarly neglected their duties. According to Mme de Lambert, who was a friend of Fénelon's, and whose *Avis à sa Fille* (written in 1709) owes something to his treatise, Molière's play did a good deal of harm. " Depuis ce temps-là on a attaché presqu'autant de honte au savoir des femmes qu'aux vices qui leur sont les plus défendus." Attacked for innocent occupations they have given themselves up to pleasure. "Has society gained by the exchange ? They have replaced learning by debauchery ; they have changed *préciosité* for indecency[1]." Mme de Lambert's remarks are pertinent enough considering that they were written during the last years of the reign of Louis XIV, but it is hardly fair to make Molière's comedy responsible for the scandalous vagaries of a decadent society.

Grimarest, as usual, gives an inaccurate account of the fortunes of *Les Femmes savantes,*

---

[1] *Réflexions nouvelles sur les Femmes*, Amsterdam, 1732, pp. 5–6. It was first published in 1727 without Mme de Lambert's permission.

saying that it was first produced at the Court, and that if it had not been for the king's good-nature it would have been a failure. As a matter of fact the play ran uninterruptedly at the Palais-Royal for eleven performances, the receipts for each of the first seven exceeding a thousand *livres*, and it was continued after Easter, though with diminished receipts, for another eight per-formances. This success is a strong testimony at once to Molière's popularity and to the in-telligence of his audience. For the play has little outward action and its comedy is of a refined type. The subject is not a great one like that of *Tartuffe* or *Don Juan* or *Le Misanthrope*, and the plot is of the simplest. But the workmanship throughout is consummate ; the characters are drawn with great delicacy, the action is developed on logical and natural lines, and if the trap set by Ariste for Trissotin provides too sudden a *dénouement*, this is at any rate neither mechanical nor conventional. Lastly the language and ver-sification abundantly prove that, given sufficient leisure, Molière could still write brilliant verse in a style which is at once lucid, vigorous, and un-failingly dramatic[1].

[1] Le plus parfait style de comédie en vers (Sainte-Beuve).

CHAPTER X

LE MALADE IMAGINAIRE

When Sganarelle, relating to his master, Don Juan, his experiences as a doctor, says that he gave his prescriptions at a venture and that it would be an odd thing if his patients recovered and came to thank him, Don Juan replies as follows ;

> Why not? Why should you not have the same privileges as all other doctors? They have no more share than you in the recovery of their patients, *et tout leur art est pure grimace.* All they do is to get the glory of successes that come from luck. So you likewise can profit by the patient's good fortune, and can accept as the result of your remedies all that comes from the favours of chance and the forces of Nature.

Chance and Nature—these according to Don Juan comprise the whole secret of the healing art. No wonder Sganarelle exclaims, "Vous êtes aussi impie en médecine."

Here Molière sounds with no uncertain note the onset of his attack on the doctors. It was delivered in force just seven months later in *L'Amour médecin* (September 1665). It was repeated in the following year in *Le Médecin malgré lui,* and again in *Monsieur de Pourceaugnac* (1669) and it was pushed home in a final charge in *Le Malade imaginaire* (1673). Why, it is naturally asked, was Molière so insistent in these attacks on medicine and the medical profession? Brunetière gives the answer with his usual confidence. Molière, he says, attacked physicians because they believed themselves to be stronger or more skilful than Nature, and belief in Nature is the key to Molière's whole philosophy. In support of the first part of this theory Brunetière puts in the foreground the speeches of Béralde in Act III, Scene 3 of *Le Malade imaginaire*, which he declares to be characteristic of Molière's attitude[1]. But except in the above-quoted passage from *Don Juan*, which we have no right to regard as an expression of Molière's own views, there is nothing in any of the other plays parallel to Béralde's contention that medicine is an interference with Nature. As for the more general part of Brunetière's theory, namely that Molière's philosophy is based on a belief in Nature, it has been so completely shattered by Faguet and is moreover on the face of it so untenable, that no more need be said about it here. As Faguet maintains, and as every one will agree, Molière's philosophy of life is founded on good sense or common sense[2], and to leave everything to Nature is contrary to common sense.

To find the principal cause of Molière's ridicule of the medical profession we need not look beyond the condition of medicine in France in Molière's day, its pedantry, its conservatism, its

---

[1] *Études critiques* IV, *La philosophie de Molière*.
[2] E. Faguet, *Rousseau contre Molière*, pp. 300 ff.

lack of science; there is an excellent guide to the whole subject in Maurice Raynaud's *Les Médecins au temps de Molière*[1]. The sovereign remedies were bleeding and purging. The favourite purgatives were rhubarb, cassia, and senna, the last a recent addition to the pharmacopeia of which the Faculty was extremely proud. From the apothecary's account in the First Scene of *Le Malade imaginaire* we learn that the purging, though frequent, was comparatively gentle and that it was tempered by soporifics and anodynes. It was far otherwise with bleeding. There was no firmer believer in its efficacy than Guy Patin (1602–1672), the friend of Molière's master Gassendi. He bled his wife twelve times for pneumonia, and his son twenty times for a fever. He bled old men of eighty years and infants of two months. He even bled an infant only three days old. Of a brother physician who died after declining to be bled he said, "May the devil bleed him in another world!" Among his patients was Gassendi, the story of whose death as told by Samuel Sorbière is well known in the annals of bleeding. Having been bled nine times, he pleaded that he could stand no more, and two of the celebrated physicians who were present were disposed to accept his plea. But a third declared energetically for more drastic measures, and the rest gave way.

---

[1] 2nd ed. 1863. See also A. M. Brown, M.D., *Molière and his medical associations*, 1897. The writer acknowledges his debt to Raynaud, which is considerable.

So poor Gassendi was bled five times more before he was allowed to die in peace[1] (1655).

When Molière returned to Paris in the year 1658 a new remedy had just achieved a signal triumph. This was the famous antimony or emetic wine. For twenty years the dispute as to its efficacy had raged furiously in the Faculty. Then during the campaign of 1658 the young king was taken ill with typhoid fever. He was moved to Calais, where for seven days he was purged and bled, but he grew steadily worse. The four Court physicians who were attending him were at their wit's end. Then they sent for Guénaut, the queen's physician, who prescribed antimony[2]. A long and solemn consultation followed under the presidency of Mazarin, who with the majority voted for its administration. They gave the king an ounce and purged him twenty-two times—and he recovered. The fortune of antimony was made.

In a letter of March 7, 1661, when Mazarin lay dying, Guy Patin relates how a similar consultation took place in the Bois de Vincennes between four of the principal Paris doctors, Guénaut, Vallot, Brayer, and Des Fougerais, and how each had a different theory as to the nature of their patient's malady. Brayer said it was the spleen, Guénaut the liver, Vallot the lungs, while

[1] Sorbière's *Life*, prefixed to *Syntagma Philosophiae Epicuri*. Amsterdam, 1684.
[2]   Il compteroit plutôt combien dans un printemps
    Guenaud et l'antimoine ont fait mourir de gens.
                (Boileau, *Sat.* IV, 32.)

Des Fougerais diagnosed an abscess of the mesentery. As this consultation was made public, it is just possible that Molière may have had it in his mind when he was writing the Fourth and Fifth Scenes of the Second Act of *L'Amour médecin*. According to the combined information of Brossette and Cizeron-Rival, the five doctors of this play represent Daquin (Tomès), Des Fougerais (Des Fonandrès), Guénaut (Macroton), Esprit (Bahys), and Yvelin (Filerin). Of these Daquin was in 1665 one of the king's eight ordinary physicians; later he became physician to the queen (1667) and first physician to the king, succeeding Vallot (1671). He was a converted Jew. Des Fougerais, whose real name was Elie Béda, was not one of the Court physicians, but he had a fashionable and remunerative practice. Guy Patin calls him "vénérable et détestable charlatan, s'il en fut jamais." The fact that he limped and that the part of Des Fonandrès was played by Louis Béjart makes the identification seem fairly certain. Guénaut was the queen's physician, and, as we have seen, had successfully prescribed antimony for the king in 1658. The name Macroton refers to his slow and deliberate way of talking, just as Bahys (from βαΰζω, to bark) is an allusion to Esprit's rapidity of utterance. "L'un va en tortue, et l'autre court la poste," is Sganarelle's comment. Esprit was physician to Monsieur, the king's brother. Yvelin was another Court physician. Raynaud suggests that the original of Tomès is Vallot, and not Daquin, who was a strong partisan of antimony and therefore opposed to bleeding. But Paul Mesnard points out that antimony and bleeding often went together, and that as a matter of fact Daquin bled with the best[1].

Apart from the personal allusions, and regarding the doctors who figure in *L'Amour médecin* merely as types of the medical profession in Molière's day, the three short scenes in which they appear are little masterpieces. Particularly admirable, because it is so perfectly natural, is the first of these, in which the two senior physicians, Des Fonandrès and Tomès, compare the merits of their respective mounts. Tomès, being conservative, rides a mule, while his colleague prefers a horse. As a matter of fact, it was Macroton-Guénaut who was the first Paris physician to take to a horse, thereby creating almost a scandal.

> Guenaud sur son cheval en passant m'eclabousse,

says Boileau in his Sixth Satire, written in 1660.

In spite of these opening amenities the two great men, when it comes to the question of treatment, contradict one another in no measured terms, Tomès being for bleeding and Des Fonandrès for antimony. Then follow the two juniors, the one speaking with exaggerated slowness, the other so fast as to be barely intelligible. In their reverence for their master, Hippocrates, in their talk about the patient's temperament and the need of expelling his peccant humours,

---

[1] *Œuvres complètes* v, 266–275 ; Raynaud, pp. 135–153.

they closely reflect the scholastic medicine of the day[1].

The same three features of scholastic medicine are made prominent in *Le Médecin malgré lui*. When that amusing rascal Sganarelle appears in his doctor's dress with an extremely pointed hat, his first remark to Géronte is "Hippocrate dit... que nous nous couvrions tous deux," and when asked in what chapter Hippocrates says this, he replies, "Dans son chapitre...des chapeaux." Later on (Act II, Scene 4) he indulges in a disquisition on *humeurs peccantes*, and in another scene (Act III, Scene 6) he speaks of "l'incongruité des humeurs opaques qui se rencontrent au tempérament naturel des femmes." Naturally he knows nothing about the subject, except the few catch-words that he had picked up when he was servant to a famous physician. His Latin is no less elementary, but when he finds that Géronte is equally ignorant of Latin, he strings together a few words which are partly of his own invention and partly a reminiscence of the Latin grammar. The use of Latin tags was one of the time-honoured pedantries of the profession. Malebranche is very severe on this harmless vanity. " Les premiers principes de ces gens-là

---

[1] In certain respects Des Fonandrès is more like Guénaut than Des Fougerais—(1) he prescribes antimony; (2) he rides a horse; (3) he is one of the two senior consultants. Now in 1665 Guénaut was 75, while Des Fougerais was only about 70, and Daquin, who married Vallot's niece, succeeded him as first physician to the king, and lived till about 1695, was considerably younger. Yet Macroton's slow speech marks him for Guénaut. Probably Molière purposely refrained from making the traits of resemblance too close.

sont cinq ou six mots latin d'un auteur, ou bien quelque passage grec, s'ils sont plus habiles[1]."

In *Monsieur de Pourcèaugnac* the two physicians who hold a solemn consultation on the case of the unfortunate provincial kindly discuss it in French *pour être plus intelligibles.* It need hardly be said that they are quite as unintelligible to the supposed patient as if they had talked Latin. But the speech of the first physician, who as the junior of the two gives his opinion first, is an admirable parody on the medical learning of the day. The "celebrated" Galen, and the "divine old man" Hippocrates are of course trotted out. In accordance with the teaching of the former the patient's malady is diagnosed as hypochondriacal melancholy, and the source of all the evil is said to be "une humeur crasse et féculente." The remedies prescribed are bleeding—"saignées fréquentes et plantureuses"—and purging. The second physician entirely agrees with his colleague, but suggests a few additional remedies, nor can he refrain from displaying his learning by the admixture of a little Latin.

An important factor, which must not be lost sight of, in determining Molière's attitude towards the medical profession was the state of his own health. The first time that we hear of his being seriously ill was in the spring of 1666, when he had a *fluxion de poitrine*—pleurisy or pneumonia—which left his lungs permanently affected. This was after the production of

[1] *Recherches de la Vérité* IV, c. iv (*Œuvres* II, 314).

L'Amour médecin, but it is very likely that he had been ill before this, and that the famous consultation of that comedy was founded to some extent on personal experience. In the spring of the following year (1667) he had another severe illness, which kept him from the theatre for nearly two months[1]. After this he had a permanent cough, to which, as we have seen, he makes allusion in *L'Avare*. It was at this time that he acquired a residence at Auteuil, and with the help of country air and a milk diet patched up his damaged constitution. He even thought of retiring from the stage altogether. But the love of his art was too strong for him, and during the next five years he worked harder than ever.

Raynaud, relying on the symptoms immediately preceding his death, believes that his malady was an aneurism of long standing. But the common view, which is borne out by the history of his illness, is that the disease was ordinary phthisis, marked by nervous irritability, a chronic cough, and occasional hæmorrhage of the lungs[2]. A remark of Grimarest's that Molière was said to be the original of his *Malade imaginaire*, combined with the title of Boulanger de Chalussay's malicious and libellous comedy, *Élomire, c'est à dire, Molière, hypocondre ou les Médecins vengés*, has led to the suggestion that Molière was at one time subject to hypochondria. But an unsupported utterance

---

[1] Though Easter was on April 10 the theatre did not open till May 15, and it was closed again from May 27 to June 10.
[2] See A. M. Brown, *op. cit.* pp. 200–201.

of Grimarest's is worth nothing, and *Élomire hypocondre*, though not printed till 1670, is shewn by internal evidence to have been written in the first half of 1666, between the time of Molière's first serious illness and the production of *Le Misanthrope*[1] (June), when to bring a charge of hypochondria against a man who had recently recovered from a serious attack of pneumonia was a piece of malicious absurdity. Possibly the illness may have left Molière nervous about his health. Like many people who suffer from a grave or distressing malady for which they can find no cure, he may have consulted various physicians and failing to get relief have conceived a contempt for the whole profession.

During the latter half of 1672 his health seems to have grown steadily worse. On August 9 and 12 the theatre was closed owing to his indisposition, and later in the year his condition caused serious alarm to his friends. It was under the shadow of approaching death that *Le Malade imaginaire* was conceived and written.

> Votre plus haut savoir n'est que pure chimère,
> 　Vains et peu sages médecins;
> Vous ne pouvez guérir par vos grands mots latins
> 　La douleur qui me désespère:
> Votre plus haut savoir n'est que pure chimère[2].

The *comédie-ballet* of *Le Malade imaginaire*

---

[1] See P. A. Becker in *Archiv für das Studium der neueren Sprachen und Litteraturen*, 1912, 174 ff. Élomire is made to say, "Dix pièces...ont depuis ce temps-là (i.e. since *Le Cocu imaginaire*) sorti de ma cervelle."

[2] Prologue to *Le Malade imaginaire*.

was presented at the Palais-Royal on February 10, 1673. It was the first *comédie-ballet* which Molière had presented at his own theatre instead of at the Court, and it was the first since *Les Fâcheux* for which Lulli had not written the music. The explanation is that the Florentine's grasping efforts to obtain a complete monopoly of music in France had led to a severance between the two collaborators. In March 1672 the king had granted to his favourite composer letters-patent for the establishment of a Royal Academy of Music which gave him at the same time a monopoly for all purely musical pieces, and soon afterwards fresh decrees rendered this monopoly even more complete. The result was that, when *La Comtesse d'Escarbagnas* was produced at the Palais-Royal in July 1672 in conjunction with *Le Mariage forcé*, music by Marc-Antoine Charpentier was substituted for Lulli's. In spite of this breach it was Molière's original intention to produce his new piece at the Court by way of celebrating the king's return in August 1672 from his first victorious campaign in Holland. But a new privilege, dated September 20, gave Lulli proprietary rights over even the verses which Molière had wedded to his music. This was more than Molière could stand; so he turned to Charpentier for help and produced *Le Malade imaginaire* at the Palais-Royal.

Regarded simply as an example of *comédie-ballet* Molière's last work is not so successful as *Le Bourgeois gentilhomme*, or even as *Monsieur de Pourceaugnac*, for the fusion between comedy and ballet is not so complete. The proof of this is that, if you drop the *intermède* between the First and Second Act and that between the Second and Third Act of *Le Malade imaginaire*, it makes no difference to the action of the play. In fact if you cut out Toinette's speech about Polichinelle at the close of the First Act, and Béralde's speech introducing the gypsies at the close of the Second Act, you would not even notice the omission of the ballets. With the final ballet it is different. Apart from its high merits, both as a piece of fooling and as a satire on the medicine of Molière's day, it serves effectually to dissipate all sense of the tragedy which underlies Argan's character. Moreover, in the Third Act the farcical element becomes more predominant. After the serious discussion between Argan and Béralde (Scene 3) we have seven scenes (4–10) of nearly continuous farce, and these are succeeded by Argan's pretended death (Scenes 11–13, and the beginning of 14) which after all is more or less of a farcical episode. But almost throughout the First and Second Acts the tone is one of pure comedy, and with this the atmosphere of extravaganza engendered by the ballets is out of keeping. Some critics, indeed, seeking to depreciate the play, have dubbed it a farce. M. Rigal, without any such intention, has accepted the term, and M. Donnay, another admirer of the play, calls it a *farce noire*. But, though there is a considerable element of farce in the Third Act, the play as a whole is certainly not a farce in the sense of being a mere parody of life. In some of its scenes it is life itself.

The whole of the First Act is admirable. First we have Argan reviewing his apothecary's account—the only instance, with the exception of *George Dandin*, of a play of Molière's opening with a soliloquy by the principal character. Then comes a scene between Argan and the servant Toinette, which, like the earlier scenes of *Le Bourgeois gentilhomme*, is remarkable for the short speeches and life-like character of the dialogue. Equally true to nature and full of quiet humour is the Fourth Scene in which Angélique, Argan's daughter, shyly confides to Toinette the state of her feelings for Cléante, while Toinette expresses her sympathy and effectually elicits her mistress's confidence by the briefest of answers. Then Argan returns and announces to Angélique that he has a proposal for her hand. Angélique is delighted, supposing that the proposal comes from Cléante, and for some time they talk at cross purposes. At last it appears that the intended husband is not Cléante, but a certain Thomas Diafoirus, the nephew of Argan's doctor, who is about to enter the profession. Here Toinette interferes, and asks why Argan, who is so rich, should want to marry his daughter to a doctor. But she is met by the immortal answer, the last word of egoism ;

C'est pour moi que je lui donne ce médecin.

Thereupon Toinette, who has taken command, defies her master, and declares that he will neither be able to force his daughter's inclination, nor have the heart to put her in a convent. Argan grows more and more angry, and at last, stick in hand, chases Toinette round and round his invalid's chair, till exhausted he sinks into it with

Ah! ah! je n'en puis plus. Voilà pour me faire mourir.

This scene again is full of humour, especially at the close when Argan's growing violence of language and final outburst of rage form an effective contrast to his character of an invalid. We have the same effect in the next scene when Toinette claps a pillow on his head, which so angers him that he flings all the pillows at her. But before this a new character has appeared in the person of Béline, Argan's second wife. She is a female Tartuffe, though without Tartuffe's ability. She has imposed upon Argan's credulity by the pretence, not of religion, but of wifely affection. Just as in the earlier play the whole household, except Orgon, see through Tartuffe, so Argan alone is blinded by Béline's hypocritical tenderness. And there is a similar reason for the credulity of both dupes. With Orgon it is an absorbing anxiety for his welfare in a future world, with Argan it is an equally absorbing anxiety to remain in this. In both alike ferocious egoism has produced a blind confidence in the individual who ministers to it.

The interested nature of Béline's pretended affection is well brought out in the Seventh Scene, between Argan, Béline, and the notary. "Non, non, je ne veux point de tout cela," says Béline, when her husband tells her of a certain sum of money which he proposes to put in her hands; and then she adds, "Ah! combien dites-vous qu'il y a dans votre alcôve?"—"Vingt mille francs, m'amour."—" Ne me parlez point de bien, je vous prie. Ah! combien sont les deux billets?"

Thus, as an 'exposition,' this First Act, save that it "lacks the accomplishment of verse," is no less admirable than the First Act of *Tartuffe*. In it we are introduced to the whole family —excepting only the child, Louison—to Argan, and Béline, and Angélique, and Toinette. We are made thoroughly acquainted with their characters, and we hear of the rival projects of marriage which constitute the plot of the play[1].

The dominant characteristic in Argan is the fear of death. It is this ever-present sword of Damocles which drives him into the arms of the physicians. He is not, like some hypochondriacs, a sufferer from minor ailments; he is not only robust, but he has a magnificent constitution, or he could not have resisted all the purgings and bleedings to which he has been subjected. But he loves life, or rather he loves being alive, and he is afraid of death. " Le plus grand faible

[1] Part of the dialogue between Argan and Toinette in Act I, Scene 5 (from "Non, je suis sûre qu'elle ne le fera pas" to "Je suis méchant quand je veux") is repeated, save for a few necessary changes, from *Les Fourberies de Scapin*, Act I, Scene 4.

des hommes," says Filerin in *L'Amour médecin,* "c'est l'amour qu'ils ont pour la vie, et nous en profitons, nous autres, par notre pompeux galimatias, et savons prendre nos avantages de cette vénération que la peur de mourir leur donne pour notre métier." That is as true to-day as it was in Molière's day. Thousands of men, for the most part those who have seldom known a day's illness, are nervous about their health. If they feel the slightest ache or pain, if they are in the least depressed or worried, they hurry off to a physician, who in these days generally earns his fee by telling them that there is nothing the matter with them. In Argan the fear of death has grown to such monstrous proportions that it has stifled his good qualities. Yet it has not, like avarice in Harpagon, completely crushed them. Though he is prepared to marry his elder daughter to a dull and pedantic fool, because he is a doctor, he is really fond of her, and when his younger daughter Louison pretends to be dead he is overcome with grief. Credulous too though he is in all matters connected with his health, he is not altogether a fool, for he has a certain shrewd insight. It is these gleams of light in his character which prevent it from being absolutely repulsive. On the stage it is the ridiculous rather than the repulsive aspect of the character that is present to us. But when we read the play a third aspect makes itself felt. We realise that Argan is at bottom a tragic figure. It is from the love of life, as

Filerin says, that he has given himself over to the physicians, but life brings him no enjoyment. He has become a miserable invalid, a ceaseless prey to unpleasant remedies. The life which he pays such a price to secure is not worth living.

With the skill of a born artist and dramatist Molière has made Toinette the exact opposite of Argan. Her gaiety, her joy in life, her perception of realities, bring a welcome current of fresh air into the sick man's chamber. "Elle n'a pas un sou d'esprit," says Sarcey, but she is alert, brisk, and quick of comprehension. She is not a *suivante*, like Dorine, but a *servante*. She is superior in status and education to Martine, and rather resembles Nicole, enjoying like her the confidence of her young mistress. There is considerable charm and some pathos in the character of Angélique. She loves her father in spite of his unpleasantness and tyranny, and she sincerely mourns his supposed death. Gentle and maidenly though she is, she is not wanting in spirit. To the importunities of Thomas Diafoirus, the commands of her father, and the malignant suggestions of her stepmother she opposes a resolute front, and her answers lack neither wit nor wisdom.

In the Fifth Scene of the Second Act we are introduced to M. Diafoirus and his *grand benêt de fils*, the priceless Thomas Diafoirus, and the satire on the doctors begins. By way of paying his court to Angélique Thomas Diafoirus presents her with his thesis against the *circulateurs*[1], as the partisans of the circulation of the blood were called, for like his father he is a staunch supporter of the ancients on all medical questions. The subject of the thesis was appropriate, for it was in this very year, 1673, that Louis XIV inaugurated at the Jardin des Plantes a special chair of anatomy for the propagation of the new discoveries. Jean Riolan, Harvey's most able opponent, a man of real learning and science, but blinded by his passionate reverence for Hippocrates and Galen, had died in 1657, the same year as Harvey, and since his death opposition to the new theory had practically died away. But as late as 1670 and 1672 contrary theses were supported at the Faculty of Medicine, so that there is nothing improbable in our friend Thomas's proceeding[2].

In the Eighth Scene of the same Act there appears a new character, and one that is quite novel in Molière's drama, the child Louison. The scene, as every one knows, was greatly admired by Goethe, and deservedly, for in its knowledge of child-nature, in its faithful rendering of it, in its simplicity and economy of language, it is a masterpiece. In the next and last scene of the Second Act Argan's brother Béralde makes a brief appearance, but it is not till the final Act that he becomes prominent, appearing in every scene.

If any of Molière's characters may be called a

---

[1] *circulator* in Latin means charlatan.
[2] See Raynaud, *op. cit.* pp. 160–172.

raisonneur, it is Béralde. He is not entirely
disconnected with the action of the play, for he
is the advocate and ambassador of Cléante in
his love-affair with Angélique, and he backs up
Toinette in her two stratagems for the furtherance of their plans. His own contribution is the
proposal that Argan should himself become a
doctor. But in the long, too long, scene with
his brother-in-law (Act III, Scene 3), his chief
function is to 'reason' with him, to present to
him the case against medicine. " Mais raisonnons
un peu, mon frere," says Argan. "Vous ne
croyez donc point à la médecine."

Béralde's argument is briefly as follows : it is
ridiculous for one man to try and cure another;
we know nothing about the working of the
human machine, the springs of which Nature has
veiled in mystery; physicians are just as ignorant
as laymen, but they conceal their ignorance by
talking Latin and holding pompous discourses.
"What is one to do then, when one is ill?"
asks Argan. "Nothing—leave Nature to herself and she will gently free herself from the
disorder into which she has fallen. It is our
anxiety, our impatience that spoils everything,
and nearly all men die from their remedies, and
not from their maladies." Then he attacks the
scholastic medicine of the day, and its meaning-
less jargon about the spleen and the liver, and
the rectification of the blood, and the preserva-
tion of the natural heat, and so on. " This," he
says, "is the romance of medicine. But when you

come to truth and experiment you will find that there is nothing in it." Far better that Argan should go and see a comedy by Molière, to which Argan replies :

"C'est un bon impertinent que votre Molière avec ses comédies, et je le trouve bien plaisant d'aller jouer d'honnêtes gens comme les médecins."—"Ce ne sont point les médecins qu'il joue, mais le ridicule de la médecine."

That is quite true of Molière's former plays. He does not ridicule doctors in the abstract, but doctors who believe in or practise the unscientific medicine of the day. But, as we have seen, Béralde goes further than this. He is opposed to all medicine, to all recourse to the physician's art. Leave Nature to herself[1]. He is of course wrong ; Nature can do a great deal to free herself from disorders, but she often wants assistance. But if Béralde, as seemingly he is, is Molière's mouthpiece, Molière's attitude is very intelligible. For several years he had been suffering from a deadly disease, and physicians had availed him nothing. Now at last he bids defiance to physicians and declines their remedies. "Cela n'est permis qu'aux gens vigoureux et robustes qui ont des forces de reste pour porter les remèdes avec la maladie ; mais pour lui, il n'a justement de la force que pour porter son mal."

[1] There is a striking similarity between Béralde's argument and Montaigne's essay *De la ressemblance des enfans aux pères* (II, 37). "C'est la crainte de la mort et de la douleur, l'impatience du mal, une furieuse et indiscrète soif de la guérison, qui nous aveugle ainsi." These words might have been addressed to Argan by Béralde.

It is a tragic confession—how tragic no one, when it was first uttered, knew.

In the next scene Béralde definitely contributes to the development of the action, for he persuades Argan to postpone the ministrations of his apothecary, and this leads to a highly amusing scene, in which M. Purgon, in a gradual *crescendo* of rage, abandons poor Argan to the alarming effects of his corrupt humours. At this juncture a new physician presents himself in the person of Toinette. The three scenes (8–10) in which she appears alternately as doctor and maid are full of verve and excellent fun[1]. But though Argan has quarrelled with M. Purgon and there is no longer a question of Thomas Diafoirus as a suitor for Angélique, Argan will not accept Béralde's candidate, Cléante. On the strength of the information that he has extracted from Louison, he is determined to send his daughter

[1] There is a first sketch of these scenes in Molière's early farce, *Le Médecin volant,* in which the valet, Sganarelle, plays a similar part to Toinette. It is developed, as we saw, from an Italian *scenario,* a fact which renders improbable Ticknor's statement, accepted by Professor Fitzmaurice Kelly, that *Le Médecin malgré lui* is taken from Lope de Vega's *El acero de Madrid.* For it is not likely that Molière should have gone to Lope, when he had already used the theme of a sham doctor in *L'Amour médecin* and *Le Médecin volant.* Besides, in Lope's comedy, though the sham doctor's prescription suggests the title and sets the action of the play in motion, it is not more than a fillip, and we hear no more of the valet—Ticknor wrongly calls him a friend of the lover—in the disguise of a doctor. A much closer resemblance to *El acero de Madrid* is afforded by *Les Bains de la Porte Saint-Bernard,* a piece by Boisfranc which was produced by the Italian company at the Hôtel de Bourgogne in 1696 (see L. Moland, *Molière et la comédie italienne,* pp. 334–6).

to a convent. Béralde hints that this is in order to
please Béline, and when Argan reproaches him
with being prejudiced against that lady, he
openly accuses her of treachery. Again Toinette
has a brilliant idea. Let Argan pretend to be
dead—" N'y a-t-il quelque danger à contrefaire
le mort?"—and he will see whether Béline is
really fond of him. The ruse is perfectly successful. Béline reveals her criminal intentions,
and Angélique her real affection for her father.
Argan's eyes are opened, and he consents to his
daughter's marriage with Cléante on condition
that he becomes a doctor. But Béralde betters
this proposal by suggesting that Argan should
become a doctor himself. This leads to the
famous ballet which represents the burlesque
reception of a doctor. Written in delightful
macaronic Latin, it is, Raynaud points out, an
abridgement made with consummate art, not
only of the ceremony of the doctorate, but of all
the ceremonies through which the candidate had
to pass from the commencement of his studies
to the final reception. It opens with the usual
address by the President of the Faculty in praise
of medicine. Then comes the examination of
the candidate, first a physiological question,
" Why does opium produce sleep? "

> Quia est in eo
> Virtus dormitiva,
> Cujus est natura
> Sensus assoupire.

Next, a general pathological question on the

treatment of lung disease and asthma. Finally, a special case is submitted to the candidate for his opinion. He knows only two remedies, bleeding and purging, but they are enough.

> Bene, bene, bene, bene respondere:
> Dignus, dignus est entrare
> In nostro docto corpore.

Then the candidate having sworn to observe the statutes of the Faculty, and to use no remedies except those prescribed by the Faculty,

> Maladus dust-il crevare
> Et mori de suo malo,

the President confers on him the doctor's cap[1].

The effect of this exhilarating ballet is to dispel any idea of tragedy which to a reader of the play at any rate is suggested by Argan's unhappy condition and character and by the sinister figure of Béline. The real tragedy of the play lies outside the play itself. It lies in the thought that the author of the play, the actor of Argan's part, was himself no imaginary invalid, but in grim reality a dying man. On the fourth day of its representation, as he was uttering the word *juro* in the final ballet, he was seized with a convulsion which was noticed by some of the spectators. Pulling himself together with a great effort, he recited the lines

---

[1] See for the ceremony Raynaud, *op. cit.* pp. 55–65, and cp. Locke's account of the conferring of a doctor's degree at Montpellier in 1676 (King, *Life of John Locke*, 2 vols., new ed. 1830, I, 119).

in which the candidate returns thanks to the
Faculty :

> Vivat, vivat, vivat, vivat, cent fois vivat,
>   Novus doctor, qui tam bene parlat !
> Mille, mille annis et manget et bibat,
>   Et seignet et tuat !

But within a few hours the ' new doctor ' was
dead, and he who had ' spoken so well,' not only
to the Paris audience but to the whole world,
was silent for ever.

CHAPTER XI

COMEDY AND CHARACTER

I HAVE said that in the opinion of some modern critics *Tartuffe* and *Le Misanthrope* are not true comedies and that Tartuffe and Orgon and Alceste are tragic rather than comic characters[1]. Granted, they say, that Molière dressed up these plays as comedies, and that he gave a comic interpretation to his own parts, this was merely for the sake of pleasing the *parterre*; his real message is for those who have sufficient insight to detect the tragedy which lies behind the comic mask. And in support of this view they allege the melancholy strain in his character, the hardships and struggles of his life, his silence in company, his seriousness, his interest in philosophy. I deny none of these characteristics, but to argue from them that Molière's greatest plays are not true comedies seems to me to labour under the misapprehension that a serious view of life is incompatible with an acute sense of the ridiculous. On the contrary, the fountains of tears and laughter lie close together, and the truest humour is often mingled with pathos. Many masters of the comic art have been of a melancholy temperament, but whether a man's bent is towards

[1] See above, pp. 110 and 175.

tragedy or comedy is a question not so much of
his temperament or his attitude towards life as
of his imagination. Molière was not blind to the
tragic issues of life—far from it—but he saw that
tragedy and evil have often a ridiculous side and
it was this side which appealed to his imagination and stimulated his creative faculties. And
realising this, he devoted himself to the study
of comedy till no secret of the comic Muse remained unrevealed to him. "S'il lui arrive d'être
tragique," says Lemaître, "c'est comme malgré
lui et par la force des choses[1]." Because he
looked deep into life and recognised its essential
seriousness, his greatest plays are serious in the
sense that they deal with serious questions. But
they are none the less true comedies. He might
have said with Figaro, "Je me hâte de rire de
tout de peur d'être obligé d'en pleurer."

Compare him with Balzac, that other great
master of the *comédie humaine*, and we at once
see the difference between the comic and the
tragic imagination. In an interesting letter to
his future wife, Mme de Hanska, Balzac gives
the sketch of a play that he is writing[2]. It is
the story of *Tartuffe*, but with this difference
that Tartuffe is a woman, the forewoman in a
big shop, and the mistress of the proprietor.
Like Molière, Balzac shews the effect of this
infatuation upon the proprietor's family, but the

---

[1] *La comédie après Molière et le théâtre de Dancourt*, 2nd ed.
1903, p. 20.
[2] *Lettres à l'Étrangère* I, 381-2.

issue is wholly tragic. One of the two daughters tries to poison the mistress. She fails in her attempt, but the mistress is sent away. Then the father, finding that he cannot live without her, deserts his family and goes off with her to America.

Take another instance. Once Balzac paid a visit to a family which consisted of a man and his daughter and his second wife. Balzac thought that he detected a latent hostility between the girl and her stepmother, and inspired by this idea he wrote *La Marâtre*, which is a grim *tragédie bourgeoise* ending in the murder of the girl by her stepmother and the suicide of the girl's lover, with whom the stepmother is also in love[1]. What would Molière have made of the same situation? We know—he made of it *Le Malade imaginaire*.

Finally compare *Eugénie Grandet* with *L'Avare*. The novel is a tragedy, the play, in spite of its sordid glimpses and its tragic suggestions, begins and ends as a comedy. And the difference between the two works is a good example of the different ways in which the imagination of the two men worked. Grandet is a man of great ability and resolute purpose. He has a real genius for business; his large commercial schemes are very different from the timid usury of Harpagon. Had his servant stolen his strong-box, detection would inevitably have followed. He is, in short, what

[1] A. Le Breton, *Balzac*, 1905, pp. 137-8, citing Spoelberch de Lovenjoul, *Histoire des Œuvres de H. de Balzac*.

Balzac loves to create—a man whose ruling passion brings misery to those about him, but success to himself. For Balzac is fascinated by the devastating power of evil, and his imagination never moves more swiftly than when it is fired by the career of a successful villain, of a Grandet, a Vautrin, or a Philippe Bridau. Molière, on the other hand, is more impressed by the limitations of criminals, by the stupidity, the timidity, or the self-indulgence which in the end trips them up. Harpagon is a man of mediocre intelligence who goes beside himself when his money is stolen. Béline falls at once into the trap prepared for her and is paralysed by detection. Tartuffe throws away his excellent chances of satisfying his ambition by making love to his patron's wife. The passions of Balzac's criminals give them genius[1]: the passions of Molière's criminals make them dupes.

Thus it is the ridiculous and not the tragic side of evil that quickens Molière's imagination. He is the lord of laughter, from the smile which shews itself only in the eyes to the convulsive merriment which shakes the sides. He can rise to the highest peaks of comedy, but he does not disdain the valleys of more elementary mirth. At the lowest point in the scale comes the comedy of action and gesture, such as Molière had learnt from the Italian *commedia dell' arte* or from the clowns of the quack vendors on the Pont-Neuf. We have an example of this in the *École des*

[1] Cp. E. Faguet, *Balzac*, pp. 121-3.

Femmes, in the first scene between Arnolphe and his servants (Act I, Scene 2). But the most obvious instance is the famous scene in *Les Fourberies de Scapin* (Act III, Scene 2) in which Scapin cudgels Géronte in the sack. Boileau thought this horse-play unworthy of Molière's genius, but there is a touch of humour in it which raises it above mere buffoonery. There is no horse-play and more humour in the scene of *Le Bourgeois gentilhomme* in which M. Jourdain exhibits his newly-acquired accomplishments to his wife and servant, and in those of *Le Malade imaginaire* in which Toinette plays the part of a doctor[1]. But in these language comes to the assistance of action and gesture, and the comic interest has a wider scope.

Elementary again, and depending entirely upon action for its effect, is what may be called the comic situation, as when Orgon and Tartuffe plump down on their knees at the same moment. This situation had already served in *Le Dépit amoureux*, in which the two old men, Albert and Polydore, go through the same performance (Act III, Scene 4). As M. Bergson points out, a situation which has little or nothing that is comic in itself may become so by force of repetition. He gives as instances *L'Étourdi*, *L'École des Maris*, *L'École des Femmes*, and *George Dandin*, in all of which the comic effect is due to repetition. He might have added *Les Fâcheux*, the whole comedy of which depends upon the repeated interruptions to Éraste's ren-

---

[1] See above, p. 284.

dezvous with his mistress. Repetition of the same phrase is another common procedure in classical comedy. Well-known examples of it in Molière are the "Et Tartuffe?" and "Le pauvre homme!" of *Tartuffe*, the "Sans dot" of *L'Avare* and the "Que diable allait-il faire dans cette galère?" of *Les Fourberies de Scapin*. M. Bergson, who denies that the repetition of words is amusing in itself, gives an ingenious explanation of the comic effect. He says that it arises from "the presence of two terms, namely a suppressed sentiment which is released like a spring, and an idea which amuses itself by suppressing it again." Thus the "Et Tartuffe?" the "Sans dot" and the "Que diable allait-il faire dans cette galère?" come automatically to the lips of the infatuated Orgon and the avaricious Harpagon and Géronte. But this cry from the inner man is immediately suppressed by the other speaker —Dorine, Valère, Scapin—who continues his narrative or his argument[1]. This is perhaps over-subtle, and it would be simpler to say that the comic effect is due to the fact that the repeated phrase reflects to perfection the ruling passion of the speaker.

A good example of the combined effect of situation and language is the excellent scene in *L'École des Maris* (II, 9) between Isabelle, Sganarelle, and Valère, in which Isabelle under colour of declaring her love for her guardian really declares it for Valère, and while pretending to

[1] Bergson, *Le rire*, pp. 73–5.

embrace Sganarelle gives her hand to her lover to kiss. As we have seen, this scene was probably inspired by Lope de Vega's *La discreta enamorada*[1].

But it is by the combination of language with thought, of words with ideas, that Molière's greatest comic effects are obtained. In these cases the language itself may or may not be comic, but the dialogue always suggests a comic idea, and generally a humorous one. An admirable example is the scene between Arnolphe and Horace (*L'École des Femmes* III, 4) in which the latter describes how Agnès had thrown down a stone on his head with a letter attached to it. The change in Arnolphe's feelings from delight at Horace's discomfiture, when he hears of the stone, to jealousy and disgust, when he hears of the letter, and the necessity which he is under of concealing his feelings, make this a scene of unsurpassable humour. Simpler, because depending on one of the most common sources of comedy, a mutual misunderstanding, but admirably worked out, is the scene of *L'Avare* (V, 3) in which Harpagon and Valère are at cross purposes, Valère confessing that he is engaged to his daughter, and Harpagon imagining that he is referring to the lost *cassette*.

Rich also in comic suggestion are the scenes between the comic hero and Sbrigani in *Monsieur de Pourceaugnac*, the great scene with Mascarille and Jodelet in *Les Précieuses ridicules*[2]

[1] See above, p. 74.
[2] See above, p. 68.

several of those in *L'Avare*, and the inimitable scene between Don Juan and M. Dimanche, which some serious-minded critic has found out of place.

Sometimes it is a common weakness of human nature which serves as the basis for Molière's humour. The whole play of *L'Amour médecin*, for instance, is an apt illustration of the theory of La Rochefoucauld, the first authorised edition of whose *Maximes* appeared in the same year (1665) as Molière's comedy, that *amour-propre* is the mainspring of human action. This note is struck at once in the opening scene, in which Sganarelle consults his friends as to the best method of rousing his daughter from her melancholy. Being a thorough egoist himself, he detects in each answer the self-interest that prompts it. "Vous êtes orfèvre, Monsieur Josse, et votre conseil sent son homme qui a envie de se défaire de sa marchandise." Similar instances are the double lovers' quarrel of *Le Dépit amoureux* (IV, 3 and 4), which Molière repeated, though less successfully, in *Tartuffe* (II, 4) and *Le Bourgeois gentilhomme* (III, 10), and the scene between Angélique and Toinette in *Le Malade imaginaire* (I, 4) with its admirable contrast between the sentimentalism of the young girl, and the common sense with a point of irony, which does not prevent real sympathy, of the servant. With them may be classed a couple of scenes in the heroic-pastoral comedy of *Mélicerte* (I, 3 and 4). In the first Lycarsis

(Molière's part) is burning to tell a piece of news, and Nicandre is equally anxious to hear it, but the news never gets told. In the second Lycarsis is besieged by two shepherdesses, who beg for the honour of an alliance with him, but who are suitors, not, as he fondly imagines, for his own hand, but for that of his son.

This last scene, however, rather tends to bring out the foible of a particular individual, than the weakness of human nature in general, and it is as revelations of individual character that a large number of Molière's finest scenes excel. In one of the encounters, for instance, between M. de Pourceaugnac and Sbrigani (I, 4) the comic effect is enhanced by the admirable portrayal of the character of the two men, the dupe and the duper, the foolish self-satisfied provincial and the wily Neapolitan intriguer. So again in *L'Avare* the scenes between Harpagon and La Flèche (I, 3), Harpagon and Frosine (II, 5), and Harpagon and his servants (III, I) are not only comic, but they are really creative. They bring before us in vivid relief not only the miser himself, but the other characters in these scenes.

It may be said that in some of these last instances there is a touch of exaggeration or farce. But there is none in the presentation of M. and Mme de Sotenville in *George Dandin*.

De la maison de la Prudoterie il y a plus de trois cent ans qu'on n'a pas remarqué qu'il y ait une femme, Dieu merci, qui ait fait parler d'elle.

Nor is there any in the opening scene of *Le*

Mariage forcé, in which Sganarelle consults his friend as to the advisability of his proposed marriage. Every link in it reveals the author's knowledge of human nature in general and of Sganarelle's character in particular. Hardly less admirable is the scene (9) in the same play between Sganarelle and the duellist Alcidas, in which the contrast between the perfect courtesy of Alcidas's language and the brutality of his actions is a finished example of true humour.

High among Molière's comic scenes stand those of *L'Amphitryon* in which Sosie is the chief figure. His soliloquy in the opening scene, and his scenes with Mercure, with Amphitryon, and with his wife, Cléanthis, are at once witty, humorous, and characteristic. But the two plays in which Molière's comic Muse keeps most consistently to the highest sphere of comedy are *Le Misanthrope* and *Les Femmes savantes*. The sonnet-scene and the scene between Célimène and Arsinoé in *Le Misanthrope* and the two scenes in *Les Femmes savantes* which centre upon Martine's dismissal for violating the laws of grammar are masterpieces of refined comedy, but they are especially noteworthy for the force and subtlety with which they bring out the characters of all the various persons who take part in them.

In hardly any of the scenes which have been cited as examples of Molière's comic genius is there any display of wit. After Molière had finally abandoned the Mascarille type of valet—his last appearance is in *Les Précieuses ridicules*—he hardly ever introduced witty remarks for their own sake, apart from the character of the person who utters them. It is true that Sganarelle, the woodcutter of *Le Médecin malgré lui*, is often witty, but then the contrast between his wit and his lazy sensuality is as essential to his character as it is to Falstaff's. That this abstinence from wit for wit's sake is not due to any lack of wit in Molière is sufficiently proved by *L'Étourdi* and *Les Précieuses ridicules*. Indeed, George Meredith, even in respect of his later plays, ranks him superior in wit to Congreve. Millamant, he declares, if more vivid than Célimène, is not her rival in wit. "What she utters adds to her personal witchery, and is not further memorable. She is a flashing portrait, and a type of the superior ladies who do not think, not of those who do[1]." This judgment may surprise some people, but what Meredith means by wit is not merely "a blaze of intellectual fireworks," but the play of mind upon mind, not merely brilliant juggling with words, but clear insight into motive and character.

We have a good instance of this superior kind of wit in *Les Fourberies de Scapin*. Scapin, in many ways, is a valet of the Mascarille type, being in fact modelled, like Mascarille, on the Italian Scappino. He is a man of action, full of resource and contrivance and prompt in execution. But he is not witty in the sense that he makes witty remarks. The scene in which he imitates Octave's father

[1] *An Essay on Comedy*, p. 41.

(1, 3), his aside remarks, and his flattery of Argante
in the scene which follows, the scene in which he
confesses his sins to his master, Léandre (II, 4), the
scene in which he gets the money out of Argante—
" Monsieur, un petit mulet " (II, 5)—the famous
galley-scene (II, 7), and the last scene of all
(III, 13), in which he pretends to be dying, are
all admirable, but in all alike Scapin shews his
superiority not in the display of wit, but in his
knowledge of character and his readiness of
resource.

Molière, then, takes a supreme interest in
character. He is before all things a creator of
character, and of comic character. This does
not mean that the outward appearance of his
characters is necessarily comic—far from it. Alceste and Don Juan are men of high birth and
breeding. They have the distinction and charm
of good looks and good manners. Arnolphe is
self-opinionated and rude when contradicted, but
he has the bearing and manners of a gentleman,
and there is certainly nothing odd in his appearance. The latter remarks apply equally to
the two other well-to-do *bourgeois*, Orgon and
Chrysale. On the other hand, Harpagon in his
old clothes, and Argan in his invalid's chair,
border on the grotesque, while M. Jourdain in
his gorgeous dressing-gown is doubtless meant
to have a comic appearance. But even in all these
last three cases it is the inward character and
not the outward fashion which furnishes the real
comedy. There remains Tartuffe. As acted by

the personable Du Croisy he no doubt had good looks of a florid type. But M. Bergson maintains with some plausibility that he is comic by virtue of his gestures, and by gestures he means his movements and even his discourse, when it is the unconscious and automatic expression of a habit of mind. He gives as an instance his famous entry, " Laurent, serrez ma haire avec sa discipline." These words may or may not be unconscious, but this much at any rate we may allow M. Bergson, that we associate with Tartuffe a certain oily unctuousness, a certain affectation of piety in his movements and gestures, which contrasted with his florid countenance and well-nourished body impart to his appearance an element of visible comedy.

But on the whole Molière's chief characters belong to comedy by virtue, not of their physical aspect, but of their mental and spiritual habit. And their comic quality arises from some exaggerated trait in their character; in Don Juan libertinism, in Tartuffe religious hypocrisy, in Harpagon avarice, in Argan the fear of death. In all these the exaggerated trait is a vice: in Alceste, on the other hand, it is a virtue—sincerity in social intercourse. All art has an inherent tendency towards simplification and accentuation. A portrait painter, for instance, must not only omit lines in his portrait, but he must strengthen those that he retains. The danger is that he may go too far in the process, with the result that the portrait becomes a caricature. It is the same with the art of the novelist and the dramatist. Balzac's great characters—Grandet, Goriot, Claës, Baron Hulot d'Ervy, Philippe Bridau—are heroic in their simplicity. They are monomaniacs, the victims of an absorbing passion. On the stage some strengthening of the lines, some accentuation of the dominant trait, is absolutely necessary. Just as the actor has to speak louder, more slowly, more distinctly than in ordinary life, so the dramatist has to emphasise the salient features of his characters in order to give the impression that they are true to life. Nearly all persons who have any character at all express themselves at times forcibly and even with exaggeration. They let themselves go, and it is when they let themselves go that they are really themselves, as nature made them, and not as they are constrained to be by the laws of society and good breeding. Now on the stage the characters let themselves go more often than they do in real life. The long intervals of ordinary routine and tranquil intercourse with their fellows are abbreviated and the revealing storms burst more frequently. The reason for this, which is only another form of simplification, is that the dramatist's aim is to reveal character, and that he has to reveal it within the space of two or three hours.

The exaggeration of a single trait is the groundwork of Ben Jonson's comedy. So far does he carry it that his minor characters are mere 'humours' or oddities, while his great characters, like Volpone, are paragons of vice. Molière has skilfully avoided this pitfall of undue simplification and exaggeration. He does not eliminate all but the salient feature. He endows his comic heroes with ordinary everyday characteristics ; he does not make them ridiculous in all things. "It is not incompatible," says Dorante in defence of Arnolphe, "that a person should be ridiculous in certain things, and a well-bred gentleman in others[1]," and Arnolphe in fact is quite a complex character. Tartuffe is a sensualist as well as an ambitious hypocrite. Don Juan is not only a libertine and atheist, but he has the courage and regard for honour of his class. Alceste, in spite of his brusqueness and his railings against social insincerity, is popular in society, especially with women. Except when he is stirred by strong feeling, he behaves with all the courtesy of a well-bred gentleman. He hates or professes to hate mankind, but he is in love with Célimène. Argan's ignoble fear of death and undisguised egoism have not entirely banished his natural affection for his children. Even Harpagon, who is less sharply individualised than the others, is in love, after his fashion, and he is very human in his vanity.

The very discussions about Molière's chief characters that have been noticed in previous chapters are a testimony at once to their com-

[1] *La Critique de l'École des Femmes*, Scene 6. (See above, p. 92.)

plexity and their truth to life. "Lorsque vous peignez les hommes, il faut peindre d'après nature." Even in those characters which are less profoundly studied than the great protagonists, such as Chrysale, Philaminte, and Philinte, the strands of good and evil are so subtly intermingled that readers are divided in their sympathy. But this is especially noticeable in the greater characters. For some persons Alceste is a tragic hero ; for a few he is a cross-grained and ridiculous prig ; the majority find him ridiculous but adorable. The courage and high-breeding of Don Juan invest him with a glamour which blinds some readers to the odious side of his character and even more to its ridiculous side. Tartuffe's resourceful and nearly successful villainy have provoked admiration. One may even be a little sorry for Harpagon and Argan. M. Jourdain, whom the average reader regards as a vain and credulous fool, has been commended for his aspirations towards education and culture. There are those who prefer Philaminte and Armande to the sensible and (as they say) commonplace Henriette.

In the days before it was the practice to prefix to each scene elaborate stage-directions touching the age, condition, dress and general appearance of each of the *dramatis personae*, a practice which seems to have been inaugurated in France by Diderot in his *Le père de famille* (published in 1758)[1], it was impossible for a

---

[1] It does not appear in *Le Méchant* (1747). In *Le Barbier de Séville* (1775) and *Le Mariage de Figaro* (1784) an annotated list of the *dramatis personae* is prefixed to the play.

dramatic author to make known to his readers
the outward aspect of his character except by
an oblique reference. Shakespeare, indeed, often
contrives to let us know in a general way what
his characters look like, whether they are tall
or short, fat or lean, dark or fair. Racine tells
us nothing; he gives us the soul without the
body. Molière does not leave us wholly without
information. We learn that Arnolphe is forty-
two, that Ariste is nearly sixty, and that his
brother Sganarelle is twenty years younger.
Harpagon owned to sixty. Toinette in her
doctor's dress looked at the most, says Argan,
twenty-six or twenty-seven. We know that Tartuffe was "gros et gras," that Orgon wore a
beard, and that Sganarelle in *Le Médecin malgré
lui* had a large black beard[1] and was dressed in
green and yellow. But we have another source
of information, though more conjectural. Molière
without writing his play for a particular actor,
as Rostand wrote *Cyrano de Bergerac* for Coquelin, took into account the physical characteristics of the actors who were to take the parts.
That gives us a clue to the age of Dorine, for
Madeleine Béjart, who played the part, was
forty-six when it was first produced in 1664.
A similar clue is furnished by the fact that
Du Croisy, who represented Tartuffe, was good
looking, rather stout, and an actor of comic parts.
Lastly, we know from the inventory made after
Molière's death that in the part of M. Jourdain he

---

[1] In both cases we must apparently understand by *beard* thick
moustaches (*Œuvres* VI, 51 n. 3).

wore a striped dressing-gown lined with orange and green silk, that in those of Orgon and Harpagon he wore black, and that Alceste's costume consisted of a doublet and breeches of grey brocade striped with gold thread and silk, lined with watered silk and decked with green ribbons ("l'homme aux rubans verts"), a vest of gold brocade, and silk stockings[1]. Argan's dress is not given in the inventory, but according to an old edition of *Le Malade imaginaire* it consisted of a red camisole, breeches and stockings, slippers, a lace handkerchief loosely tied round the neck, and a nightcap with a lace lining (*coiffe*). This is confirmed by two contemporary engravings, so that there is no authority for the dressing-gown of tradition[2].

The complexity that we have noticed in Molière's characters and the divergent views that are held about them are sufficient answers to the charge that Molière creates types rather than individuals, a charge which seems largely to have arisen from the titles of some of his comedies—*Le Misanthrope, L'Avare, Le Bourgeois gentilhomme, Le Malade imaginaire*, not to speak of *L'Imposteur*, the alternative title of *Tartuffe*. M. Bergson, indeed, bases partly on these titles and on those of Molière's successors—*Le Joueur, Le Distrait, Le Glorieux, Le Méchant*—a theory that it is the aim of comedy to present types, a theory which he at once proceeds to qualify by adding that "it will even create, if need be, new types." On

---

[1] E. Soulié, *op. cit.* pp. 275–6.   [2] *Ib.* p. 88.

the other hand, he says, tragedy, like all art *except comedy*, creates individuals—characters that are unique. Hamlet is unique. If he resembles other men in certain characteristics, it is certainly not by reason of those characteristics that he interests us most. Yet every one regards him as a living character, and it is only in this sense that he is universally true[1]. But the answer is that Hamlet does interest us, and that in no slight degree, by the characteristics which he shares with other men, and it is just these characteristics which help to make him a living man instead of an abstract humour. Alceste is every whit as unique as Hamlet, and he is equally alive. But both are universally true, not merely in the sense that they are universally regarded as alive but because they are types as well as individuals, types not indeed of average commonplace humanity, but of what human beings might become under certain aspects and conditions, and if certain characteristics were developed in an unusual degree. There is a vast difference between types of humanity and social types ; the latter are confined to one age and one place, the former are eternal. For all Molière's interest in social relations it is types of humanity that really interest him and call forth his fullest powers. Of social types he only gives sketches.

It is easier to agree with M. Bergson when he says that "the comic character is unconscious; contrary to the wearer of Gyges's ring, he is in-

[1] Bergson, *op. cit.* pp. 167–9.

visible to himself, while he is visible to all the world[1]." Tartuffe at first sight may seem to be an exception, but Vinet is right in pointing out that "though he is not naive relatively to Orgon, he is naive relatively to us," and he might have added to the rest of Orgon's household. For it may be contended—and M. Bergson in conformity with his theory of automatism as a source of the comic does so contend—that Tartuffe's hypocritical gestures and utterances had become so much of a professional habit that he was no longer conscious of them. In another passage M. Bergson insists on what he calls *l'endurcissement professionnel* as a common source of comic effect[2], and he gives as an example Molière's doctors, " who treat their patients as if they had been created for the sake of the doctor and as if Nature herself were a dependence of medicine."

All this argument of M. Bergson's as to the unconsciousness of comic characters in general, and of Molière's characters in particular, may be summed up in the statement that many of Molière's characters are humorous. For it is the sign of a humorous character that he is unconsciously ridiculous. If Harpagon, says M. Bergson, had known that he was a laughing-stock to his neighbours, he would at least have tried to conceal his avarice. True, and just because Harpagon is unconsciously ridiculous, he is humorous. So with Tartuffe and Arnolphe and Argan; all four are instances of characters who are both

---

[1] *Ib.* p. 17.   [2] *Ib.* pp. 183 ff., and cp. pp. 48 and 55.

humorous and disagreeable. Alceste, on the other hand, is humorous and loveable, for his creator loves him while he laughs at him. So in the same play Oronte and Acaste are humorous because they are perfectly unconscious in their fatuity, and one may add to the list Chrysale, M. Jourdain, M. and Mme de Sotenville, M. de Pourceaugnac, and in a lower sphere of life Sganarelle the servant of Don Juan, and Sosie the servant of Amphitryon. It is noteworthy that most of these humorous parts, in fact all the important ones, were played by Molière himself. If one remembers that among his other parts were the three Sganarelles of *Le Cocu imaginaire*, *L'École des Maris*, and *Le Mariage forcé*, one recognises that, like all masters of the comic spirit who are also creators of character, he was a great humorist.

In all these humorous characters, and in those of Mascarille, Sganarelle the woodcutter, Hali the valet of *Le Sicilien*, and Sosie (all Molière's parts), the comic effect is greatly enhanced by the comicality of their speech. In real life a comical individual generally expresses himself in comical language. But dramatists often fail in reproducing this characteristic. Plautus excelled in this form of the *vis comica*, and so did Molière. Labiche has shewn the same power in modern times, but while, as a writer of vaudeville, he used it unsparingly, Molière, except in *Les Précieuses ridicules*, restrained himself within the limits of true comedy.

Another characteristic of Molière's creative power is the rapidity with which he creates. The speech in which Acaste complacently describes his personal advantages to his brother Marquis, ending up with

> Je crois qu'avec tout cela, mon cher marquis, je crois
> Qu'on peut, par tout pays, être content de soi,

makes him as alive to us as a portrait by Vandyck of one of the young courtiers of Charles I. Another good instance of lightning portraiture is Mme Pernelle in *Tartuffe* with her

> Allons, Flipote, allons, que d'eux je me délivre.

A single speech suffices to delineate Argatiphontidas, one of the four captains in *Amphitryon*, as a type of the choleric warrior who strikes first and listens to explanations afterwards. Even *Psyché* with its magnificent ballets and elaborate machinery, in which one would hardly expect to find portrayal of character, can furnish a couple of instances. In the Prologue, Venus in her very first words appears, as she has never appeared before, as a celebrated beauty who sees her empire passing from her,

> Toutes les choses ont leur tour,
> Et Vénus n'est plus à la mode.
> Il est d'autres attraits naissants
> Où l'on va porter ses encens:
> Psyché, Psyché la belle, aujourd'hui tient ma place;
> Déjà tout l'univers s'empresse à l'adorer,
> Et c'est trop que, dans ma disgrâce,
> Je trouve encor quelqu'un qui me daigne honorer.

Equally characteristic is the scene between Psyché's two sisters (I, I) in which their vanity and their jealousy of Psyché are depicted with the same power of penetrating at once to the recesses of the heart. Nor is it only in the portrayal of minor characters that Molière shews this power. As soon as his chief characters appear on the stage they at once display certain superficial traits which are indications of their real nature. Thus Arnolphe is rude and positive at the very outset of his conversation with Chrysalde, and Alceste in his first words with Philinte is brusque and unreasonable.

PHILINTE

Qu'est-ce donc? qu'avez-vous?

ALCESTE

Laissez-moi, je vous prie.

PHILINTE

Mais encor, dites-moi quelle bizarrerie.

ALCESTE

Laissez-moi là, vous dis-je, et courez vous cacher.

PHILINTE

Mais on entend les gens au moins sans se fâcher.

ALCESTE

Moi, je veux me fâcher, et ne veux point entendre.

Another good example is the entry of Agnès with her needlework in her hand and the four and a half lines in which she reveals her untutored simplicity. "Oui, Monsieur, Dieu merci"—"Hors les puces qui m'ont la nuit inquiétée"—"Vous me ferez plaisir"—"Je me fais des cornettes. Vos chemises de nuit et vos coiffes sont faites."

This power of rapid creation is all-important

in drama. It is one of the many weaknesses in Augier's comedies, once so much admired and now fallen out of favour, that he develops his characters too slowly. The gradual method is all very well in a novel, but in a drama it is essential that an actor should give at the outset some hint of his character, and that its development should keep pace with the action of the play. Even Macbeth and Néron, to take two great examples of development, one from the English romantic school and the other from the French classical school, are no exceptions to this principle.

Molière's comedy then is essentially a comedy of character. But it is also social comedy, and he paints his characters against a social background. In the majority of his social comedies the unit of society is the family, the chief exceptions being *L'École des Femmes* and *Le Misanthrope*, in both of which the principal character is a bachelor. As a rule the head of the family is a well-to-do *bourgeois* (Orgon, Géronte, M. Jourdain, Chrysale, Argan). He is for the most part selfish and tyrannical; he has little education and a limited outlook; he is shrewd and thoroughly alive to his own interests, but the ridiculous mania by which he is obsessed makes him a ready dupe in the hands of a clever intriguer. Molière in short has taken the conventional self-seeking and tyrannical father of classical and Renaissance comedy, and given him the variety and complexity of real life. Chrysale, for instance, in his tenderness to his daughter

and his abject submission to his wife, is far removed from the ordinary type. In my account
of Molière's life I mentioned that his father is
said to have been the model for his money-loving
Harpagons, and Argans, and Sganarelles. But in
reality the groundwork of their character is the
typical father of classical and Renaissance comedy.
I also pointed out that there is just as little truth
in the statement that Molière's stepmothers are
more conspicuous than his mothers, and that by
the side of Elmire and Béline you must put
Mme Jourdain and Philaminte. But these four
names practically complete the list of Molière's
mothers, so far as his social comedies are concerned, and it will be seen that they have nothing
in common. Mme Jourdain is sensible but acidu-
lous, Philaminte is masterful but devoid of common sense, Elmire is charming in her placid
rectitude, Béline is a Tartuffe in petticoats.
It is in his Court plays, *Les Amants magnifiques*, *La Princesse d'Élide*, and *Psyché* that, as
M. Lafenestre points out, we find really affection-
ate and indulgent parents—in the first-named a
mother, in the other two a father.

Though Molière generally takes a love-story
for his plot, for the obvious reason that it provides a simple and natural *dénouement*, love
cannot be said to play a prominent part in his
comedies. His young men and maidens are not
great lovers—had they been so his picture of
society would not have been a true one—nor
are they strongly individualised. But they have

sufficient charm to enlist our sympathies, and they diffuse an atmosphere of innocence and purity over Molière's comedy which keeps it sweet and healthy. The men are honest and honourable, and if their love stops short of passion, it is at any rate courageous and sincere. But the majority are mere types, and it would require a very subtle reader of character to retain a distinct image of Valère in *Tartuffe*, Cléonte in *Le Bourgeois gentilhomme*, and Cléante in *Le Malade imaginaire*. The only two who really stand out are Horace the *beau blondin* of *L'École des Femmes* with his misplaced confidences, and the well-bred, sensible, outspoken, and generous Clitandre of *Les Femmes savantes*.

There is more variety in Molière's young girls. They vary, for instance, in the degree of resistance that they offer to their father's choice of a husband. The most submissive is Mariane in *Tartuffe*. The most determined in her resistance is Élise in *L'Avare*, but then like her brother Valère, who should have been mentioned above as a lover of some individuality, she has been brought up in a hard school, with no mother and an unnatural father. Angélique in *Le Malade imaginaire* has to contend against a hostile stepmother, but though her father is thoroughly selfish in his ridiculous valetudinarianism, he is not wholly unnatural, and therefore, while she is firm in rejecting the husband that he thrusts upon her, she retains her affection for him. But the two young girls who are the most firmly

drawn and the most admired in Molière's gallery
are Agnès and Henriette. It is a sign of their
excellence as portraits and of their truth to
nature that both have been variously judged.
To some Agnès is a model of simplicity and
purity; others see in her the makings of a *rusée*
coquette. Henriette with her good sense and
clear-sightedness is in the eyes of some a charming example of Gallican femininity, whereas
others find her commonplace and wanting in
delicacy. Among these latter is J.-J. Weiss, one
of whose critical oddities it was to have an
unfavourable opinion of Molière's women in
general, excepting only from his condemnation
Elvire, Don Juan's neglected wife, and the
submissive Mariane of *Tartuffe*. He compares
Angélique with Rosine of *Le Barbier de Séville*,
greatly to the advantage of the latter[1], but the
comparison is unfortunate, for it may be remembered that Rosine became a "Mère coupable."

In the three most important of Molière's family
plays, *Tartuffe*, *Les Femmes savantes*, and *Le
Malade imaginaire*, the family group is completed
by a brother or brother-in-law of the head of the
family. He has little to do with the action of
the play, and his main function is to give advice.
Hence he is often described as "le sage de la
pièce" or in modern terminology "le raisonneur."
Ariste, as we saw, plays only a subordinate part
in *Les Femmes savantes*, but Cléante in *Tartuffe* and Béralde in *Le Malade imaginaire* are

[1] *Molière*, pp. 64–81.

characters of considerable importance. The business of all three alike is to help to bring about a happy *dénouement*, that is to say, the marriage of their niece with the man of her choice, and, as a means to this end, to reason with the brother or brother-in-law whose weakness or folly is making for a contrary solution. It is characteristic of Molière's sense of reality that in no case have their arguments the slightest effect. Chrysale does not become any more courageous in the presence of Philaminte, Orgon and Argan are only confirmed in their obstinate credulity[1]. But Cléante and Béralde have this dramatic value, that they serve as foils, that they help to bring out in sharper relief the particular folly which Molière is ridiculing. The same dramatic purpose is fulfilled by Chrysalde in *L'École des Femmes* and Philinte in *Le Misanthrope*, both of whom have the effect of supremely irritating the hero of the play, and thus of moving him to state his opinions with exaggerated emphasis. But neither Chrysalde nor Philinte can be called "le sage de la pièce." Their standpoint is that

[1] Cp. Nicole, *Essais de Morale* III, 23, "Il se trouve quelquefois des gens assez charitables, pour essayer de nous tirer de l'illusion où nous vivons à l'égard de nous-mêmes. L'amour-propre fait donc son possible pour éloigner cet inconvénient, et il ne manque pas encore de voies pour y réussir. Car il témoigne tant de chagrin et de mauvaise humeur à ceux qui nous voudroient rendre ce bon office ; il trouve tant de prétextes pour ne pas croire ce qu'on nous découvre de nos défauts ; il est si ingénieux à en trouver de plus grands dans ceux qui remarquent les nôtres, et à faire passer pour malignité les jugemens qu'ils font à notre désavantage, qu'il n'y a presque personne qui se veuille hasarder à nous les dire" (*Traité de la connaissance de soi-même*).

of tolerant and slightly cynical men of the world, who, taking a pessimistic view of human nature themselves, counsel their friends to make the best of a society which they are unable to reform. It is true that this view of Chrysalde's character depends largely upon whether the advice that he gives Arnolphe in Act IV, Scene 8 is meant to be serious or whether, as Faguet—arguing partly from Arnolphe's "Mais cette *raillerie*, en un mot, m'importune," and partly from the exaggeration of some of his remarks—maintains, it is mere banter[1]. If Faguet is right, we must add Chrysalde to the list of *raisonneurs*. On the other hand Ariste, in *L'École des Maris*, cannot fairly be brought under this category, for he not only acts as well as preaches, but he is one of the principal characters of the play. We may even admit that Cléante and Béralde are *raisonneurs* in the sense that they are the mouthpieces of Molière's own sentiments. But when Faguet goes on to suggest that a similar *raisonneur* would not be out of place in *Don Juan*, *L'Avare*, *Le Bourgeois gentilhomme* and even in *Le Misanthrope*[2], lovers of Molière must firmly protest. Molière is before all things a dramatist, and Cléante and Béralde are the two least satisfactory characters in the whole of his drama.

Passing from the masters to the servants, we note that, after Ergaste in *L'École des Maris*, Molière made little use of the conventional valet of comedy with his miraculous resourcefulness

---

[1] *Rousseau contre Molière*, p. 240 n. 1.   [2] *Ib.* p. 145.

and gift for intrigue. The only examples in his later plays are La Flèche (*L'Avare*), Covielle (*Le Bourgeois gentilhomme*), and that amusing rascal, Scapin. In place of this type of valet we have either a less gifted, but more humorous and natural type of man-servant—Sganarelle, Sosie, and Maître Jacques—or we have those delightful servants of the other sex whom Molière has stamped with his immortal genius almost more convincingly than any other class of his characters. From Dorine the confidential *suivante* of *Tartuffe*, with her many years of faithful service, to Martine the ungrammatical kitchenmaid of *Les Femmes savantes* all alike are honest, good-tempered and out-spoken, racy of the soil, embodiments of shrewdness and common sense. Their special idiosyncrasies have been pointed out in the preceding chapters and they are too well known to need further praise in this.

In the same degree that Molière loved simplicity and natural wit, he hated pedantry and affectation. Thus the pedantry of philosophy is held up to ridicule in the portraits of Pancrace and Marphurius, the Aristotelian and the Pyrrhonist of *L'Amour médecin*, and in M. Jourdain's teacher of philosophy, while Vadius represents the pedantry of learning, and the doctors the pedantry of medicine. Lysidas (*Critique de l'École des Femmes*) is the pedantic author, Trissotin the affected author, while the various *Marquis* stand for the affectation of the man of fashion.

Le marquis aujourd'hui est le plaisant de la comédie. Et, comme dans les comédies anciennes on voit toujours un valet bouffon qui fait rire les auditeurs, de même dans toutes nos pièces de maintenant il faut toujours un marquis ridicule qui divertisse la compagnie[1].

In spite of this statement the only comedies of Molière in which the *Marquis* is held up to ridicule are *Les Fâcheux*—and that only in Éraste's narrative, and not as a character in the play—the *Critique de l'École des Femmes* and *L'Impromptu de Versailles*, in both of which Molière was paying them out for their attacks, and *Le Misanthrope*. On the other hand Éraste, the hero of *Les Fâcheux*, Dorante in *La Critique* and Clitandre in *Les Femmes savantes* are examples of well-bred frequenters of the Court who are both sensible and natural.

Molière's peasants deserve a special notice, for it is a class which finds very scanty representation in the literature of the reign of Louis XIV. In fact during the great years of the reign La Fontaine's sympathetic portrait of the poor woodcutter weighed down by family cares, soldiers, taxes, creditors, and forced labour, is almost the only reference to them outside Molière. It is not till we come to La Bruyère with his famous "L'on voit certains animaux farouches, des mâles et des femelles, répandus par la campagne, noirs, livides et tout brûlés du soleil &c.," to Fénelon's letter to the king, and to the writings of Boisguilbert and Vauban, that the miseries of the unhappy peasant of the *Grand Siècle* begin to be vocal in literature. Meanwhile Molière represents, not unsympa-

---

[1] *L'Impromptu de Versailles*, Scene I.

thetically, his more amusing side. Alain and Georgette, the two servants to whom Arnolphe has entrusted the care of Agnès, are chiefly characterised by their stupidity and their love of money. But in *Don Juan* we have admirable portraits of Pierrot and Charlotte, the realism of which is increased by their speaking in the patois of the neighbourhood of Paris, a patois which had already been used by Cyrano de Bergerac in *Le Pedant joué.* It is used again by Molière for the peasants of *Le Médecin malgré lui*, Lucas, Thibaut, and Perrin. The account which Thibaut gives to Sganarelle of his wife's malady and Sganarelle's pretended inability to understand him until Perrin hands him his fee is a piece of first-rate comedy.

Molière knew the provinces as well as he knew Paris, and though he has used his knowledge sparingly, he has used it with excellent effect. M. and Mme de Sotenville are immortal examples of the lesser French nobility who lived in poverty on their own estates and seldom came to Paris. M. de Pourceaugnac is an equally delightful specimen of the official class as represented at Limoges, and through him we are introduced to all his relations, to his brother the consul, his nephew the canon, and his cousin the assessor. In *La Comtesse d'Escarbagnas* Molière takes us to Angoulême, and in the salon of the countess, who is a provincial *précieuse*, we find M. Tibaudier, a councillor, and M. Harpin, a tax-collector, from whom Lesage borrowed some touches for his *Turcaret*.

Such are the secondary characters, some clearly individualised, others mere types, whom Molière has grouped round his chief figures. But he has not like his great successor in the portraiture of the *comédie humaine* attempted to give a complete picture of the society of his day. He could not have boasted, like Balzac, that he had "fait concurrence à l'état civil." In *Les Fâcheux*, indeed, he had shewn remarkable skill in sketching a variety of social types, but after that experiment he became more and more absorbed in the intensive study of character. Nor can his comedies, though they naturally throw much light on contemporary manners and morals, be described, with the solitary and brilliant exception of *Les Précieuses ridicules*, as comedies of manners. Molière left it to Dancourt, under the influence of La Bruyère, to inaugurate in a gay but superficial fashion this particular class of comedy. He left it to Lesage to work up the sketches that he had carelessly introduced in *Le Bourgeois gentilhomme* and *La Comtesse d'Escarbagnas*, and to produce in that terrible winter which followed the disastrous campaign of 1708 the first great French comedy of manners. For it is as a study of social types, or in other words as a comedy of manners, that *Turcaret* has achieved and deserves its reputation.

CHAPTER XII

CONSTRUCTION, STYLE, AND MORAL TEACHING

MOLIÈRE'S interest in plot was in inverse ratio to his interest in character. In some of his plays he takes an old plot or story and shapes his characters to fit it. Thus *L'Étourdi*, the *Dépit amoureux* and *Sganarelle* are founded on Italian comedies, *Amphitryon* and *L'Avare* owe their origin to Plautus, *L'École des Maris* and *Les Fourberies de Scapin* to Terence, *Le Médecin malgré lui* and *George Dandin* are developments from farces, probably French in their ultimate origin, *Don Juan* goes back to the popular play of Tirso de Molina, and the idea of *L'École des Femmes* is probably taken from Scarron's novel of *La Précaution inutile*. But this does not account either for *Tartuffe* or *Le Misanthrope* or *Le Bourgeois gentilhomme* or *Les Femmes savantes* or *Le Malade imaginaire*, or for the one-act comedies, *Les Précieuses ridicules*, *Le Mariage forcé* and *L'Amour médecin*. In all of these Molière starts either from a character, or more often, it may be supposed, considering that he is a social moralist, from some social or moral problem. But in either case the conception of the living character precedes the search for a plot. This plot is always of the simplest. In *Tartuffe*, *Le Bourgeois gentilhomme*, *Le Malade imaginaire*, and *M. de Pourceaugnac* it is the time-honoured theme of the selfish and tyrannical father who tries to force his daughter into a marriage of his own choosing, and who is ultimately outwitted by the other members of his household. This also forms part of the plot of *L'Avare*. In *Les Femmes savantes* it is the mother who plays the tyrant, while in *L'Amour médecin* the father's tyranny takes a different form, for he does not want his daughter to marry at all. In *Le Sicilien* we have the equally old theme, which is only another variation of the former one, of the guardian who wants to marry his ward. In *Les Précieuses ridicules* there is practically no plot; the play is little more than a *tableau*. *Les Fâcheux* is a simple *pièce à tiroirs*, a succession of scenes loosely strung together. Simple though the plot of *Le Misanthrope* is, the love of a man who hates all shams and insincerities for a woman of the world who is a coquette, it is admirably suited to its purpose, and the construction of the play is firmer and more logical than is usually supposed.

Even in those comedies in which Molière has made use of a borrowed plot it is the characters and not the plot that interest him. This is notably so in *Don Juan*. He had chosen the play on account of its popularity, which was due partly to its romantic character and partly to its use of machinery and spectacular effect. But while he keeps, as he was bound to do, to the main outlines of the story, and does not discard the machinery, his whole interest is in the character of Don Juan, with Sganarelle as his Sancho Panza. It is the same with *L'Avare*. He found a gay comedy, with a simple but suitable plot, and he turned it into a comedy which sometimes borders on tragedy, and which has for its main interest the profound study of a soul-destroying vice.

In both *L'École des Maris* and *L'École des Femmes* the interest is not so much in the plot as in the characters and the social problem. *L'Étourdi* is a succession of episodes which serve to shew off the fertile resourcefulness of Mascarille. In the *Dépit amoureux* Molière has blended with the Italian original a simple study of human passions founded on first-hand observations. *Le Médecin malgré lui* and *George Dandin* betray their medieval origin, for the plot, such as it is, is as old as the hills, and the play is little more than a succession of scenes, in which observation and comic humour go hand in hand. Lastly, *Les Fourberies de Scapin*, based on Terence's *Phormio*, is a more or less conventional comedy of intrigue, but again Molière is far more interested in the character of Scapin than in the working out of the plot.

Critics from Boileau[1] downwards have found fault with Molière's *dénouements*, but he would have listened to their criticisms unmoved. He would have laughed at a modern author who

---

[1] *Correspondance entre Boileau et Brossette*, ed. A. Laverdet, 1858, p. 516.

writes his Fifth Act first, and he would have scoffed at the superstition of the *pièce bien faite*. Among the weakest of his *dénouements* in the eyes of modern readers is that of *L'École des Femmes*. He does not refer to it in *La Critique* —possibly because it was not criticised by his contemporaries—but had he cared to defend it, he might have pointed out that it is far more difficult to end a comedy than a tragedy. For Tragedy which finds its materials in history has a *dénouement* already to hand by which it is more or less bound. Moreover death, which is the favourite ending for a tragedy, is at once dramatic and natural. For Comedy, no doubt, the appropriate *dénouement* is marriage, which, if it is often only the beginning of life, is the end of an episode. But this supposes that the two lovers are the principal characters in the play, and though love may furnish Molière with a plot it is with him of secondary interest.

Caring then little about his plot, Molière was equally indifferent to its *dénouement*, but he had to end his comedy somehow. The difficulty was to devise an ending which should serve as an appropriate punishment for the principal object of his satire, in other words, for his comic hero. In *L'École des Femmes* he had recourse to the stale device of the lost child and the parent who has suddenly returned from beyond the seas, and he repeated it in *L'Avare* with the addition of a romantic story of shipwreck and corsairs. The only defence that can be offered is that in the seventeenth century such moving incidents were not so rare as they are now. Only ten years after the production of *L'Avare* no less a person than Jean-François Regnard, the future comic poet, was captured by pirates in the Mediterranean, and sold as a slave at Algiers. Moreover, while Molière in the earlier play had conformed to the rules of the stage by preparing us for the *dénouement* in the First Act, in *L'Avare*, in defiance of all tradition, he springs it upon us without any preparation.

But there was a deeper reason than mere indifference which led Molière to avoid striking *dénouements.* The mechanical ending which is furnished by some unexpected incident may be indifferent art, but it is not contrary to nature. Children may find their parents after many years' absence ; they may even find them at an extremely convenient moment. But what does not happen in nature is the sudden conversion of a man in whom some vice or folly has assumed the proportions of monomania. Against endings of this sort, the refuge of the ordinary playwright, which at once lower comedy to the level of farce, Molière resolutely set his face. " Lorsque vous peignez des hommes, il faut peindre d'après nature." Had he accepted these easy *dénouements* he would have painted not men, but '*portraits à plaisir.*'

Thus the general principle which guides him in the choice of a *dénouement* is that his comic hero should receive appropriate punishment, but

that he should not be converted. Tartuffe and
Don Juan, who are real criminals, are punished
as such. Tartuffe is carried off to prison, but
though he is confounded he does not repent.
Don Juan meets his terrible fate—here Molière
had no choice—with an impenitence equal to
his courage. Arnolphe, who is no criminal, but
merely obstinate and arrogant, is punished by
the loss of his bride, to whom, in his queer selfish
tyrannical fashion, he is really attached. But he
is forced to yield to circumstances ; he has learnt
no moral lesson. The end of *Le Misanthrope*
is better than any *coup de théâtre*, for it is perfectly natural. It has been said that it is not an
end, but it is the end of a phase in Alceste's
life ; he and Célimène are parted. Whether he
will banish himself to his estates, whether he
will relax something of his stiff idealism, whether
Célimène will become less heartless in her
coquetry, is left to the imagination of Molière's
readers. The beauty of the ending is that it
leaves us to dream our dreams and to weave
our own sequel. But so far as Molière has left it,
Alceste is still the generous, impractical idealist,
Célimène is still the fascinating embodiment of
cool common sense.

Harpagon and M. Jourdain, Philaminte and
Argan suffer, like Arnolphe, the traditional
punishment of comedy. Harpagon loses his bride,
the others lose the son-in-law of their choice.
But they come off more lightly than Arnolphe,
who has to witness the downfall of a vaunted

system, the shipwreck of long-cherished hopes. Harpagon will console himself with the recovery of his *cassette* ; M. Jourdain will still ape the aristocracy, and fall a prey to a more unscrupulous Dorimène ; Philaminte will still neglect her household duties for the fringes of learning and science ; Argan will still go in terror of death and put credulous faith in the behests of a new physician.

It is a mistake to suppose that because Molière took but a languid interest in his plot he did not understand the art of constructing a play. We must not judge him by comedies like *Don Juan* or *Le Bourgeois gentilhomme*, which were put together in a hurry, or by *L'Avare*, which bears so many marks of haste that we safely include it in the same category. We must judge him by the great verse comedies —*L'École des Femmes*, *Tartuffe*, *Le Misanthrope*—which he conceived and built up at leisure. In all of these the construction is admirable. We have seen that *L'École des Femmes* was criticised as lacking action, and that Molière rightly defended it on the ground that the narratives of Arnolphe and Horace are true actions, because they reciprocally affect the speakers, and so lead to the development of the plot. We have seen too that this development is worked out with gradually rising interest, as the advantage of the contest between the two protagonists shifts from one side to the other, but in so well-ordered and logical a fashion, that at the end of each round the younger rival is always one stage nearer to victory. The merit of *Tartuffe* as a well-constructed play has always been recognised and needs no further commendation. *Le Misanthrope*, on the other hand, has sometimes been described as a mere succession of *tableaux*, but I have tried to shew that this is a mistake, that there is really more action in it than is commonly allowed, and that those scenes which are often regarded as episodical, or at least as devised purely for the sake of illustrating character, are nearly all connected with the development of the simple plot. The construction of *Les Femmes savantes* is weaker than that of the other three masterpieces. The amusing scene (II, 6) which centres round Martine, admirably though it serves to shew up the folly of the learned ladies, has no connexion with the plot, which is the attempt of Clitandre to win the hand of Henriette. Moreover, although Martine has definite notice to quit, in which Chrysale acquiesces, she reappears in the Fifth Act as if nothing had happened.

Molière's devotion to nature and to truth of representation is nowhere better shewn than in his avoidance of unnatural situations and unnatural incidents. One of the commonest faults of modern dramatists is that they bring their characters together in convenient but impossible meeting-places. This at once gives an air of unreality, an air of farce or *vaudeville*, to what is meant to be a comedy of real life. Molière is

saved from this largely by his own feeling for
truth of representation, but partly also by the
necessity of conforming to the unity of place.
This, indeed, at first brought with it its own improbabilities. In *L'Étourdi, Sganarelle, L'École
des Maris, Les Fâcheux, L'École des Femmes*
and *Le Mariage forcé* the scene, in accordance
with classical and Renaissance convention, is
in the street, and, as in *Le Menteur*, all the conversations, in which sometimes several persons
take part, are carried on in a public thorough-
fare. But in *Les Précieuses ridicules*, which has
only three scenes of any length, and which, regarded as a whole, has very little action, Molière
transferred the scene from the street to the
house, and then developing this idea in *Tartuffe*
he made nearly all his characters members of the
same household. This was a master-stroke, which
gave solidity and reality to the whole action of the
play. Twice he varied his procedure by bringing
his characters together, not as members of the
same family, but as frequenters of the same salon.
This is what happens in *La Comtesse d'Escarbagnas* as well as in *Le Misanthrope*.

As for the unity of time he treats it in the
same way as Racine. Except in *L'École des
Femmes*, in which, as we learn from Act v,
Scene 6, the *dénouement* takes place the day
after the opening of the play—but presumably
within the twenty-four hours—and in *Don Juan*
and *Le Malade imaginaire*, Molière makes no
reference to time, and the acts as well as the

scenes follow one another without any apparent interruption. No doubt this rule, like the unity of place, leads to improbabilities, and it may be said of *Le Misanthrope* as of *Le Cid* that the day spent in Célimène's salon was a *journée bien remplie*. But the answer to a criticism of this sort, and the answer stands good for Racine as well as for Molière, is that, when the dramatic interest depends less on external action than on the action of the mind, less on the working out of an intrigue than on the development of a character, we do not think of the time.

It is only on rare occasions that Molière relaxes the strict observance of the rules. In *Le Médecin malgré lui* the scene is changed from the country-side (Act I) to a room in Géronte's house (Acts II and III). In *Le Malade imaginaire* a night elapses between the First and the Second Acts, but the whole action takes place within little more than twelve hours, for it is evening when the play opens—too late to send a message to Cléante—and it is morning at the beginning of the Second Act. "Monsieur Purgon," says Argan, "m'a dit de me promener le matin dans la chambre douze allées et douze venues." In the same play the *liaison des scènes*, that is to say, the rule that at least one character must remain on the stage at the end of each scene so as to connect it with the next, is broken between Scenes 7 and 8 of Act I. But even here the breach is in the letter rather than in the spirit, for Argan, Béline, and the notary merely withdraw to Argan's 'petit cabinet,' and can be seen from the adjoining room. " Les voilà avec un notaire," says Toinette. Similarly in *L'Avare* there is, strictly speaking, no *liaison* between the scene in which La Flèche appears with the money-box under his arm (IV, 6), and the sudden return of Harpagon from the garden after his discovery of its loss. But here the breach of continuity was inevitable. The one real exception to the observance of the rules is, as we have seen, *Don Juan*, in which the unity of place is wholly abandoned, and the unity of time is relaxed by extending the action to a couple of days. It is a romantic play treated on romantic lines.

Besides Boileau's criticism of Molière's *dénouements*, Brossette has also recorded criticisms by him on his language and versification[1]. But these were only directed against particular passages. The criticism of La Bruyère is more sweeping. "Il n'a manqué à Molière que d'éviter le jargon et le barbarisme[2], et d'écrire purement." He was followed by Bayle who says, "Il (Molière) avait une facilité incroyable à faire des vers, mais il se donnait trop de liberté d'inventer de nouveaux termes et de nouvelles expressions : il lui échappait même fort souvent des barbarismes." Sixteen years later (1713) Fénelon wrote as follows :

En pensant bien, il parle souvent mal; il se sert des phrases les plus forcées et les moins naturelles. Térence dit

[1] *Op. cit.* p. 515.
[2] The words *et le barbarisme* were added in the sixth edition of *Les Caractères* (1696).

en quatre mots, avec la plus élégante simplicité, ce que celui-ci dit qu'avec une multitude de métaphores qui approchent du galimatias. J'aime bien mieux sa prose que ses vers. Par exemple, *L'Avare* est moins mal écrit que les pièces qui sont en vers[1].

Vauvenargues quotes these remarks of Fénelon's in support of his own opinion, which is that "on trouve dans Molière tant de négligences et d'expressions bizarres et impropres, qu'il y a peu de poètes, si j'ose le dire, moins corrects et moins purs que lui." In comparatively recent times these criticisms were repeated and developed by Édouard Scherer in an article in *Le Temps* entitled *Une hérésie littéraire*, which aroused the indignation of all faithful Moliéristes.

It would be impertinent in a foreigner to attempt to defend Molière against these criticisms. Happily there is no need to make the attempt, for the task has been performed in a masterly and definitive fashion by Brunetière[2]. He begins by admitting, almost unreservedly, that the charges of negligence and incorrectness (*barbarisme*), of the use of jargon, and the abuse of metaphor are from the reader's point of view perfectly justified. He further admits that frequent *chevilles* or padding are to be found in Molière's verse. Moreover, rejecting the explanation that Molière's faults of language are mainly due to the haste in which some of his

---

[1] *Lettre sur les occupations de l'Académie Française.*
[2] *Études critiques* VII, 85–132.

plays had to be written, he gives instances of incorrect constructions, *chevilles*, mixed metaphors and *galimatias* from *L'École des Femmes*, *Tartuffe*, *Le Misanthrope*, *Amphitryon* and *Les Femmes savantes*, the plays upon which Molière lavished the greatest care. He points out, indeed, that sometimes when Molière is supposed to be incorrect he is merely conforming to the usage of his own day, but admits that, after making all allowance for this, there remain plenty of instances of incorrect language.

The real defence is that Molière is incorrect because spoken language is often incorrect, and Molière before all things aims at being natural. The same defence is offered by Dumas *fils*. "Ce langage du théâtre a-t-il besoin d'être correct? Non, dans le sens grammatical. Il faut, avant tout, qu'il soit clair, coloré, pénétrant, incisif," and he quotes the admirable line of Racine,

Je t'aimais inconstant; qu'aurais-je fait fidèle?[1]

Brunetière rightly rejects the view of M. Servois and others that by *jargon* La Bruyère means the use of patois by Molière's peasants : La Bruyère, he says, means the *jargon précieux*, the conventional language of gallantry in Molière's day. He might have added that we find this language not only in *Tartuffe* and *Le Misanthrope* and *L'Avare*, but in Racine's *Andromaque*. And the explanation surely is that Molière puts this

---

[1] Preface to *Le Père prodigue*.

conventional language in the mouth of lovers, because it was the fashion.

> Et sans pointe un amant n'osa plus soupirer

was as true when Molière wrote *L'Avare* as it was of the earlier period of which Boileau is speaking.

As for Fénelon's objection to the 'multitude of metaphors,' or, as we should say, to mixed metaphors, Brunetière shrewdly points out that it is just this mixture of metaphors that is natural, whereas it is the laborious chase of a single metaphor that is affected and precious. And he quotes eight lines from *Les Femmes savantes* in which Trissotin delivers himself of a carefully worked-up but utterly ridiculous metaphor. Of course it is easy to go to the opposite extreme, and a 'multitude of metaphors' may be as ridiculous as a single one, but we have only to turn to Montaigne to realise that a change of metaphor is natural to an imaginative mind. To the charge of employing *chevilles* Brunetière again pleads guilty on Molière's behalf. But he maintains that these are necessary in a spoken dialogue in order to give relief to the listener and to allow him time to follow the speaker's thought. It may be added that so scrupulous a master of technique as Théodore de Banville declares that *chevilles* are necessary in all verse, and that there are as many *chevilles* in a good poem as in a bad one[1].

---

[1] *Petit traité de poésie française*, p. 21.

Sarcey is no less decided than Brunetière in his approbation of Molière's style. " ' Molière writes badly,' says M. Scherer. In any case he does not write badly for the stage." And he goes on to say with perfect truth that if you have movement, relief, colour, sincerity, then, in spite of faulty constructions, improper words, incoherent metaphors, archaic turns of phrase, you are a writer for the stage, even a great writer. He quotes the actor Provost, who was professor of diction at the Conservatoire, as saying to him that "Molière is the only dramatic author, the only one, mark you, whose words are always easy to speak, because both his prose and his verse lend themselves so readily to the tone of conversation." Then Provost quoted eight lines of *Tartuffe*, which seem to the reader on a first perusal singularly ill-written and disjointed:

> Ce fut par un motif de cas de conscience.
> J'allais droit à mon traître en faire confidence;
> Et son raisonnement me vint persuader
> De lui donner plutôt la cassette à garder,
> Afin que, pour nier, en cas de quelque enquête,
> J'eusse d'un faux-fuyant la faveur toute prête,
> Par où ma conscience eût pleine sûreté,
> À faire des serments contre la vérité[1].

But the old actor pointed out that the phrase beginning with *afin que* is an answer to a gesture of the speaker's (Orgon) interlocutor; that the line

> J'eusse d'un faux-fuyant la faveur toute prête

is a superb one; and that the prolongation of

[1] Act V, Scene I.

the period in the next two lines, which seems indefensible from the reader's point of view, is admirable on the stage. For firstly, the repetition of the same thought in different words is perfectly natural in conversation, and secondly, such repetition helps to impress the idea upon the mind of the audience[1].

There is no doubt that all actors, dramatic authors, and dramatic critics agree with Provost, Dumas *fils*, and Sarcey in praising unreservedly the dramatic qualities of Molière's style. His critics of the seventeenth and eighteenth centuries were men who had little or no knowledge of the stage. La Bruyère's lack of dramatic experience is amply shewn by his portrait of Onuphre as a corrective to Tartuffe. Admirable for its just observation, it is absolutely undramatic. Fénelon, whose appreciation of Molière generally—" Encore une fois, je le trouve grand "—is in marked contrast to the attitude of his brother ecclesiastics Bossuet and Bourdaloue, had of course never been inside a theatre. Vauvenargues's ill-health similarly incapacitated him. At any rate, he judges dramatic literature solely from the point of view of a reader.

But even to a reader who does not study Molière with the meticulous censoriousness of a grammarian or a verbal critic his style is not among the least of his charms. For its supreme merit is that it is a living style, a style by virtue of which the puppets of the stage become living men and women. It is a style that one

[1] Sarcey, *op. cit.* pp. 24-28.

naturally compares to that of Fielding and
Scott and Thackeray and Cervantes. They
too, especially Scott, are sometimes careless and
involved, but they write with the easy confidence of men whose knowledge of language is
derived, not from the dictionary or the grammar,
but from life itself. And when they give their
minds to it, or when they are unconsciously up-
lifted by their subject-matter, they display a
royal mastery of phrase and diction that cannot
be surpassed.

The impression of life that we get from Molière's style is greatly helped by the fact that it
varies with the speaker. All Molière's more
important characters have their distinctive modes
of speech, even their little tricks of phrase and
expression. It is not easy to point to any specially
characteristic phrases, for the individuality of
speech which is so marked in Molière's characters depends rather upon the subtle turns
that make themselves felt almost unconsciously.
But Alceste's favourite *Morbleu*[1] at once occurs
to one, and he is fond of beginning with an
abrupt *Oui* or *Non*, and of using trenchant
expressions like *Je veux, Je vous déclare net, Je
vous parle net*. It is a weak point with many
dramatists, and one of the chief causes of their
comparative failure, that they do not differentiate
their characters by their speech[2]. The reason is

[1] See especially the opening scenes with Philinte, and cp. *ante*,
p. 161.
[2] Moratín in the *Discurso preliminar* prefixed to his *Comedies*
has some pertinent remarks on this head. "This defect [i.e. that

that they think more of their literary style than
of their characters. Molière, on the other hand,
is above all things interested in his characters.
It is to give them life that he shapes his language
in the first place, and it is only in the second
place that he takes thought for his style. His
style, in short, is dramatic before being literary.

In this fitting of speech to character Molière
surpasses Corneille, who in other respects
had furnished him with an excellent model in
Le Menteur. That gay and attractive comedy
charms by the sparkle and vivacity of its dialogue, the ease and brilliance of its language.
But there is little portrayal of character, and
that partly because the language does not
vary sufficiently with the speaker. Moreover,
though the comic effect is often of a high order,
it is produced rather by the ideas than by the
language. Corneille is not, like Molière, a great
master of comic speech. He could not have
created Sosie or even the Sganarelle of *Le
Médecin malgré lui.* Cliton is less brilliant than
Mascarille. Yet one play of Corneille's may have
given Molière hints for style, namely *Nicomède.*
We know that during the visit of Molière's
company to Rouen they played it several times,
and that it was the piece selected for their first

of making all the characters speak alike] abounds in our old
comedies and is very common in the modern ones of other
nations. It cannot be disguised either by delicate sallies of wit,
or by wealth of epigram, or by purity of language, or by excellence of style, or by sonorous or flowing verse. Without due expression of passion or character, all is lost."

performance when they came to Paris. Its style is a model of easy, nervous and dignified language, and the tone of its quieter and more conversational passages is very similar to that of the more serious passages in Molière's comedies, especially in *Tartuffe*.

In conformity with the practice of his day it was Molière's usual habit to write a five-act play in verse and a three-act or one-act play in prose. But when he was pressed for time, as in the case of *Don Juan* and *L'Avare*, he used prose even for a play of five acts. *Le Bourgeois gentilhomme* is another instance, but an imperfect one, for, as we saw, in the libretto which was distributed to the audience at the Court performances the play is divided into three acts. Another exception is *Amphitryon*, which, though only a three-act play, is written in verse.

It is commonly assumed that prose has at least this advantage over verse as a medium for comedy, that it is nearer to nature, and that therefore the dramatist who uses it is more likely to make his play a faithful reflection of real life. But if one asks oneself whether Molière's plays in prose are closer to life than his plays in verse, whether *L'Avare* and *Le Malade imaginaire* give a greater impression of fidelity to nature than *Tartuffe* and *Le Misanthrope*, one is forced to answer in the negative. It is sometimes forgotten that, though prose is the natural speech of man, the prose of the stage is not an exact copy of the prose of ordinary conversation. For instance, M. Jourdain's language is so perfectly simple and natural that it seems to be the language of real life. But one may be quite sure that in real life M. Jourdain's language would neither have been so correct, nor so precise, nor so much to the point. Neither would the whole conversation in which he takes part have been conducted on such orderly lines. The stage, like every form of art, is subject to certain conventions, from which it cannot escape. Its business is not to copy real life, but to give the illusion of it. And this illusion in the hands of a great artist can be given just as well through the medium of verse as through the medium of prose. For the expression of ordinary sentiments and ideas prose is no doubt better, especially in the hands of an average dramatist. But for more complex or deeper ideas and feelings verse lends itself to greater clearness and precision. The very difficulty of verse compels the dramatist to be clear and precise, and sometimes, if the expression is really poetic, suggests to the imagination a deeper truth. For there is a danger of confounding realism with truth, or scientific truth with imaginative truth.

Even for the purpose of ordinary everyday conversation the use of prose is very far from insuring an impression of reality[1]. There comes

[1] "No es fácil embellecer sin exageración el diálogo familiar, cuando se han de expresar en él ideas y pasiones comunes." Moratín, *Discurso preliminar*.

into one's mind memories of many comedies, written in excellent prose and possessing other admirable qualities, which fail in this respect. It is a great testimony to Molière's mastery over the medium of verse that his masterpieces produce this illusion of reality. By the side of this rare gift, such imperfections as *chevilles* and intricacy of phrase sink into insignificance. " J'aime bien mieux sa prose que ses vers." Fénelon was wrong. From the dramatic point of view Molière's prose is wonderful, but his verse is more wonderful still.

When we examined the reason why Molière wrote *L'Avare* in prose, we saw that it was most probably because he was pressed for time, and not because he was making an experiment. But still there are features in it which suggest that Molière was moving unconsciously in the direction of a form of comedy different from classical comedy and more resembling that of modern *drame*, a form of comedy which does not exclude pathos, or even a hint of tragedy. Brunetière, indeed, maintains that *Tartuffe* is a *drame*, and that the comedy of character, whenever the study of character becomes profound—such as the study of a misanthrope, a miser, or a hypocrite can hardly fail to be— tends inevitably to become drama, and a particular form of drama, the *tragédie bourgeoise*, as it was understood by Diderot and Sedaine and Mercier and Beaumarchais[1]. I have given

[1] *Les Époques du théâtre français*, pp. 147–51.

my reasons for disagreeing with this view so far as *Tartuffe* and *Le Misanthrope* are concerned, but there are certainly scenes in *L'Avare* which are more suggestive of modern drama than of classical comedy. But Molière invariably saves the situation by introducing after such scenes an extra dose of comedy, and thus prevents his play from becoming a *tragédie bourgeoise* or even a *comédie sérieuse*. *Le Malade imaginaire*, being a three-act play, was naturally written in prose, and, so far as the evidence goes, was conceived and completed at leisure. The ballet which is interspersed between the acts effectually prevents the play from becoming anything but a comedy—it has even, as we saw, been called a farce. But like *L'Avare* it contains elements which make for drama. Probably Molière did not mean the scene in which Angélique finds her father apparently dead to be really pathetic, but when Mlle Baretta (Mme Worms) imported into it all the pathos that the situation seems to require, she fell into a very natural error of judgment[1]. Again, when in the previous scene Béline, labouring under the same mistake as Angélique, proceeds to pillage her husband's property, we are on the verge of serious drama. Béline is in intention just as much of a criminal as the stepmother in *La Marâtre*. Finally, in the scene between Argan and Béralde (III, 3) the discussion is carried on in a grave and serious tone, and Béralde plays the part of a

[1] F. Sarcey, *op. cit.* pp. 220–2.

modern *raisonneur*. And this comedy, with its possibilities and its suggestions—I do not say more—of a modern *drame*, is written in prose which from its care and breadth and variety is eminently suited to that type of play.

Another feature which *L'Avare* has in common with two other of Molière's prose plays, the romantic drama of *Don Juan* and the *comédie-ballet* of *Le Bourgeois gentilhomme*, is the increased number of *dramatis personae*. In *Don Juan* there are sixteen, besides the spectre and the suites of Don Juan and of Don Carlos and Don Alonse; in *L'Avare* there are fifteen; in *Le Bourgeois gentilhomme* seventeen, not counting the musicians, who take part not only in the ballet but in the comedy itself. In *Le Malade imaginaire* there are only twelve—one less than in *Les Femmes savantes* and the same as in *Tartuffe*. One notices, too, that Molière, especially in *L'Avare* and to a less extent in *Le Malade imaginaire*, has a tendency to bring more characters on the stage at once than was customary in classical drama[1].

If it cannot be said that in all this Molière was deliberately moving towards the modern *drame*, his innovations at any rate indicate a tentative groping in that direction. Like most true artists he loved experiment. We see this in the many various types of his plays—Italian comedy in

---

[1] Faguet regards *Tartuffe* and *Don Juan* as *comedies sérieuses* or *drames* (*Rousseau contre Molière*, p. 172) and *L'Avare* as on the borderland.

L'Étourdi, social farce in *Les Précieuses ridicules*, tragi-comedy in *Don Garcie*, gallant comedy in *La Princesse d'Élide* and *Les Amants magnifiques*, romantic drama in *Don Juan*, pastoral comedy in *Mélicerte*, the libretto for a musical comedy in *Le Sicilien*, mythological comedy in *Amphitryon*, comédie-ballet in *Le Bourgeois gentilhomme* and many other pieces, *tragédie-ballet* in *Psyché*. Then there are his metrical experiments—*vers blancs* in *Le Sicilien*, *vers libres* in *Amphitryon* and *Psyché*. But through all these experiments he remained true to that type of comedy which he created for the modern world, the social comedy of character. It is therefore to a consideration of Molière as a social moralist that my final pages must be devoted.

Though Molière was supremely interested in character, he was, unlike Shakespeare, less concerned with its growth and development than with its effect on a man's fellows. In fine, he studied man above all things as a social animal, man in his relations with his family, or with that larger organism which is called society. Thus, while Shakespeare chooses for the setting of his tragedies more or less barbarous ages in which the elemental passions are unrestrained by social laws, Molière makes social law the touchstone of character. Harpagon's avarice, Orgon's infatuation with Tartuffe are bad in themselves, but they are doubly bad because they tend to disintegrate the family. Alceste's exaggerated sincerity of speech is ridiculous because it is incompatible

with the *bienséances* of society, and it is chiefly
from the social standpoint that Molière arraigns
vice and folly. The one exception, in this as in
other respects, is *Don Juan*. This profound study
of an atheist and libertine has no social background. Our interest is wholly in the man himself, not in the bearing of his actions on any
social group. His character is not, like Alceste's,
conditioned by his relations to society, or, like
Tartuffe's, by his relations to a family.

Yet, none the less, it is as a social moralist
as much as a student of individual character that
Molière is interested in Don Juan. In its bold
attack on the social vices of the day the play
of which he is the hero forms a trilogy with
Tartuffe and *Le Misanthrope*, in which, as we
have seen, Molière shewed no less prescience
than courage. The vices which he attacked in
these plays were vices not only of his own age
but also of the two or three generations which
came after him. Religious hypocrisy was ram-
pant during the last thirty years of the reign of
Louis XIV. "Le courtisan d'autrefois," says La
Bruyère, "avait ses cheveux, était en chausses
et en pourpoint, portait de large canons, et il
était libertin. Cela ne sied plus; il porte une
perruque, l'habit serré, le bas uni, et il est dévot."
This is an apt commentary not only on *Tartuffe*
but on *Don Juan*. Don Juan himself stands, not
only for the Vardes and Guiches and Lauzuns
of Molière's own day, but for the libertines and
debauchees who frequented the supper parties of
the Temple in the last years of the reign of

Louis XIV, and who under the Regency and Louis XV became a real social danger. Such a man was the Duc de Richelieu, the friend of Voltaire, the professional seducer of women, vain, heartless and cruel, who lived up to the very eve of the Revolution. So, too, we have seen that the love of evil-speaking which Molière—for here at least he is in full sympathy with Alceste—attacks in *Le Misanthrope* developed in the eighteenth century, with the growth of the salon, into a serious evil. Had not Jean-Jacques Rousseau been blinded by his lack of humour and his self-conceit, he might have realised that the insincerity and artificiality which he hated in French society had been arraigned by the very man whose plays he attacked as immoral.

If *Tartuffe* is an attack on religious hypocrisy as a danger to the whole social fabric, it is also a criticism on the religious director as a menace to the unity and discipline of the family. *L'Avare* shews us that avarice in the head of a family is no less hurtful than bigotry, for it makes the children deceitful and disobedient. It is equally prejudicial to the well-being of the family when the husband indulges in absurd social aspirations, or gives himself up to the nursing of imaginary ailments, or when the wife dabbles in learning and science to the neglect of her children and her household[1].

But the welfare of the family is based on a

---

[1] Balzac agrees with Molière as to the importance of the family. "Aussi regardé-je la Famille et non l'Individu comme le véritable élément social." Preface to *La comedie humaine*, 1855.

well-assorted marriage, and Molière is never tired of inveighing against parents who sacrifice their daughters to their own interests, who give their daughters in marriage without consulting them, or even in spite of their reasonable opposition. We saw that on his very first appearance as a moralist, namely in *Sganarelle*[1], he took up this position, and he recurs to it again and again—in *Tartuffe*, in *Le Médecin malgré lui*, in *George Dandin*, in *L'Avare*, in *Le Bourgeois gentilhomme*, in *Les Femmes savantes*, and in *Le Malade imaginaire*. In fact, in six of these eight plays the whole plot turns upon the daughter's resistance to her father's choice of a husband. It is true that this plot is a conventional one, but it is equally true that in all these plays Molière treats it not merely as a playwright but also as a moralist. He puts the woman's point of view most forcibly in that curious mixture of boisterous farce and serious comedy, *George Dandin*. "M'avez-vous," says Angélique to her husband, "avant le mariage demandé mon consentement, et si je voulois bien de vous? Vous n'avez consulté pour cela que mon père et ma mère; ce sont eux proprement qui vous ont épousé[2]." And she says to her lover: "Pensez-vous qu'on soit capable d'aimer de certains maris qu'il y a? On les prend, parce qu'on ne s'en peut défendre, et que l'on dépend de parents qui n'ont des yeux que pour le bien[3]."

[1] See above, p. 71. [2] Act II, Scene 2.
[3] Act III, Scene 5. For Molière's campaign against this domestic tyranny see Weiss, *Molière*, pp. 162–70. The Spanish follower of Molière, Moratín, takes the same line in his master-

Molière regarded it as essential to a well-assorted marriage that there should be no great disparity of condition between husband and wife. A noble might marry the daughter of well-to-do and well-bred *bourgeois* parents (Clitandre and Henriette), but a marriage between a yeoman and the daughter even of a petty provincial noble was bound to end in disaster (George Dandin and Angélique). As regards the relative ages of a married couple Molière's views seem to have been biased first by his hopes and then by his experience. In *L'École des Maris*, when he was meditating on his own marriage, the great disparity of age between Ariste and Léonor is not referred to as an objection. Even in *L'École des Femmes*, which was produced just after his marriage, Agnès reproaches Arnolphe not with being double her age but with never having made an effort to win her affections. But in his later plays Molière, moved apparently by his own matrimonial failure, is all for youth marrying youth. One thing, however, is necessary besides youth, and that is mutual inclination. It need not be a romantic passion, but liking there must be. That is a condition even more essential in his eyes than equality of age and rank.

> ...qui donne à sa fille un homme qu'elle hait
> Est responsable au Ciel des fautes qu'elle fait[1].

In thus insisting on the claims of affection and

piece, *El st de las niñas*. "This is the result of the abuse of authority, of the oppression from which youth suffers," says Don Diego at the close of the play.
[1] See *Tartuffe* II, 2 (Dorine to Orgon).

on the right of a young girl to be consulted as to the choice of her future husband, Molière was by no means in accord with the general practice of his day. A striking instance of this practice is afforded by Mme de Caylus, the author of the well-known *souvenirs*. One of the most attractive women in France, the relative and *protégée* of Mme de Maintenon, she might have made a happy as well as a brilliant marriage. Yet, when she was barely thirteen, she was married to the Comte de Caylus, a hardened drunkard, rough, brutal, and quarrelsome, of whom Saint-Simon wrote that his death, which occurred eighteen years later, "gave pleasure to his whole family." Another striking instance of this arbitrary treatment of daughters is Mme Guyon's marriage in 1664. She had to sign the contract without even being told who her future husband was, and she only saw him for the first time two or three days before the marriage. She was fifteen; he was thirty-eight and a martyr to gout. It is then in no spirit of empty compliment that Lagrange and Vinot claim on Molière's behalf that "jamais homme n'a su mieux que lui remplir le précepte qui veut que la comédie instruise en divertissant." This must not, of course, be pushed too far. Molière was, in the first place—and he never forgot it—the manager of a theatrical company, for the financial success of which he was responsible; secondly, he was a dramatic artist, concerned to make his work as perfect as circumstances permitted. It was only in the third place that he was a moralist. In this he differs from modern writers of problem-plays, who are moralists in the first place, and dramatists only because the drama is a convenient and lucrative method of propagating their doctrines.

But it is said that Molière also writes problem-plays. "*L'École des Femmes* est notre première comédie à thèse," says Brunetière, though why *L'École des Femmes* and not *L'École des Maris* is not very clear. He thus puts *L'École des Femmes* in the same category with *Les Idées de Madame Aubray* and *Le Fils naturel* of Dumas *fils*, with Augier's *Madame Caverlet* and *Les Fourchambault*, with M. Brieux's *La Robe rouge*, with Mr Galsworthy's *Strife* and *The Eldest Son*. Now in nearly all these plays the chief interest is in the problem and not in the plot or the characters. This is more especially the case with *Les Idées de Madame Aubray*, *La Robe rouge* and *The Eldest Son*. Let us hear the critic of the *Times* on *La Robe rouge*. "The author is so filled with his subject"—the French judicial system and professional bias—"that he has poured more ideas into his play than any play will bear," and again, "Most thesis-plays, certainly M. Brieux's, are actor-proof. It is upon the clear statement of their ideas, the cogency of their arguments that they depend for their main effect; and so long as the players speak the words set down for them with intelligence all goes well."

Now let us look at Molière's plays. What is the thesis of *L'École des Femmes*? Brunetière says it is "Follow Nature," but in our consideration of *Le Malade imaginaire* the fallacy of Brunetière's views about Molière and Nature has already been pointed out. The thesis of *L'École des Femmes* is rather, "Do not think yourself cleverer than all the world, and if you determine to marry when you are past forty do not prepare a girl for the part of your wife by bringing her up in seclusion and ignorance." The comedy agrees with a discussion between Arnolphe and his friend Chrysalde in which Arnolphe proclaims that

Épouser une sotte est pour n'être point sot.

But from the first our interest is engaged not in the abstract discussion, but in Arnolphe's character and in the fate of his scheme. And it is the failure of this scheme that is the real *dénouement* of the play. Similarly the interest of *L'École des Maris* lies less in the problem as to whether strictness or indulgence is the better method of winning the affections of your ward than in the character of Sganarelle and in the efforts of Isabelle to outwit him.

Le Misanthrope, like the two *Écoles*, opens with a discussion, and the question is, "how far is sincerity in social intercourse possible?" There is, however, this difference between *Le Misanthrope* and the two earlier plays that Molière does not take a side, and the question is left unanswered. But here again, the interest of the play is not in the thesis, but in the characters of Alceste and Célimène and their relations to one another. *Tartuffe* is an attack on religious hypo-

crisy, just as *Le Misanthrope* is an attack on
back-biting as a social amusement. But it also
contains a problem, namely the effect of a director
of conscience upon family life. Once more the
play opens with a discussion, this time in full
family conclave, and once more we lose sight of
the problem in our interest in the characters and
in the success or failure of Tartuffe's schemes.
Thus we see that though Molière often takes
a moral or social question as the starting-point
of his play, and indeed emphasises the fact by
casting his opening scene in the form of a discussion, yet from the first he creates his characters and plans his action. The result is that
the play becomes a drama and not a mere debate.
In the words of George Meredith, Molière's
"moral does not hang like a tail or preach from
one character, incessantly cocking an eye at the
audience." It is no doubt partly owing to this
fact that there has been a tendency of late
among French critics to depreciate Molière as a
moralist. "La morale de Molière," says M. Lavisse, "est très modeste. On ne trouve pas dans
tout son théâtre un devoir qui commande un
renoncement à soi, même un effort qui coûte."
Then, after an absurdly unfair reference to *La
Princesse d'Élide* and *Amphitryon*, he complains that Molière preaches the right of women
to be unfaithful to tyrannical husbands, and says
that with him

L'amour est une loi de la nature....Molière prend parti pour
elle contre les gêneurs de l'amour, les pères, les tuteurs, les
maris...comme aussi contre les médecins...comme encore

contre tous ceux, Tartuffes, femmes savantes, cuistres des lettres, qui l'offensent par des manières, des grimaces, et des faussetés. La nature doit être tempérée par la raison—mais la raison est naturelle aussi—et par les convenances de la société—mais la société aussi est naturelle, l'homme étant un être sociable[1].

It will be seen that in making Molière a follower of Nature M. Lavisse is in agreement with Brunetière, but he gives so wide an interpretation to the meaning of that comprehensive term that the agreement is more apparent than real. M. Lavisse in fact uses the term Nature more or less in the Stoic sense, as equivalent to Reason.

Faguet, while he has exposed the absurdity of the view that Molière's moral is that of "Follow Nature," is hardly just to him as a moralist. He declares that he is neither patriotic nor "civic" nor religious, nor a lover of virtue, at any rate of heroic virtue[2]. And, as has been said, he regrets that Molière did not introduce a *raisonneur* into *Don Juan*, *Le Misanthrope*, *L'Avare*, and *Le Bourgeois gentilhomme*, in order to make his meaning more clear, and to blow the trumpet of virtue with a more certain sound. But these views seem to imply a complete misunderstanding of the functions of the comic drama. In the first place a dramatist is not bound to express his own opinions, and in the second the very nature of comedy, at least as Molière understood it, is opposed to the utter-

---

[1] *Histoire de France* VII, 113-4.
[2] *Rousseau contre Molière*, pp. 206 ff.

ance of lofty sentiments. Comedy "instructs men by amusing them"; her business is not to preach virtue, but to ridicule vice and folly. She deals, not with heroes and saints, not with Cids and Polyeuctes, but with ordinary men.

Yet Faguet is on the right track when he declares that Molière's guiding star is not Nature but common sense, by the light of which he steers his path as a moralist. For common sense is the soul of comedy. Thus when Molière attacks vice and folly in the name of common sense, he is fulfilling the true function of a comic dramatist. M. Jourdain is ridiculous because he is devoid of common sense. It is the want of common sense that makes Alceste, whom we all love and admire, say and do ridiculous things. On the other hand, Dorine is "common sense incarnate." It is in the name of common sense that Sganarelle protests against the view of Don Juan that the mystery of the universe can be explained by the law of four and four make eight. "La belle croyance et les beaux articles de foi que voilà! Votre religion, à ce que je vois, est donc l'arithmétique." Sganarelle's reasoning may have its nose broken, but his common sense triumphs.

Molière, it has often been remarked, is fond of choosing valets and women servants as the representatives of common sense. He recognised that common-sense is not a monopoly of the well-born and well-educated, but that it may be found in an illiterate kitchen-maid as well as in a learned man of letters, in a poor valet as well as in a great noble. Thus it is often the valets or the maid-servants who point the moral —witness Sosie in *L'Amphitryon*—and point it more effectively than any *raisonneur*. It is because Molière believed in common sense and simplicity and straight-forward speaking that he had a peculiar aversion to all singularity and pretension, to all claims to be an *être à part*, to all anti-social vices and follies.

It may be said that common sense morality is not the highest type of morality, that common sense alone will not make a saint or a hero. This is quite true, and it follows that Molière's morality is not of the highest type. It is only in *Le Misanthrope* that we have glimpses of a loftier ideal. But, once more, the answer is that the home of comedy is not on the austere heights, but in the smiling valleys.

If Molière's morality is modest and unambitious, it is at any rate sound and wholesome[1]. Those who see in *Amphitryon* a fulsome compliment to Louis XIV's intrigue with Mme de Montespan, or in *Don Juan* a defence of atheism, shew themselves to be as ignorant of Molière's methods as Jean-Jacques Rousseau, when he complained that *Le Misanthrope* ridiculed virtue and that *L'Avare* preached disobedience to

---

[1] Cp. H. Davignon, *Molière et la vie* [1904], p. 229, "Il est impossible de fermer les yeux sur la conception de vie normale et regulière, faite d'honnêteté et de droiture, qui se dégage de son œuvre."

parents. I have noted in connexion with *Tartuffe* and *Don Juan* and *Le Misanthrope* how nearly Molière agrees with Bossuet and Bourdaloue. It is a striking testimony to the soundness of his morality that it should be possible to illustrate his attitude towards vice and wrongdoing from the sermons of the two great preachers who attacked his comedies with such uncompromising severity.

INDEX

For EU product safety concerns, contact us at Calle de José Abascal, 56–1°,
28003 Madrid, Spain or eugpsr@cambridge.org.

 www.ingramcontent.com/pod-product-compliance
Ingram Content Group UK Ltd.
Pitfield, Milton Keynes, MK11 3LW, UK
UKHW012329130625
459647UK00009B/159